Troilus and Criseyde

Troilus and Criseyde

by

GEOFFREY CHAUCER

TRANSLATED INTO MODERN ENGLISH,
WITH PREFACE, INTRODUCTION,
APPENDICES AND NOTES, BY

MARGARET STANLEY-WRENCH

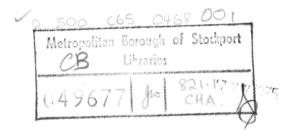
CENTAUR PRESS LTD.

This translation first published 1965
by Centaur Press Ltd., 11-14 *Stanhope Mews West,*
*London, S.W.*7 *and Fontwell, Sussex*

Second impression 1971

SBN 90000055 4

Printed by Unwin Brothers Limited.
The Gresham Press, Old Woking, Surrey, England.
A member of the Staples Printing Group.

FOR BILL

Preface

Chaucer's Canterbury Tales are familiar to nearly everyone, but his great poem, *Troilus and Criseyde,* which has been called the first psychological novel, a story about men and women in love, as true today as it was in the Fourteenth Century, is far less widely known than it deserves to be.

It is not a 'difficult' poem, yet because modern readers are held back by Chaucer's idiom and the language of the Fourteenth Century, I have tried to turn it into modern English, in a way that retains something of Chaucer's own music, yet can give a sense of its wholeness, the quick moving, yet leisured story, subtle characterisation and comedy of the original.

The translation was started to help my own students, and they have been the most patient of guinea pigs. We worked through *Troilus and Criseyde* together, and from them I discovered just what was difficult and what needed explaining. The translation has been a real labour of love, and of pleasure, too. No one who reads Chaucer can fail to be aware of his personality, humorous, half sly, twinkling, warmly human. At the same time he is a poet whose craftsmanship and skill is most delicate, and to keep the music of Chaucer's own verse is almost impossible. Middle English, with its French pronunciation, its lengthened vowels, was a more dancing and light-hearted language than ours. It has also been impossible to retain all Chaucer's rhymes, although at times I have used the mediaeval trick of rhyming words which have a different sense yet the same sound. I have also followed Chaucer's own stanza, the beautifully interlaced Rime Royale, which he himself introduced and used so often. It has dignity and decorum, in the full mediaeval sense of the words, and gives exactly the right music for a poem which is a dance, as well as a tragedy of love.

This 'translation' is not intended as a crib. Its aim is to give an impression of Chaucer's masterpiece, and to point the way to *Troilus and Criseyde* in the original Middle English. The notes, also, are meant as brief explanations, and to refer readers to other more scholarly works.

It is in the spirit of humility, but with love and joy that I undertook this task, and I offer it in the same spirit, directing the reader to read, but to be unsatisfied until he or she has tried Chaucer's own delicate and gracious poetry.

My thanks are due to the various Chaucerian and mediaeval scholars whose works are listed in the bibliography, and should be read by all who wish to understand more of Chaucer. I also owe a debt of gratitude to my students, colleagues and friends, whose patience, advice and help has been inexhaustible.

M.S.W.

May, 1964.

Introduction

Troilus and Criseyde is a mature work. Even if one did not know that it was written by Chaucer in middle life, the poem bears all the marks of maturity, a deep, humorous understanding and acceptance of life as it is; wit; judgement; and the most exquisite skill and craftsmanship. Its date is about 1382-1385, and although neither the plot, nor the characters and situations, are invented by Chaucer, it is as great a poem as the better known *Canterbury Tales*.

As will be seen from the notes, the tale of *Troilus and Criseyde* is one which a mediaeval audience would know well, being one of the many apocryphal Troy stories which had been the subject of poems and stories in France and Italy. Among these were the *Roman de Troie,* by Benoit de Sainte-Maure, written in the 12th Century, and the *Historia Trojana,* by Guido delle Colone, written in the 13th Century. Chaucer's immediate source was Boccaccio's *Il Filostrato,* written about 1338. He may have first read this in Italy, to which he travelled on missions for the King in 1372 and 1378, perhaps without even knowing that it was by Boccaccio. In mediaeval days authors were inhibited by no rules of copyright, nor felt a sense of guilt over possible plagiarism. A good story was free for all.

Yet Chaucer, of all mediaeval poets, deserves the title of Innovator. What he does is fresh, new, modern. If he uses a well-worn plot, his treatment of it is original, and whatever he writes has the distinctive, unmistakable print of Geoffrey Chaucer. In his own day he was famed as the poet of love, and as the translator of that most popular mediaeval poem, the courtly and allegorical *Romance of the Rose*. But even in his translations, and in what we now regard as his minor poems, he shows superlative skill, introducing new metrical forms, together

9

with new literary themes and conventions. He also did something which few other mediaeval writers wholly succeed in doing, (with perhaps the exception of William Langland in *Piers Plowman,* and the unknown author of *Sir Gawayne and the Grene Knight*), that is, he writes for his time, of his time, and yet for eternity. He is mediaeval, but he has an outlook which we like to think of as 'modern', an analytical eye for the psychological quirks and oddities of human nature, and a sophisticated yet innocent acceptance of life as a whole. We can appreciate and enjoy the *Canterbury Tales* or *Troilus and Criseyde* with next to no knowledge of mediaeval conventions, ideas and attitudes, although such knowledge will of course add greatly to such enjoyment. But to approach many of Chaucer's contemporaries we need much specialised knowledge, for they are much more 'mediaeval' writers.

Gower; Robert Manning; and those unknown poets who wrote *Pearl, The Owl and the Nightingale,* the minstrel romances such as *King Horn, Havelock, Sir Orfeo,* and the splendid alliterative poem, *Sir Gawayne and the Grene Knight,* are unknown to many modern readers, not merely because of language difficulties, but because a barrier of belief, a gulf separates us from the moral, religious and social climate of the Middle Ages.

But Chaucer is also 'modern' in his treatment of the English language. He entrusted his work to the graceful speech of the well educated, aristocratic Fourteenth Century Englishman, a type of Middle English spoken in and around London, embellished with French words, and with something of the sophistication and elegance of courtly music and dance. Gower, and other 'learned' writers, played for safety by writing in Latin, or the Romance languages, French or Italian. Others, such as Langland, or the poet of Sir Gawayne, clung to an older style of writing, strongly alliterative, with much of the virility and vigour of Anglo-Saxon, blustering as a north-easterly wind. Chaucer poked fun at such writers when, in the Prologue to the Parson's Tale, this 'southren man' said that he could not "geeste

'rum, ram, ruf by lettre' ", that is, write the strongly alliterative
verse of the midlands and the North.

Chaucer made fun, too, of the sing-song minstrel romances
and ballads in his own *Rime of Sir Topas,* and of the learned
and classical 'tragedies' in the *Monk's Tale,* whilst the Man of
Law, in his Prologue, said of Chaucer, his creator,

> "Chaucer, thogh he kan but lewedly
> On metres and on ryming craftily
> Has seyd hem in swich Englissh as he kan
> Of olde tyme, as knoweth many a man."

It is done with the same delicacy and grace as Mozart quoting
in Don Giovanni from Figaro, laughing at, yet honouring the
gift!

Aware of the changing nature of the English language, how
"Forme of speche is chaunge", Chaucer also prayed that none
might misunderstand his "litel myn tragedye" of *Troilus and
Criseyde,* nor "mysmetre for defaute of tonge"; yet chose
fallible, changing English in which to write of fallible, changing
human nature.

Even in the poems of Chaucer which are most markedly
mediaeval, full of the various allegorical and courtly conven-
tions of the Middle Ages, such as the *Book of the Duchess, The
House of Fame,* or the *Parliament of Fowles,* one is aware of
that Chaucerian voice, distinctive, humorous, humane, yet
urbane and highly sophisticated. It is strange that the critics
of the 17th and 18th Centuries considered Chaucer to be a
simple, 'rude' and primitive poet, although the corrupt texts,
which made it impossible to scan his work correctly, were in
part responsible for this view. In everything he wrote there is
worldly-wise urbanity, breadth and balance, the skill of a con-
scious literary artist, one of the most well read, civilised and
courtly of all poets.

Although *Troilus and Criseyde* is, for its modern readers, a
psychological novel, it is also a mediaeval poem, and so the

lovers in it, though human, and behaving as men and women in love always have behaved and always will, are also a well-bred, courtly pair, bound, to a certain extent, by the rules and conventions of courtly love, and a closely knit and somewhat artificial section of society. The poem is literature for the court, its tone is romantic, sophisticated, philosophical and moral, and Chaucer keeps to the rules of rhetoric, and uses the digressions, quotations and allusions, 'sententiae' and 'exemplum', to please his mediaeval audience, who expected instruction mixed with their entertainment.

He also keeps closely to his source. The story follows the course of Boccaccio's poem, and the characters are the same. Chaucer differs from Boccaccio, however, in making them warmer and gentler, in stressing the fallible human element, and so creating greater humanity, perhaps less 'romance'. *Troilus and Criseyde* has in it something of that ominous, storm-cloud threat of Greek Tragedy; from the beginning, the lovers' happiness is underlined by tragic irony; it is fussy, well-meaning Pandarus, delighting to arrange the lives of other people, yet wanting their happiness more than anything on earth, who destroys those he loves best. Fortune, playing with the fates of men like a cat with mice, turns her wheel, and it is she who stands out, dark and tall and menacing, mutable, yet unmovable, the one character who remains untouched and unchanged.

This allegorical conception of Fortune is common in mediaeval literature and art, and persists through the poetry of Spenser, and the plays of Shakespeare, right into the 17th and 18th centuries. But, as Shakespeare did in *Romeo and Juliet,* Chaucer makes the coldness and indifference of Fortune so much the more terrible through contrast with the robust, sensual, warm-hearted characters, whose lives she twists and ruins. Juliet's Nurse and Pandarus, like those earthy, practical Nurses in Euripides' Hippolytus or Medea, make darker the implacable iciness of Fate and Doom. And only in a Scottish Chaucerian poet like Henryson, who deliberately 'follows up' *Troilus and Criseyde* with his *Testament of Cressid,* does one get the same sense of 'lacrimae rerum', the pity of it all.

There is nothing else in mediaval literature quite like the comic scenes when Pandarus runs with a cushion to save Troilus' knees from the hard floor as he kneels, a correct and lowly lover by his mistress' bed; when he 'pokes' his niece, or teases his friend, or makes fun of his own unluckiness in love. There are lively human touches in *Sir Gawayne and the Grene Knight*, tenderness and pathos in *Sir Orfeo*, robust yet bitter humour in *Piers Plowman*, but not this particular blending of warmth and tenderness with what is robustly comic and down to earth. Chaucer and Shakespeare alone can do this, showing life as it really is, yet isolated, selected through conscious artistry and skill into what are the situations of drama and the greatest tragedy.

M. STANLEY-WRENCH.

Troilus and Criseyde

Book One

1   The double sorrow of Troilus to tell,
    He who was son of Priam, King of Troy,
    In love, how his adventures grew and fell
    From woe to well, then after out of joy
    My purpose is: I'll rhyme and time employ.   5
    Thesiphone, Muse, help me to endite
    This woeful verse. I weep even as I write!

2   To you I speak, O goddess of torment,
    You, cruel fury, sorrowing ever in pain.
    Help me, the most compassionate instrument,   10
    Longing to help poor lovers to complain.
    For it is right (I make this very plain,)
    For woeful folk to wear a dreary face,
    And sorrowful tales must move with mournful pace.

3   For I, who serve the servant of great Love   15
    Dare not pray to him in my wretchedness
    For help in telling what he should approve,
    Not even if I'm slain. In dumb darkness
    I'm cooped, yet if my work brings any gladness
    To those in love, helping them to prevail   20
    I'm glad, for them I'll labour and travail.

4   But happy lovers, who in gladness swim,
    If there is any pity left in you,
    Think back to all those days when hope was dim,

17

And have in mind the bitterness and rue   25
Of other folk, and think with kindness, too,
How once you felt when love did not so please,
Or you have won his joys with too much ease.

5   And pray for all those wretches in the plight
Of Troilus, which you shall shortly hear,   30
That love may bring them soon to heavenly light.
And pray also for me to God most dear,
That I may have the strength, in some manner
To show the pain that all Love's folk endure,
Through Troilus story and his adventure.   35

6   And also pray for those locked in despair,
Who love, and never will their joy recover.
Also for those whom slander's shameful spear
Has torn and wounded, he or she, poor lover.
Beg God that in his mercy he will sever   40
The bonds that bind them in this world and place,
Setting free those whom Love will never grace.

7   And pray also for those who are at ease,
That God will grant they may endure so still,
And send them strength their ladies well to please,   45
So that their hearts with pleasure love may fill.
And as for me, my profit and my skill
Will be to pray for lovers pityingly,
And write their woes, and live so, lovingly.

8   And may I have compassion for each one   50
As if I were his brother, close and dear.
So listen, for my prologue now is done.
I plunge straight to the point of my matter,
In which you may the double sorrows hear
Of Troilus, all his loving of Criseyde,   55
And how his lady left him ere she died.

9   It is well known how that the Greeks, most strong
    In arms, and with a thousand ships set sail
    For Troy, and there beseiged the city long.
    Nigh on ten years before they could prevail.   60
    And so with many blows they hit one nail,
    One thing alone, revenge for ravishment,
    For Helen's rape through Paris' blandishment.

10   Now it fell out that in the town there was
    Dwelling a lord of much authority,   65
    A priest, a great one, and his name, Calchas,
    That so expert in knowledge was, that he
    Knew well and truly Troy destroyed should be
    Through his god's oracle, whose title, thus,
    Dan Phoebus, or Apollo Delphicus.   70

11   So when this Calchas knew by calculation,
    Also by oracle of this Apollo,
    The Greeks should come, so fierce and great a nation,
    And cast down Troy without much more ado,
    He made his plans to leave the town and go,   75
    For gazing in his magic crystal ball
    He saw that, willy-nilly, Troy must fall.

12   So, for this reason, and to get away
    Unheard, unseen, this wise, foresighted man
    Slipped over to the Greeks, and kindly, they   80
    Received him courteously, and bowed, and ran
    To do his bidding, for their trust and plan
    Was, he in wisdom should direct and guide them
    Through every terror that might well betide them.

13   Such din arose when first it was made known   85
    Throughout the town, and rumours flew about
    That Calchas had turned traitor and had flown,
    He'd joined the Greeks. "Revenge, revenge," all shout.

"He's broken faith, and we're betrayed, no doubt.
We'll have his blood, Calchas, and all his kin,   90
Burn up the lot of them, flesh, bone and skin!"

14   Now Calchas, acting so, had left behind
     His daughter, who knew nothing of his deed.
     And now, in great distress of heart and mind
     She even feared for life, thought she might bleed   95
     To expiate his sin. Poor girl, indeed
     She did not know what way to turn, alone,
     Widowed, without one friend to whom to moan.

15   Criseyde was this lady's name aright,
     And I believe that throughout Troy's city   100
     None was so fair, surpassing every sight,
     So angel-like was her own fresh beauty
     That like a thing immortal so seemed she,
     A perfect, flawless, lovely, heavenly creature
     Sent down to shame and mock flawed human nature. 105

16   This lady, who all day heard at her ear
     Words beating of her father's treacherous shame,
     Was almost driven mad with sorrow and fear,
     And in her dark brown widow's habit came
     To Hector, there excused herself from blame,   110
     And kneeling, with her tremulous, tearful voice
     Begged for his mercy with most piteous noise.

17   For Hector was compassionate by nature,
     And saw that she was in most sore distress,
     And also that she was so fair a creature,   115
     And so he made her glad by his goodness.
     "Forget your father's treason. Wretchedness
     Like this is mischance only. Stay in Troy
     So long as you desire, with us, in joy,

18 And men shall do you every courtesy,   120
    And honour you, as they have done before
    Whilst here in Troy your father lived, for we
    Will care for you, protect you as of yore."
    She thanked him with humility, and bore
    Herself with calm and lovely dignity,   125
    And took her leave, went home, lived quietly,

19 With staff and servants and in such a style
    As it was fitting for her rank to hold,
    Running her house discreetly all the while
    She stayed in Troy. And both by young and old   130
    She was well loved. Good things of her all told.
    But whether she had any child or no
    Books do not tell, therefore I let this go.

20 Matters fell out, as things do so in war
    Between the folk of Troy and the Greeks oft.   135
    Some days the Trojans bought it very dear.
    Next day the Greeks found not a thing was soft
    About the men of Troy. Fortunes aloft,
    And then pushed down, as Luck's wheel spun and turned
    Giddily whirling as their anger burned.   140

21 But how the town was conquered and laid low
    Is not my purpose or my task to tell.
    I must not let such long digressions grow,
    Or keep you idly waiting here as well.
    All that happened, or to Troy befell   145
    Is found in Homer, Dares' works, or Dyte,
    And who so wishes may read all they write.

22 But though the Greeks shut in the men of Troy,
    Beseiged their city, circling it about,
    The Trojans still kept up old rites with joy,   150
    Honouring the gods with holy prayers devout.

They reverenced first and foremost, out of doubt
A trusted relic called Palladion.
In her their faith was, more than any one.

23 And so it happened, when once more the time   155
Of April came, when fields are robed and bright
In fresh, new green, and spring is in his prime,
And sweetly smelling flowers, red and white
Were scattered here and there, my authors write
That as of old Troy's people crowded, gay   160
And ready for Palladion's holy day.

24 And to the temple in their best attire
To hear the service, join the holy rite
Went many people, crowding and on fire
For praise and worship. Many a lusty knight,   165
And many a lady fresh and maiden bright,
All elegantly dressed, both most and least,
Yes, fitting both the season and the feast.

25 Among these other people was Criseyda
In sable widow's weeds, yet none the less   170
Even as the first of letters now is 'A',
Even so in beauty she stood first, I guess,
Her loveliness made happy all that press.
Never was any precious thing so right,
Nor under a black cloud a star so bright   175

26 As was Criseyde, so folk said, each one
Who saw her there, black robed and full of grace,
Yet she stood humbly, quiet and alone,
Behind a crowd, and in a narrow space
Close to the door, still shamefast was her face.   180
Discreet in dress, well bred and poised she stood,
A lovely creature, debonaire and good.

27   But Troilus, as was his custom, led
      His band of young companions up and down.
      All through that temple's aisles he stalked ahead   185
      Staring at every lady of that town,
      Now here, now there, for he had no devotion
      For any girl, no love pangs spoilt his rest.
      Heart-free, his roving eye ranged round with zest!

28   And as he strolled he glanced around to spy   190
      If any knight or squire of his young band
      Dawdled, sighed, or long and amorously
      Looked at any woman. There he'd stand
      Mocking their love-lorn state, assured and bland.
      "Lord, you can bet she's sleeping extra well   195
      Whilst you, poor wretch, toss to and fro in hell!"

29   Then he went on, "By God, I've often heard
      About a lover's life, how you go on,
      How much you sweat to get one kindly word,
      How hard you toil to bask in love's brief sun.   200
      Oh, and what fuss and tears when love is done!
      What fools you lovers are, in blind distress,
      Nor warned by seeing others in this mess!"

30   He raised his eyebrows smugly as he spoke
      As if to say, "How very wise am I!"   205
      At which the god of love looked black as smoke,
      And thought about revenge for treachery.
      He showed that bow of his was whole and spry.
      A bull's eye hit! The arrow sped to kill.
      Though proud as peacock, Love can pluck him still!   210

31   O blind, blind world, how often, all awry
      Intentions go contrarywise. Proud crest
      Of arrogance goes tumbling from on high.
      Caught is the cocky one, the self possessed.

Troilus, who climbs so high with so much zest,   215
He has no thought of stumbling headlong down.
Yet each day withers seeds which fools have sown!

32   And as proud Dobbin starts to buck and skip,
Full-fed and overheated by his corn,
Until he gets a lashing from the whip,   220
And then he thinks, "Although I prance and scorn
My trace and chain, and glisten, sleek and shorn,
Yet am I but a horse, and horse's dull
Laws I must keep, and with my team mates pull."

33   Just so it happened with this fierce, proud knight,   225
Though he could call a worthy king his sire,
And thought in arrogance that nothing might
Hinder or keep him from his heart's desire,
Yet one glance, and his heart was all afire
With dread that he, who had been proud and free   230
Was subject to love's rule most suddenly.

34   Let this man be a warning to you all,
You wise, proud, worthy folk, all scorning love,
Love, which so soon can all your hearts enthrall.
So it has always been, so it will prove   235
Right to the end of time, in this same groove,
That love enthralls and binds each man, each creature,
And none may fight against the laws of nature.

35   That this is right and true has been well proved,
And this you know quite well, both one and all,   240
The wisest are not those who never loved.
The mightiest champion, sinewy, strong and tall
Love overcomes and brings him to a fall
With those of worth and wealth and high degree.
This was, and is, and yet is still to be.   245

36   And that this thing is so is very well.
The wisest men have been made happy so,
And Love has comforted with his sweet spell
Every sad heart once sunken deep in woe.
And in the cruel heart made kindness grow.   250
Love makes the good more worthy of that name
Since through his power they shun all vice and shame.

37   Now, since one may not easily withstand
Love, in itself so excellent and kind,
Do not refuse Love's light and tender band,   255
For when he chooses he will seize and bind.
The yielding branch is strongest, that you'll find
Than one which breaks. And so I council you
To follow Love, or else he'll capture you!

38   Now to my special point, to Troilus,   260
The prince I spoke about, King Priam's son.
I mean to tell his life without more fuss,
He is my hero, so no more digression,
His joys, his cares, here, in this single session
I mean to tell, so back to my beginning,   265
The thread thus twisted I must go on spinning.

39   Inside that temple, gay and light of heart,
Pleasing himself by glancing to and fro
At this and that girl, musing from what part
She came, from suburb, east, or west end, so   270
It happened that in staring high and low
His gliding glances came to rest at last
On Criseyde, and there they were held fast.

40   He was quite overcome, thrown back, astounded,
And unobtrusively tried hard to see   275
Her better. "God", thought he, by love sore wounded,
"Where have you been, so fair in your beauty?"

His heart swelled with his longing powerfully,
But dreading lest men heard his little sigh,
Acting, he once more strolled half mockingly.   280

41   Criseyde was not too short, nor yet too tall,
Her limbs and all about her feminine,
Nothing aggressive, masculine at all,
But delicate and elegant and fine.
Candour was in her face and its pure line,   285
Shining so clearly that all men could see
Breeding and womanly nobility.

42   Troilus, half dazed in his astonishment
Began to like her air and gracious way
Which had a trace of arrogance, she bent   290
Her head askance, frowning as if to say
"Why do you stare so? What, can I not stay
Here in this spot?" And then she smiled, so light
He thought he had not seen a fairer sight.

43   And from that glance of hers, alive and quick   295
A seed of hot desire and burning love
Rooted into his heart to grow and stick
With deep impression nothing could remove.
And though before he'd liked to range and rove,
Now he was glad to shrink back in his shell   300
Shy as a snail and hesitant as well.

44   And yet this man who thought himself so clever,
Who scorned all those made dry by love's hot flame,
Still did not realise Love hovered ever
There in the subtle glance that darting came   305
From her two shining eyes. So he was slain
There, with that look of hers, this quelled his heart.
Blessed be love, who thus can folk convert!

45 She, this girl in black, to Troilus
    Was now more precious than all else beside,   310
    Yet he gave not a sign why he stood thus,
    Nor said a word of his desire, but tried
    By feigning ease his whirling thoughts to hide.
    And now and then he gazed at others there,
    Then, whilst the priests droned on, back, back to her. 315

46 Then afterwards, still not quite overcome,
    Easy and self-possessed, homeward he went,
    Yet now repenting all that he had done
    In mocking lovers, dreading the descent
    Of showers of scorn upon himself. He meant   320
    To keep as secret his own love-lorn heart,
    His pain and sorrow hidden and apart.

47 He left the temple, with his once proud heart
    Shot through and through by those fair glances, sent
    From his love's eyes, like a keen, pointed dart.   325
    Back to his palace cheerfully he went.
    Jesting, he feigned he was on pleasure bent,
    And though he was among Love's servants now,
    To tease himself, and them, he was not slow,

48 And said, "Lord, lord, you lovers! Every man   330
    Of you, even he who hardest of all tries
    To serve and please must suffer harm and pain,
    Servants who get no wages, hire nor prize.
    Scorn's the reward you get for good service!
    Cruelty repays a deed that's kindly done.   335
    A fine, well-ordered Guild you lovers run!

49 Nothing about your rules is set or plain.
    You fuss about such foolish, trifling things.
    And yet to keep your laws is toil and pain.

You make such great demands, to join you brings   340
Troubles unending. Well you know the stings
Of love, yet grumble and look melancholy
If I should scold you for your faults and folly.

50   Believe me, friends, whatever things you do
Or else do not do, and with what intention,   345
Your lady will perversely misconstrue
Saying you're in the wrong. And, let me mention,
She can be angry, pay you no attention,
Flout you and scorn. You've no redress at all.
Lord, who would be a servant in Love's hall!"   350

51   For all this talk, he had to bide his time.
There was no remedy, he had been caught.
Love had him trapped there in the thick birdlime!
Now he was ill at ease, troubled, distraught.
And so, pretending to his friends he sought   355
Other distractions, one and all sent packing,
Although to him all peace and quiet was lacking.

52   Then Troilus in his room, quite, quite alone
Sat down upon his bed's edge quietly.
And first he sighed, then afterwards a groan   360
Racked him. He thought of her unceasingly,
And as he sat entranced, half dreamingly
He saw her in the temple, and her fair
Looks, and each feature he had fed on there.

53   And so he made a mirror of his mind   365
In which her whole sweet figure was reflected.
His heart now satisfied and pleased to find
It right to love one such, his life directed
To serve her, and if things fell so, perfected
By being her true knight, or else, low bent   370
In humbleness becoming her servant.

54 Labour, cost and trouble, he'd not spare
    These for such a goodly one, nor feel
    A trace of shame for his desire of her,
    Even if this were known, but think it real,   375
    A badge of true love, shining bright as steel.
    So with himself he argued at the start
    Of love, not guessing at its bitterer part.

55 So he proposed all love's craft to pursue,
    To follow, hoping that in secrecy   380
    The hawk Desire he could keep close in mew,
    Hiding her from all others utterly
    Until his heart healed by her help could be.
    And he remembered love that's overblown
    Gives bitter fruit although good seed was sown.   385

56 And much more, above all, deliberated
    What things he should, and what he should not say.
    And how to raise love's spark in her debated.
    Then he began a poem, a lover's lay,
    Crying aloud, as sorrowing lovers may.   390
    Yes, with Criseyde headlong in love he fell
    Without repentance, and with hope as well.

57 The sense and sentence of his poem is found
    In him I follow, he, my author, Lollius.
    Only the difference of our language's sound   395
    Comes between what I and Troilus
    Say and said. See, every word here, thus,
    As I translate them. If you wish to, read
    In this next verse his very words indeed.

                    SONG OF TROILUS

58 "If there's no Love, O God, why feel I so?   400
    And if there's Love, what thing, or who is he?
    If Love is good, from whence comes all my woe?

If he is wicked, strange it seems to me
That every torment and adversity
That springs from Love, I find most palatable.   405
The more I thirst, the more to drink I'm able.

59   And if for my own pleasure I feel pain
From whence comes all my wailing and complaint?
If I enjoy my wound, why then complain?
Why, when unwearied, should I fail and faint?   410
O lively death, O hurt, sweet and yet quaint,
Why do I feel such things so frequently
Unless with my consent they breed in me?

60   And if I will them, then I wrongfully
Complain. And yet so battered to and fro,   415
All pilotless on shipboard tossed am I,
On the sea's midst by winds conflicting so
That rage and counter rage incessant grow.
Alas, what is this illness, strange, yet sweet?
I die from burning cold and icy heat!"   420

61   Then to the God of Love so piteously
He cried and said, "O Lord, yours my soul is,
Yours with each thing that owes you loyalty.
I thank you, Lord, that you brought me to this.
Yet is she mortal or divine, my bliss,   425
She whom you bid me serve obediently,
And as her man for ever live or die?

62   Love, you are there in her bright shining eye,
A place fit for your grace, O lord divine,
Wherefore, O Love, if my service or I   430
May please you, be to me kind and benign,
For all my royal rank I here resign
Into her hand, and humbly kneeling here
Become her man, make her my lady dear."

63   Love's fire did not abate for royal blood   435
     In Troilus' veins, nor spared him any pain
     For all his deeds of valour brave and good.
     Thank God, he felt it all, the fiery chain
     That binds us all, enslaved him, and again
     Burned him and galled him so, his cheeks turned grey, 440
     All colour ebbing sixty times a day!

64   Day after day his thoughts so dwelt on her,
     And his desires so quickened and increased,
     All other duties now neglected were.
     He hoped, by seeing her, pain might be eased   445
     Through her sweet looks. And yet to see her teased.
     The more he looked upon his love he learned
     The nearer that he was, the more he burned.

65   For greatest heat is nearest to the fire.
     All of you folk know this, I'm very sure.   450
     But I know also, were he near or far,
     At night, by day, wise, foolish, ever there
     His heart, the eye of love, with its fixed stare
     Turned always to his lady, lovelier
     To him than Helen or Polixinia.   455

66   And not an hour there passed in any day
     That to himself a thousand times he said,
     "Good goodly, whom I serve obediently
     Well as I can, now would to God, Criseyde
     You would have mercy on me ere I died.   460
     Dear heart, alas, gone are my hue, health, wit, I
     Lose life itself unless you will have pity."

67   All other fears had fled, however dire.
     He had no dread of war, nor yet of hell.
     The only offspring of his hot desire   465
     Were arguments whose lines to one knot fell,

If she would pity him, all would be well.
He was her man, her knight, and he was sure
Love was all life, and only love death's cure.

68   The sharp and showering arrows, deeds of arms   470
     Done by his brothers, Hector and them all,
     Stirred Troilus at last. In war's alarms
     He was among the bravest, towering tall
     Wherever dangers were most great, the call
     To battle made him labour with such skill   475
     That to think on his prowess cheers me still.

69   Yet he fought, not because he hated Greeks,
     Not even to redeem his native town,
     This did not madden him, nor make his cheeks
     Burn. One thing only made this warrior frown,   480
     That she should like him for his brave renown !
     And so from day to day in arms he sped
     So well that Greeks held him, like death, in dread.

70   From this time on love drove his sleep away,
     Made him hate food, caused worries to increase,   485
     So that, however hard he tried to say
     Nothing was wrong, his health showed such decrease
     That he was forced to say some real disease
     Tormented him, lest friends should tease and say
     Love was the fire that burned his life away.   490

71   He told them he had caught a tiresome fever
     And was not well. Whether his lady knew
     And guessed his trouble, seeking to discover
     What ailed him, I'm uncertain. Give her due,
     Nothing I've read ascribes indifference to   495
     Criseyde. She did not know he suffered pain,
     Was not aware of him, in bliss or bane.

72   Then Troilus began to feel such woe
      That he was almost driven mad. His dread
      Was that his lady loved some other so   500
      That she would never take him or give heed
      To his desire, and this made his heart bleed.
      But, not to win the world, could he confess
      To any friend his worry or distress.

73   But when he had a moment free from care,   505
      Troilus to Troilus started to complain.
      "Fool, now, you're truly trapped within the snare,
      You, who teased poor lovers torn by pain.
      Now you are caught and gnaw at your own chain,
      You, who scolded lovers for what now   510
      Takes all your strength away and lays you low.

74   Now what will every lover say of you
      If this comes out? They'll laugh behind your back,
      Jeering and saying, "There he goes, who knew
      So much, and scorned us lovers with no lack   515
      Of mockery and mirth. Now pay him back
      Love, let him limp, and in your merry measure
      Dance without profit, skilfulness or pleasure!"

75   But oh, poor Troilus, God has planned it so
      That since you have to love, your destiny   520
      Is this, to have your bitterness and woe
      Scorned by a girl who shows you no pity,
      And to her man so cold, so cruel is she,
      The frost beneath a winter moon is so,
      Destroying me, as fire licks up the snow.   525

76   Oh, would to God I were safe in the port
      Of death, to which my grief and sorrow lead.
      Oh, Lord, to me it would be much comfort

c

To shed my woes, my languishing in dread.
For if the love I hide should burst and spread   530
Its flaunting petals, they will make more jokes
About me than men do of fools in books.

77   Now help me, God, and you, sweeting, for whom
I cry, well trapped. Never was man trapped so.
Oh, mercy, dear heart, save me from the doom   535
Of death, for, lady, while I breathe and go,
More dearly than myself I will love you.
Sweet, give me one look like a loving friend,
Though you give nothing more until life's end."

78   These words, and many more aloud he said   540
In his complaint, calling on her dear name,
Wishing to tell her all his woe and dread.
His salt tears almost drowned him. All in vain.
How could she hear an unknown love complain?
And as he realised his foolishness,   545
Greater a thousand times was his distress.

79   As he was wailing in his room alone,
In slipped a friend of his, Pandar his name,
And he, unnoticed, heard poor Troilus groan,
And saw his great distress, his tears, his shame.   550
"Good God, what is the matter? Who's to blame?
Have the Greeks worn you down so soon? You seem
A shadow of yourself, so wan and lean.

80   Or have you something on your conscience pressing,
And have become religious suddenly,   555
Wailing for sins and wanting heaven's blessing?
Has panic seized upon you quietly?
God save our foes, besieging this city,
Who through their deeds can joyful folk depress,
And bring our gay lads to such holiness!"   560

81 He spoke in this way to provoke his friend,
    To rouse and make him angry, that he might
    In flare of fury make his misery end,
    And once more see unsheathed his courage bright.
    For he knew well that near, or out of sight,   565
    No one was braver, or bore such a name
    For deeds of arms, or more desired such fame.

82 "What bad luck or what twisted trick of fate"
    Said Troilus, "Has brought you here today
    To see my loneliness and sorry state?   570
    For God's sake, and for mine, go, go away,
    Or else my death, or this, my slow decay
    Will make you most unhappy. Truly, I
    Am sick and worn, and soon enough will die.

83 But if you think that I'm made ill through fear   575
    This is not true, and so do not despise
    Your friend. There's something else I heed, more near
    Than Greeks and all their havoc. For this dies
    My heart, for this tears stream down from my eyes.
    I cannot tell what lies within my breast.   580
    Do not be angry. Secrecy is best."

84 This Pandar, so compassionate, his tears
    Melted him almost, said again, again,
    Troilus, what is it? What distress and fears
    Torture you? If ever there has been   585
    Friendship between us, tell me of your pain,
    Don't hurt me by this wounding secrecy.
    Its only your friend Pandar, only me!

85 And I'll divide your sorrow here, I'll take
    The greater part, to comfort you, for so   590
    Its right for friends to do, for friendship's sake
    To share between them every care and woe.

Why, all my life, and this is truth, I know,
I've loved you, rich or poor, for ill, for well,
So do not hide your trouble now, but tell—"   595

86 Then sorrowing Troilus sighed and said, "My friend,
God grant I'm doing right to tell you this,
Yet I please you by telling in the end.
If my sad heart should break, I must confess,
And if I don't, I know your merciless   600
Nagging. And so, to show how trustingly
I treat you, friend, here's how it stands with me.

87 Love, against whom those who the most defend
Themselves, the least redress and help obtain,
Does with despair and woe my heart offend,   605
Till I am close to death's most bitter bane.
Desire and longing burns me with such pain
That to be killed would be a greater joy
To me than rule as King of Greece and Troy!

88 My dear friend, Pandar, let this satisfy   610
You, this, that I have told you of my woe
And my cold care, concealed from every eye.
And if by chance more folk should hear and know
The truth, then truly, trouble might well follow.
Be glad I told you, and then let me be   615
To die of unknown sorrow quietly."

89 "You stupid man, how long have you hid this
with such unfriendliness?" said Pandarus.
"You might have thought that when things go amiss
Advice can help, and mine may well aid us."   620
"You help us! That is news!" said Troilus.
"Your love affairs go wrong and out of line,
So how the devil can you help with mine?"

90 "That's true enough," said Pandar. "Though I be
    A fool in love, yet one who's deep in muck   625
    Up to the neck in trouble, cannily
    Can stop his comrade from becoming stuck.
    Why, I have seen a blind man walk with luck
    Round pitfalls into which the sighted fell.
    Fools can sometimes guide a wise man well!   630

91 A whetstone is no carving instrument,
    And yet it serves to make sharp carving tools.
    And if you've seen how far astray I went,
    Beware of straying likewise. That's your school!
    And so the wise may be taught by a fool.   635
    Sharpen your wit by looking at my folly.
    All things are sharpened by what's contrary.

92 How could the taste of sweetness ever please
    Unless the taster first knew bitterness?
    Nor can a man be truly well at ease   640
    Unless he first feels sorrow or distress.
    White shows up black, and badness reveals goodness.
    Each sets the other off, seems much more plain.
    The truth of this the wise man will explain.

93 So I, who have so often felt love's pain,   645
    And know its woes so well, can help you better
    Than one who has not felt its bitter bane.
    I can advise you how to bear your fetter.
    Who, more than I, can teach you love's own letter?
    Sharing your heavy burden, I shall make   650
    Your chain and charge seem less, and the weight take.

94 I know my case is like one you know well,
    That of Oënone, the shepherdess,
    Who loved your brother, Paris, and it fell

That she wrote to him of her heaviness.   655
You saw the letter that she wrote, I guess?"
"No, no, I never saw it," said Troilus.
"You didn't? Listen, then, for she wrote thus—

95   "Maker of medicine, Phoebus, fount of healing,
     Who knew the virtues of all herbs, their care,   660
     The remedies their sap is rich and real in,
     He, though physician, could not find a cure
     For his own illness, bound within the snare
     Of love, for King Admetus' lovely daughter.
     That wound he could not heal, and hopeless,
                                        sought her."   665

96   This is the case I'm in, unhappy me,
     I love a lady, and that love hurts sore.
     Yet I can counsel others cunningly,
     Though not myself. So scold your friend no more.
     I have no further cause away to soar   670
     Than does a hawk who wants to flirt and play.
     And yet a few more wise words I can say.

97   And of this one thing certain you can be,
     That even should men torture me, I would
     Not say a word of what you have told me,   675
     Now, by my life, I would not if I could,
     Restrain your love, or hinder if I should!
     Not even if the lady be another's,
     Or Helen, and more properly your brother's!

98   And therefore reassure me as a friend,   680
     And tell me plainly who has caused your woe,
     What's at the root of it, and who can mend
     Your misery? I long to help and show
     My sympathy, not rant and scold. I know
     One cannot cure a man from love, until   685
     The man himself desires to end his ill!

99   Now, know this well—there are two faults, two ways
Of going wrong, to trust all, or trust none!
Follow the middle course, and earn high praise.
They will reward you if you trust someone!   690
Because of this I wish you would have done
With all your wrong ideas, and trust in me.
Tell me your sorrow, please, and speedily!

100   The learned say, 'Pity a lonely man,
For, should he slip, no one will help him rise.'   695
But as for you, you have a friend who can!
Tell me your troubles, let me help. The wise
Teach us that love's not won by weeping eyes,
By wallowing like tearful Niobe
In grief, and turned to stone eternally.   700

101   Be done with moaning and with dreariness,
And let us lessen woe with cheerful speech.
So, in this way, your sorrow will seem less.
Don't take perverse joy in the pain of each
Unhappiness and pang, as fools who reach   705
For some new sorrow when they're in distress,
And won't heed those who seek to cure the mess!

102   Men say, 'A sufferer finds true consolation
Sharing his pain and sorrow with a friend.'
And that should be our true determination,   710
For you and I are both in love, and find
The state a sad one. Certainly my mind
Is woeful, and indeed there's no more room
On me for further roosting flocks of gloom!

103   God knows you cannot be afraid I'll steal   715
Your lady from you! Well enough you know
With whom I am in love, with love that's real,
And for how long, and with what progress slow.

Since I've no axe to grind, (that you'll allow,)
And since I am the friend you trust, then tell
Me something of your cares. You know mine well."

104 Yet for all this Troilus was silent still,
And lay as quiet as if he were dead,
Then suddenly sat up and sighed his fill,
And to the voice of Pandar gave good heed. 725
Yet rolled his eyes and looked so strange indeed
That Pandarus was fearful lest in frenzy
He should fall down, or else take sick and die.

105 So he cried out, "Wake up!" aloud and sharp,
"What, are you sleeping in a lethargy? 730
Or are you like a donkey when the harp
Is played, who hears the sound, yet knows not why,
And nothing of the lovely melody
Sinks in his ears to gladden him, for he
Is so dull in his bestiality?" 735

106 And Pandar, with these words, ended his say.
But Troilus answered not a word again,
Telling his troubles so was not his way.
He feared to speak to others of his pain.
For it is said, 'Those men who cut a cane 740
Find often it is used to beat their back',
(So say the wise) 'Till it is blue and black.'

107 Especially he felt it wrong to speak
Of love, which should be secret, private, hid.
Only if Love is bridled, tame and meek 745
Will he spring gaily at his rider's bid.
Also it's wise to seem as if one did
Seek to escape when one in fact gives chase!
Of all this Troilus thought with worried face.

108   Yet when he heard Pandar, his friend, cry out   750
     "Wake up!" he sighed and sat up in his bed.
     "My friend, though I lie still, no need to shout,
     I am not deaf. I heard the words you said,"
     Cried Troilus. "Be peaceful now instead,
     Let me alone, my troubles to bewail.   755
     To help me all your proverbs won't avail.

109   There is no other cure will do for me,
     And I will not be cured, I mean to die.
     What do I care about queen Niobe!
     Those old examples, let them be, I pray!"   760
     "No, that I won't," said Pandarus, "I say
     Fools wallow in their woe, and weep and wail,
     But will not seek the cure that could avail.

110   And so I see that you are quite demented!
     All the same, tell me if I know your dear,   765
     She who has wounded you, she you lamented.
     I dare say if I whispered in her ear
     Of your deep love, how you yourself from fear
     Dare not tell her this, she would pity you."
     "No, no," cried Troilus. "God, this you shan't do!" 770

111   "What? Can't I set about your work as well
     As if my own life hung upon this deed?"
     "No, friend, you can't." "Why not?" cried Pandar, "Tell."
     "Because I know your plan would never speed!"
     "Oh, so you think so?" "I am sure indeed.   775
     In spite of all your uppish certainty,
     I know she'll never love a wretch like me."

112   Said Pandarus, "Alas, how can this be,
     And why so needlessly do you despair?
     Is she not living? Benedicite!   780
     Why are you sure you have no redress there?

For wounds like yours there's healing, hope, repair.
So do not think for you there is no cure.
What is before us lies in luck and venture.

113   I grant you that you're now enduring pain   785
      As sharp at Tityus does deep down in Hell,
      His belly torn by birds with might and main.
      (These are called vultures, or so the books tell)
      But I, I cannot bear that you should dwell
      In such a foolish state of mind, still feeling   790
      Your ills cannot find medicine or healing.

114   But you won't have it so, your coward heart,
      Bad temper, and most foolish wilfulness,
      And your mistrust all keep alive your hurt.
      You will not help yourself, your cussedness   795
      Won't let you even tell me your distress.
      You lie down here, not caring what you do.
      How could a woman love a wretch like you!

115   And then, what will she think about your death
      If you die so? She will not know the reason,   800
      But think for fear you yielded up your breath,
      Because the Greeks besiege us for a season.
      Fine credit then you'll have to take your ease on!
      Your lady and the whole of Troy will shout
      "He's dead, the wretch, and fries in Hell, no doubt!" 805

116   Ah, you can weep alone here, cry and kneel,
      But if you love a girl, and do not tell,
      She, in return, will see you do not feel!
      Not known, not kissed, and you'll lose love as well!
      Why, many a man has pined in his love's spell   810
      For twenty years, yet thought himself in bliss
      To serve her, though she gave him never one kiss!

117   In his position, should he then despair
Or turn a traitor to his own dear love,
Or kill himself because his lady's fair?   815
No, no, it will his love much fresher prove,
And his heart's queen to worship much more move.
He'll think it is reward enough to serve
His lady, far more than he can deserve!"

118   Troilus at last took in these words, and thought   820
How stupid was the state he now was in.
Pandarus spoke the truth, and if he sought
To kill himself, it would be cowardly sin.
And even if he died, what profit then?
Criseyde would not hear of it, and she   825
Little enough knew of his misery.

119   And as he thought of this, he deeply sighed
And said, "Alas, what had I better do?"
Then Pandar answered, "Speak. No longer hide
Your troubles. Talk, and tell me all your woe.   830
You have my word of secrecy, and so
Trust me. If I don't help you now, and heal,
Hang me when I've been broken on the wheel!"

120   "That's what you say now," said Troilus,
"And easier said than done. Mine's a hard case.   835
Why, Fortune is my foe, I find. Alas,
For no one, high or low in rank or place
Can fight with Fortune, or avert disgrace.
We can't escape her cruel wheel. With all
Of us she plays as cat with mouse or ball."   840

121   Pandar said, "You blame Fortune now,
For you have lost your temper. Can't you see
That she dispenses favours, and will show
Her warmth and love to all in some degree?

Yes, you have this much comfort, seriously,   845
That, even as the joys which Fortune brings
Fly quickly, so her sorrows, too, have wings.

122   And if her wheel should stop and cease to turn,
      Why, then she'd not be Fortune any more.
      So, since her wheel will never halt, then learn   850
      All that you long for may well be in store,
      Whirled to you by the change you now deplore!
      At any moment now she'll be helping.
      Your luck is on the turn, so rise and sing.

123   Now do you see just what I ask of you?   855
      Be done with hang-dog looks, moaning and woe.
      He who wants his doctor's aid must do
      Something to help, unbind his wound and show
      It freely, and—may Cerberus sieze me now—
      If my own sister caused this love-lorn sorrow   860
      I'd give her to you as your girl tomorrow!

124   So face me squarely, tell me who she is,
      Then I can get this business of yours done.
      Do I know this lady? Tell me this,
      For when I know her, then I can get on!"   865
      He hit him on the quick, made the blood run,
      A bull's eye. Troilus blushed in shamed alarm.
      "Ah ha," said Pandar, "Now we're getting warm!"

125   And as he spoke these words he shook him hard.
      "Wretch, you shall tell me who and what she is."   870
      Yet still that ninny Troilus, like a coward
      Shook as if going off to Hell, not bliss!
      And said, "Alas, greatest of woes is this!
      My darling enemy is called . . . Criseyde."
      And as he spoke that word he almost died.   875

126 When Pandar heard her name spoken aloud,
Lord, he was glad, and said, "My friend most dear,
For God's sake now be happy, gay and proud,
Love is on your side, be of good cheer.
In breeding, wisdom, poise, she has no peer,   880
Endowed with all this, and with gentleness.
You know yourself if she is fair, I guess!

127 I never saw a lady of her rank
More generous, more gay, nor in her ways
More friendly, gracious, quick to give or thank.   885
No one more apt to do good things always.
Nothing about her that one cannot praise.
Honoured by all. Look far and near, you'll find
Her queenlier than a queen, kinder than kind.

128 Therefore be cheerful, be of good comfort.   890
The most important thing in life is this,
To have good courage, and to be well taught,
In ordering one's days at peace, in bliss
With one's own self. So you should be, it is
Nothing but good to love well and love right.   895
To do so is not chance, but grace and light.

129 Be thankful, then, be glad and cheerful, too,
Because your lady is all goodness, she
Has every attribute of great virtue,
And with all these is sure to be some pity.   900
As for yourself, act with sincerity.
Ask nothing of her that will soil her name,
For virtue never stoops to deeds of shame.

130 I bless the day that ever I was born,
Now that I see you in so fine a place.   905
For, by my soul, in love, I could have sworn
You never would have fallen with such grace!

And you know why! You used to pull a face
At love in scorn, and in your malice call
The god 'Saint Idiot, lord of fools and all.'   910

131   How often you have made your foolish jokes,
And said that Love's true servants, every one
Were in their folly monkeys and dumb mokes!
And some, you said, lay munching meals alone
Tucked up in bed, and trying hard to groan.   915
And some of them, you swore, were white with fever,
And in your malice hoped they'd be so ever!

132   Others, you said, piled on against Love's cold
More than enough to guard their shivering skin.
And some, you said, pretended, lied and told   920
Their friends they could not sleep, yet deep in sin
Slept soft and sound! And so these thought to win
Good luck in love, yet were laid low at last,
Or so you said, jeering and mocking fast.

133   You also added, they, for the most part   925
Generalised about their woes and such,
And most of them to cure a wounded heart
And gain success hit out too hard, too much.
Now it's your turn. I'll jest at you and touch
Your wound, although I grant as yet you're not   930
Amongst those feeble lovers, that poor lot!

134   Now beat your breast, say to the god of Love,
'Forgive me, Lord, for now I do repent
All my misspoken words. Indeed I prove
Truly in love myself.' With good intent   935
Say this sincerely." "Cupid, I consent."
Said Troilus. "Lord, all my scorn forgive.
I'll never mock again, not whilst I live."

135 "You have said well," cried Pandar. "Now I hope
     Your meekness Cupid's anger has appeased.   940
     And since you've sept so much and seemed to mope,
     And shown repentance, that your lord is pleased.
     Now my sole wish is for you to be eased.
     May she, from whom has come your wound and woe
     Hereafter health and comfort send also.   945

136 For the same soil from which spring wicked weeds
     Bears healing herbs which spread in wholesomeness.
     Next to the rough, wild nettle gently feeds
     The soft, sweet rose with her smooth loveliness.
     Hills tower above the vale in loftiness.   950
     After the dark night dawns a golden morrow,
     And joy will end the tyranny of sorrow.

137 Now see that you ride with an easy rein,
     Sail with the tide, for that is always best,
     Else are we two both labouring in vain.   955
     He who is patient gets there with the rest.
     Be most discreet, true, diligent, with zest
     Live free and easy, persevere to serve
     Your love, and all will be as you deserve.

138 But he who's here and there and everywhere   960
     Is nowhere whole, or so write learned men.
     No wonder such folk fail in each affair!
     In other walks of life you'll find this happen.
     Watch! Those who plant a young tree in the garden
     Then dig it up to see if it is growing   965
     Will find there's never a bud or blossom showing!

139 So, since the God of Love has planted you
     Here, in this place, to suit your worthiness,
     Stay firmly rooted, this is where you'll do
     Best and prosper. And should heaviness   970

Oppress, be hopeful, and if dreariness
Or hurry puts our joint work to confusion,
I'll try to bring it to a good conclusion.

140   And do you know why I am not afraid
       To talk about this matter with my niece?   975
       Because I think of words wise scholars said,
       'As yet no living man or woman's peace
       Has not been ended as love's fires increase,
       Either of heavenly or the human kind.'
       And so I hope in her some grace to find.   980

141   But thinking of her in particular,
       So beautiful and young, the kind of love
       To suit her should be earthly. Though, so far,
       Her tastes and loves may quite well pious prove!
       Yet for a girl like her, warm as a dove,   985
       Better to take some lusty knight to tame her,
       And if she does not do so, I will blame her!

142   And so I am, and always will be, ready
       To take much trouble over helping you.
       Hoping to please you both, as I have said, I   990
       Look on you both as wise, and know you do
       Keep council in such wise that when you woo
       No one will be the wiser. And we three
       Will hug ourselves in happy secrecy!

143   Now, my opinion of you is so good   995
       That, by my soul, I think you so improved,
       Converted, made a new man, new in mood
       And action and demeanour since you loved.
       Love, in his goodness, has your worth approved,
       And made you his supporter, true and firm,   1000
       Whose solid strength will make his foemen squirm!

144   For an example, think of those wise men
Who formerly were pagans, steeped in sin,
Yet when converted from their wicked heathen
Ways, through God's grace blessedly begin   1005
To be most holy, and more converts win,
Strongest in faith are such as these, I know,
And best of all can errors overthrow."

145   When Troilus heard how Pandar had consented
To help him with his love toward Criseyde,   1100
His woe was healed, he felt quite untormented,
Yet his love burned much hotter, and he said
In sober wise, (although his gay heart played!)
"Now, joyful Venus, help me ere I die.
And Pandar, thank you, true and heartily.   1015

146   Yet, my dear friend, how will my woe grow less
Till all this has been done? Oh good, good Pandar,
What will you say of me and my distress?
I am afraid she will be moved to anger,
Refuse to listen or believe. And far   1020
Worst of all I dread and fear lest she
Will not take you, her uncle, seriously."

147   Said Pandar, laughing, "Are you sure you don't
Worry in case the Man in the Moon falls down?
What a fuss-pot you are! And I say, don't!   1025
Don't meddle, leave it all to me, you clown!
For God's sake, and I'm praying, act full grown!
Let me do things my own way, that's the best."
"All right," said Troilus, "Just as you request,

148   Only, one word more before you go.   1030
Don't misunderstand me, don't believe
I mean her any harm, or plan to do
Anything shameful that could hurt or grieve

D

My lady. I would rather die than live
To have her think I mean ought else but good　　1035
Towards her. And let this be understood."

149　Then Pandar laughed, "Ho, ho," and then answered,
"Am I your pledge, your pawn? Why, all act so!
I wouldn't care if she stood here and heard
All that you say. But goodbye, I will go.　　1040
Be glad I do. God speed us both also!
Give me the busyness, the toil and sweat.
From my success may you the sweetness get."

150　Then Troilus fell upon his knees, and gripping
Pandarus closely, cried most valiantly,　　1045
"Confusion to the Greeks! And in God's keeping
Be our affairs. And while I live I'll be
A scourge to those same Greeks if God helps me.
And yet I think I boast too much, my words
May come to roost again like boding birds.　　1050

151　Pandar, my friend, nothing more can I say.
You, all wise, know all, can do all, are all!
My life, my death, whole in your hands I lay.
Help me now," said he, "By my soul, I shall."
"God shield you, friend, and give help most especial 1055
In this, when you me to her recommend,
Criseyde, who can my life, or death command."

152　Then Pandar, greatly wanting now to serve
His greatest friend, spoke loud and clear his views.
"Goodbye. I soon shall all your thanks deserve.　　1060
Here is my hand. You soon shall have good news."
Then went his way, thinking how best to choose
A way to ask Criseyde for her grace,
And how to find best time for this, and place.

153 For every man who has a house to start   1065
    Makes no rash haste to build without a plan,
    But waits and thinks, makes blueprints in his heart,
    Feels, tests out all the ways and means he can,
    Building slow, step by step, and span by span.
    So Pandar in his mind worked it all out,   1070
    And, before moving, mapped a detailed route.

154 And Troilus lay no longer on his bed,
    But straightaway mounted upon his bay,
    And like a lion into combat sped.
    Woe to the Greeks who met with him that day!   1075
    Then, back in Troy, his manner was so gay,
    So pleasant, courteous, and so full of grace
    That all loved him who met him face to face.

155 For he was now of men the friendliest,
    The gentlest, the most generous and free,   1080
    Of all knights most successful and the best
    Of those who lived then, or might ever be.
    Gone was his mocking and his cruelty,
    His proud, disdainful looks and manner strange.
    And each fault to some virtue seemed to change.   1085

156 Now we'll have done with Troilus for a spell.
    For he is like a man, who, wounded sore
    Still limps with aching limb and is not well,
    Eased, certainly, but healed as yet no more.
    Yet, a good patient, waits to learn the lore   1090
    From him who is to set about a cure.
    So Troilus waited on for his adventure.   1092

Book Two

1   On, on, out of these black waves for to sail,
     O wind, O wind, the weather now blows clear,
     For in this sea the boat has such travail
     That with my skill I scarcely can it steer.
     This sea is what I call the troubles where   5
     In storm of deep despair sank Troilus.
     But these new times I think will be propitious.

2   O lady mine, whose name I know, Cleo,
     Sped me upon my way, and be my Muse.
     Help me to rhyme and finish what I do.   10
     No other craft or art I need to use.
     And so myself to lovers I excuse,
     Because this poem is not my fancy's song,
     But a translation from the Latin tongue.

3   And so for it I need no praise, nor blame
     For this whole work, but beg you, very meek
     That you'll excuse me if the words are lame,
     For what my author says, I, too, must speak.
     If what I say of love seems wan and weak,
     Remember, after all, it is not news!   20
     Also that those who're blind cannot judge hues!

4   You also know that forms of speech do change
     Within a thousand years, and words change, too.
     Those which were current years ago seem strange

To us today, yet once they spoke them so, 25
And sped as well in love as men now do.
Yet ways of winning love in different ages
And different lands change, too, in style and stages.

5 So, if it should fall out that any lovers
Listen to this my story, how it goes, 30
How Troilus sped, and what the tale discovers
Of how he won his lady's grace, and those
Lovers who listen, think, "Little he knows!"
I would not act so in my love affair!"
They must not doubt me though I was not there. 35

6 For everyone who makes his way to Rome
Does not go by the self same road or way.
And in some countries no success could come
To lovers if our customs they'd obey,
Did all the things we do, don't do or say! 40
For different people and for different places
Are laws and habits different as faces!

7 And, among my listeners, I dare say
There are not three who've said and done alike
When they were deep in love! And what well may 45
Suit one, will not fit others. One will write
His lady's name in trees, another strike
Initials deep in stone. But as for me,
I'm following my author carefully.

8 In May, mother of all the months of mirth, 50
When the fresh flowers of blue and white and red
Which winter slew, spring up into rebirth,
And in the meadows balmy airs are shed
Floating and soft, and the sun's plumes outspread
Tell how Taurus rules, it happened so 55
On May the third, as I am telling you,

9   That Pandarus, despite his wise words, felt
     The pangs of love himself so deep and strong
     That, though he'd preached of love, found his heart melt,
     His colour fade away, and before long   60
     He was so crossed in love, so vexed, he flung
     Himself upon his bed, yet before morning
     He lay tired out with tossing and with turning.

10   The swallow, Procne, with her sorrowful song
     As soon as it was light, began to mourn   65
     Of her sad fate. And Pandarus lay long
     In bed, half dozing, half awake and worn,
     When right into his ear her chittering on
     Of how Tereus ravished Philomel
     Dragged Pandar from his dreamy slumbering spell.   70

11   He called his servants and began to dress,
     Remembering what errand must be done
     For Troilus, and his serious business.
     Then cast a horoscope, and found the moon
     Favoured a journey, so he set out soon,   75
     And to his niece's palace made his way.
     Guide him, Janus, god of gates, I pray.

12   When he had reached his niece's house that day,
     "Where is your lady?" to her men said he.
     They told him, and he went in straightaway,   80
     And found two other ladies there, and she
     Sat with them in a cool paved room, the three
     Listening to a tale they wished to hear,
     "The Siege of Thebes", which a maid read out clear.

13   "Madam, God be with you all," he cried.   85
     "With you, your reader, book and company."
     "Why, uncle, welcome, welcome now indeed,"
     Said she, and rose, and talking cheerfully

His hand in hers, added, "And merrily
This evening will go on, since we have met."   90
Then by her on the seat her uncle set.

14   "Indeed, my niece, if God wills, all the year
You will do better!" said he, cheerfully.
"But I am sorry if my coming here
Has interrupted this fine history!   95
What is your book? Oh, tell us! Can it be
Something of love, so good for me to hear?"
"Uncle," she teased, "Your mistress is not here!"

15   And then they laughed together, and she said,
"The romance that we read tells about Thebes,   100
And of King Laius' death we have just read,
Of Oedipus, his son, and such sad deeds.
And here we stopped, look, at these letters red,
Just at the point where down Amphiorax fell,
Bishop though he was, right into Hell!"   105

16   Pandarus yawned and said, "All this I know,
And all about the siege of Thebes. So far
Twelve books about it have been written now!
No more of this. Now tell me how you are.
Take off your veil, and let your face be bare.   110
Shut up your book, get up and let us dance.
Its time we gave to May true observance."

17   "God forbid!" said she. "Are you quite mad?
Is this the way a widow should behave?
By all the gods, you frighten me, you bad   115
Wild man, it seems to me as if you rave!
Far better that I should sit in a cave
Anchoress-like, and read the good saints' lives.
Let maidens dance, and with them gay young wives."

18 "Now, as I live," then said this Pandarus,   120
    "There's something I could tell to make you gay!"
    "Now, uncle dear," she said, "Please tell it us,
    For God's love, say, is the siege done away?
    I'm so afraid of Greeks I almost die!"
    "No, by my soul," he said, "Not this, no no,   125
    Five times much better is the thing I know!"

19 "Oh, God," she said, "What ever thing is that?
    What, five times better! Uncle, now you tease.
    For all the world I cannot guess just what
    This thing could be! You're joking, uncle, please   130
    Tell me what is it, for I'll have no ease
    Unless you do, and I'm too dull to guess
    What are you thinking of, that I confess."

20 "As I am pledged to you, my niece most dear,
    And for my life, I cannot, will not tell!"   135
    "Oh, Uncle, why so?" said she. "Ah, you'll hear.
    Because if I should tell you, I know well
    You'd be the proudest woman of them all,
    Proudest of all who are in Troy alive.
    If I am joking, may I never thrive!"   140

21 Then she began to puzzle more and more
    A thousandfold, and looked down pensively,
    For never since her birth had she before
    Been so on fire with curiosity.
    Then sighed and turned towards him winningly.   145
    "Dear uncle, now I won't keep on or tease you,
    Nor ask more tiresome questions to displease you."

22 So after this, with cheerful jests and chat,
    And stories told in friendship and good cheer,
    They both amused themselves with this and that,   150
    Discussing what was strange, profound or queer

As friends do, talking of the things they hear,
Until she asked how Hector did, for long
Troy's bulwark, but to Greeks a scourge most strong.

23   "Thank God he's doing well," said Pandarus,   155
    "Save in his arm he has a little wound.
    Also his brisk young brother, Troilus—
    You may say he is Hector the second.
    In him all virtues that there are abound,
    Such as truth, and noble gentleness,   160
    Wisdom, honour, frankness, worthiness."

24   "Indeed," said she. "Uncle, that's good to hear.
    And God bless both of them. May they do well.
    Truly, I think it very right and proper
    For a King's son in battles to excel,   165
    And be well bred. For all too seldom dwell
    Together in one person, bravery,
    Goodness and knightly true nobility."

25   "Indeed, that's very true," said Pandarus.
    "But I can swear the King has two good sons,   170
    That is to say, Hector and Troilus,
    And even if I die for it at once
    I swear they've not a fault, and for the nonce
    There are no better men under the sun.
    All know their valour and what they have done.   175

26   There is no need of Hector's fame to tell.
    In all the world there is no better knight.
    He is, in fact, of all good things a well.
    He well may have more valour than he might!
    And this knows many a wise and worthy knight.   180
    The same is true of Troilus, and I swear,
    God help me, there's no peer for this good pair!"

27 "By all the gods," said she, "That's very true
    Of Hector, and of Troilus certainly.
    I hear on all sides of his valour, too,   185
    The fearless way he fights, so gallantly,
    And in this town behaves so very gently
    To everyone, that he must win the prize
    Amongst those men I feel deserve most praise."

28 "That's very true indeed," said Pandarus.   190
    "For yesterday whoever was with him
    Must have been quite amazed at Troilus,
    For like a swarm of bees, in fighting grim
    Before him flew the Greeks with trembling limb.
    All through the battle field, in every ear   195
    Rang one cry only, "Troilus is here!"

29 Now here, now there, he hunted them so fast,
    All flowed with Grecian blood, and Troilus
    Harried them sorely, down the foe were cast.
    Wherever he was fighting it went thus.   200
    Death he brought to them, but life to us.
    Throughout the day no one dared him withstand
    So long as that red sword smoked in his hand.

30 Yet with all this he is the friendliest man
    For someone of his rank, that ever I met.   205
    And when he wishes with good fellowship can
    Honour the friends on whom his favour's set."
    With these words Pandar, quick as he could get,
    Began to take his leave. "Now I must go."
    "It's my fault, uncle," said she, "if you do,   210

31 Why, what's the matter than you've tired so quickly,
    Especially of women! Must you go?
    No, sit down, uncle. There are matters prickly,
    Business affairs I must discuss with you."

Then all her friends and servants hearing so,   215
Went further off to give them privacy,
So any serious talk might secret be.

32   Then when she'd told him all she wished to do
Of her affairs, estate, and legal ties,
Said Pandar, "Now it's time for me to go,   220
But first, let's dance a little. Come, arise,
Take off your widow's veil, let's see your eyes.
Why do you make yourself an old scarecrow
Now that adventure's on the way to you!"

33   "Adventure! For the love of God!" she said   225
"What do you mean?" Why, aren't you going to tell?"
"No," he replied. "Theres no time now. We need
Leisure for that. Moreover, you might well
Take what I say amiss, and make me quell!
Better for me to hold my tongue than say   230
True words that might upon your conscience weigh.

34   For by Minerva, niece, I swear to you,
By Jupiter, who makes the thunder ring,
By joyous Venus, whom, as lovers do,
I worship, you're the only woman living   235
(Apart from mistresses) to my knowing
That I love best, and am most loath to grieve.
Of that you're well aware, so I believe!"

35   "Yes, uncle," said she, "And I thank you, too.
You've always been my firmest, truest friend.   240
I've trusted no man quite so much as you,
And given you so little in the end.
Yet, by God's grace, I hope my wit to mend.
Not for all the world I'd cause you pain,
And if I have, I'll make it right again.   245

36   So, for God's love, I beg you and beseech,
     For you are he whom I both love and trust,
     Please, please explain your strange and curious speech.
     Uncle, speak out to me, your niece. You must!"
     She cried. Her uncle took and kissed her first,   250
     Then said, "Most certainly, Criseyde, my dear.
     I speak now for your good, all that you'll hear."

37   So modestly she looked down at the floor,
     And Pandar coughed and cleared his throat a little,
     Then said, "My dear, in telling tales, before   255
     Men reach the point, they circle, twist and whittle
     Their words with subtle art and conceits brittle,
     Yet, for all that, their whole design is tending
     To one thing, one thing only, to the ending!

38   And since the ending gives each tale its strength, 260
     And since to help's my story's point and end,
     Why should I paint, or draw it out at length?
     Certainly not to you, my niece and friend."
     He, as he spoke, began to stare and send
     Most penetrating looks into her face,   265
     Then added, "In such mirror there's much grace."

39   Then to himself he said, "If I spin out
     My tale, or make it difficult or long,
     She'll not enjoy its savour, and will doubt
     My good intentions, taking me all wrong!   270
     Innocent, simple minds suspect the strong
     Involved discourse they cannot understand.
     My tale I'll soften so it fits her hand!"

40   Then he looked hard at her in eager wise,
     And she knew well that he was staring so, 275
     And said, "Lord, lord, you peer so with your eyes,
     Is it the first time you've seen me, or no?"

"Yes, and you'll seem much better when I go!
If luck was in your face most anxiously
I sought to find. Soon all this luck will see!   280

41   For luck, good luck comes swimming to us all
In turn, if we are ready to receive it.
Yet he who turns away and will not haul
The proferred fish, but stupidly will leave it,   285
Well, niece, good luck and fortune don't deceive, it
Is his own folly and crass laziness
Which brings down on his head deserved distress.

42   And you have such good luck, my lovely girl,
Sailing towards you, and can catch it now.
So, for God's love, and mine, take up the pearl   290
Before it's gone. This, niece, I beg of you.
Why should I make my story longer grow?
Give me your hand. In all the world there's none
Luckier than you, if you'll take what you've won.

43   And since I speak with every good intention,   295
As I have told you many times before,
And have in mind your honest reputation
Better than any other man, therefore
I swear by every oath I ever swore,
If you are angry, or believe I lie,   300
I'll never see you more before I die!

44   So don't be scared. Why do you tremble so?
Don't look aghast, or lose your lovely hue,
The worst part now is past and done, you know,
And though the story that I tell is new,   305
Trust in me, niece, and you will find me true.
If I believed this news I have unfitting
For you to hear, d'you think I would it bring?"

45 "Oh, uncle dear, now, for God's sake, I pray,"
    Said she, "Come off it, tell me what it is!   310
    For I'm so terrified of what you'll say,
    And yet so curious to know what this
    Thing of yours can be, good or amiss.
    Do speak, don't let me in such terror dwell."
    "So I will do. Then listen, and I'll tell.   315

46 Now, my dear niece, the King's beloved son,
    Good, fresh and generous, wise and truly worthy,
    Who, throughout all his life kind deeds has done,
    Noble Prince Troilus loves you so entirely,
    That if you do not pity, he will die,   320
    And this is all. Now what more can I say?
    Your choice will give him life, or death today.

47 But if you let him die, I'll perish, too.
    I swear to you, Criseyde, and it's no lie,
    With this knife here I'll cut my throat right through!" 325
    And with these words the tears poured from his eye.
    "And if through you the pair of us must die,
    Both guiltless, then you will have had good sport!
    What use to you the two dead fish so caught!

48 Alas, the prince, my lord and friend most dear,   330
    That good, true man, that gentle, noble knight,
    Who only wants your friendship and good cheer,
    I see him failing as he walks upright.
    Hurrying towards his death with all his might,
    If it is Fortune's and your will he die.   335
    Why did the gods give you such fatal beauty?

49 And if you are so heedless and so cruel
    As not to trouble more about his fate,
    A man like this, so worthy, such a jewel,
    Than for the death of wretches fit for hate,   340

If you're so hard, your beauty won't equate
For all the cruelty of such a deed.
Of deep and wise reflection you have need!

50   The loveliest gem, if flawed, is valueless.
      A herb which holds no healing is a weed.   345
      Beauty without some pity cold and useless,
      And wretched they who scorn all things, indeed.
      And you, the sum of beauty, flower and seed,
      If there is no compassion found in you,
      I say your life brings harm, and evil, too.   350

51   And do not think I'm talking lightly now.
      I'd rather, niece, that we were hanged, all three,
      High up, in view of all, than stoop so low
      As to be procurer for him! For see,
      I am your uncle, and the shame for me   355
      Would equal yours, if, through a near relation
      You lost your honour and your reputation.

52   Now understand, that this is all I ask,
      No promise, nothing binding, and no vow,
      But only that you smile on him, a task   360
      That's light indeed; be friendlier, kinder now.
      At least to save his life some liking show!
      This sums and totals up my whole intent.
      God help me, nothing more than this was meant!

53   And I have cause enough for this request,   365
      And reason, too, in making it to you.
      I can see clearly how, within your breast
      Doubts war with fears. You're scared of gossip. True,
      They may talk, but, take my assurance, do,
      No one with sense will say he comes to see   370
      You but in friendship and civility.

54 For even when men haunt the temples daily
    Nobody thinks the gods they there devour!
    And he, your Troilus, also will not fail. He
    Governs himself so well by sheer will power   375
    That all men praise him as of knights the flower.
    Besides, he'll visit you so seldom here
    That if all Troy should watch, you need not fear!

55 Love between friends, this is the custom here!
    So wrap and wear this pleasant cloak also,   380
    And as God is my judge, Criseyde dear,
    As I have said, it's best to do just so,
    Remember, my good niece, to ease his woe,
    Pour sugar in the sourness of your fear,
    Lest through your scruples die my friend most dear!" 385

56 Criseyde, who heard him speaking in this wise
    Thought, "Soon enough I'll feel and know his meaning,"
    "Now, uncle," said she, "What do you devise?
    And what advise me? Which way are you leaning?"
    "Well said, my girl. It's best for you, I'm feeling, 390
    To love him in return. That way, the gains
    Of love for love win Love by skilful games.

57 Think also, child, how age wastes, hour by hour
    In all you girls a part of your beauty,
    And so, before old age can you devour,   395
    And with it, chance of love, give generously
    In love, and let this proverb precept be—
    'Too late', said Beauty, when her fairness passed
    And old age mocked her cruel disdain at last.

58 At court the King's Fool jeers and cries aloud   400
    Whenever he sees women's pride flare high.
    "Oh, you may live long lives and puff up proud
    Until crows' feet are growing round your eye.

E

Then may you have a glass in which to pry
And see your face, and with it all tomorrow." 405
Ah, niece, I wish you no more care and sorrow!"

59   Pandar was silent then, and hung his head.
Criseyde burst into tears, and weeping, cried,
"Alas, woe, woe, why am I not struck dead?
I can trust no one now, all faith has died.   410
To danger, strangers, all doors open wide—
For he I thought to be my dearest friend
Tells me to love, when he should me defend.

60   Alas, I would have thought, and never doubted
That if I, through misfortune, fell in love   415
With Hector, or Achilles so stout hearted,
Or even with Troilus, you would disapprove,
Reproach in anger, and with frowns reprove,
No moderation and no mercy showing.
But this false world, who knows what way it's going! 420

61   Why, is *this* thing the joy and celebration,
Is *this* your council, this my happy fate!
Is this the sum of all your protestation
About which you made so much song of late?
All to this end! Oh, Pallas, now my state   425
Is cruel. Uncle, how could you so place me
In dread and danger that must soon disgrace me?"

62   With that she sighed in deep and gloomy sorrow.
"Ah, must you view it so?" said Pandarus.
"By God, I'll come no more today, tomorrow.   430
Since in God's sight I am mistrusted thus.
Little enough you care for both of us!
Whether we live or die—O cruelty—
Let him live, niece, no matter about me!

63 O cruel god, unpitying, wicked Mars.   435
    O furies straight from Hell, to you I cry,
    Let me not leave this house, O evil stars,
    If I meant any harm or villany.
    But since I see my lord and friend must die,
    I, too, I here confess, with my last breath,   440
    You wickedly condemn us both to death.

64 But since you clearly want me to be dead,
    By Neptune, watery god of the whole sea,
    From this day forth I'll eat no crumb of bread
    Till I my own outpouring heart's blood see,   445
    For truly I will die as well as he."
    Then up he sprang, to rush away pell mell,
    Until she caught him by his coat's lapel.

65 Criseyde, who almost died with pangs of fear,
    For she was the most fearful of the race   450
    Of women, heard these words beat at her ear,
    And saw her uncle's earnest, careworn face,
    Yet thought the thing he asked of her disgrace,
    And terrified of this, and that, and more,
    Began to fear and fret and worry sore.   455

66 She thought, "Why do these sad misfortunes happen
    Continually in love? And in this way?
    Alas for all the wickedness of men!
    Now if my uncle Pandarus should slay
    Himself before me in my house today,   460
    What will folk say, whatever will they think?
    I must tread carefully round this slippery brink."

67 Sighing again, she said, three times in all—
    "Lord, Lord, I'm so unhappy, feel such grief.
    The choice, to lose my good name, or let fall   465
    The balance, and then lose my uncle's life.

Yet, with God's help there'll be an end to strife.
I'll work it so that I my honour keep,
And he his life." And so she ceased to weep.

68   "Faced with two harms, the lesser one must choose.   470
       Better for me to give encouragement
       With honour, than my uncle's life to lose.
       You're sure that nothing more than this was meant?"
       "No, no, dear niece," said he in great content.
       "That's good," she cried. "Then I will do my part,   475
       And counter to my will constrain my heart.

69   Yet I'll make no false promise to a knight,
       Nor love him, not unless love comes to me
       Of my free will. In other ways I might,
       Safeguarding reputation, pleasantly   480
       Meet and talk with him. Fears alone, and shy
       Dread kept me back, made me say 'No' to you.
       Yet when cause ceases, illness ceases, too.

70   And here I make my open protestation.
       In this affair if you should deeper go,   485
       Not even for your rescue, or salvation
       Of you, if you should kill yourself, you two,
       Not even if the whole world turned my foe,
       Will I grant more to him than I have said."
       "Well, I agree," said Pandar. "True indeed.   490

71   But can I trust you'll keep your word?" said he,
       "And will you hold to what you've promised here,
       And not go back on what you've said to me?"
       "Why, certainly," cried she, "My uncle dear."
       "And I will have no cause in this matter   495
       To grumble or complain of you, or preach?"
       Certainly not! No need for further speech."

72   So then they gaily talked of this and that,
     Till at the last, "Good uncle," cried Criseyde,
     "For love of God who made us, tell me what   500
     And when you first knew of his woe. Beside
     You, do men know of it?" "No," Pandar cried.
     And then she asked, "Can he speak well of love?
     Tell me, then I'll prepare, and ready prove!"

73   Then Pandarus, giving a little smile   505
     Said, "Niece, now to you everything I'll tell.
     The other day, in fact, not a long while
     Back, in the palace garden, by a well
     Troilus and I were loitering for a spell,
     Planning strategy, and how we could   510
     Defeat the Greeks with plans both neat and good.

74   Soon afterwards we started exercise,
     And practised casting darts and spears, until
     Troilus was tired, said he would sleep, his eyes
     Were heavy. On the grass he slept his fill,   515
     Whilst I walked up and down, debating still,
     Until I heard, as I paced there alone
     How he began to toss and turn and groan.

75   So I crept up, and tiptoeing behind
     (For certainly, I'll tell you truthfully   520
     Exactly how I call it all to mind),
     I heard him cry to Love most ruefully.
     He said, 'Lord, pity all my misery.
     Although I have been rebel in intent,
     Now, mea culpa, Lord, I do repent!   525

76   O mighty God, by whose true disposition
     The strongest men are led, through whose just hand
     All find their place, hear this, my meek confession,
     And send me fitting penance, yet command

Me not to hopelessness, but bold to stand.   530
Then shall my happy spirit go from thee.
Be thou my shield in all benignity.

77   For truly, Lord, she has me deeply wounded,
      She, who stood in black, with her bright eye,
      That to the bottom of my heart it sounded,   535
      And through this wound I feel that I must die,
      This is the bitterest stroke, I'll not deny.
      For hotter seem those embers glowing red
      When they are mixed with ashes pale and dead.'

78   When he had said these words, he hung his head,   540
      And muttered, what, I know not truthfully.
      So then I tiptoed off with quiet tread,
      As if I'd not heard his soliloquy.
      But came and stood close by, and quietly
      Said, "Wake up, you are sleeping far too long.   545
      You're not in love, to snooze and snore so strong,

79   And sleep so soundly that you I can't wake!
      Who ever saw so dull and doped a man!"
      'Yes, yes, my friend,' said he, 'Your head may ache
      For love, but let me live as best I can!'   550
      But though with sorrow he was pale and wan,
      He put on such a cheerful countenance,
      As if about to lead the latest dance!

80   Nothing more happened till the other day.
      It happened I was going all alone   555
      Into his room, and there I saw he lay
      Upon his bed, and there gave such a groan
      As never yet I heard, and what his moan
      Was of, I did not know, for as I came
      He ceased to sigh, to weep and to complain.   560

81   This made me feel suspicious, so I crept
     Nearer, and found that he was weeping sore,
     And, as God is my judge, so much he wept,
     I never pitied any creature more,
     Hardly by ingenuity or lore   565
     Could I from death this wretched Troilus keep,
     And even now to think of him I weep!

82   And yet, God knows, never since I was born
     Was I so careful not to scold or preach,
     Nor had so many oaths of friendship sworn   570
     As I to him, before he'd tell or teach
     Me of his troubles. But that woeful speech!
     Don't ask me to recall his sad complaint
     Unless you want to see me droop and faint!

83   And yet to save his life, and this alone,   575
     Not to harm you, my dear, I am thus driven,
     So, for God's love, who made us, skin and bone,
     Be kind to him, that way, life will be given
     To us. Now I've confessed, may I be shriven!
     And since you know that my intent is clean   580
     And innocent, note I no evil mean.

84   Good luck and fortune may the gods prepare
     For you, who've caught such fish without a net.
     And may you be as wise as you are fair,
     More firm within the ring than ruby set.   585
     Never before were lovers so well met
     As will be when you're his as he is yours.
     God grant I see that happiest of all hours!"

85   "I never said a thing of that!" said she.
     "Now you've spoilt everything, and shamed the rest!" 590
     "Oh, please have mercy, dear niece," then said he,
     "Those things I said, I meant them for the best,

By Mars, the god of war, in cold steel dressed.
Niece, don't be angry, for we're kin, we two."
"Oh, well," she cried, "Then I'll forgive it you."   595

86 With this he took his leave and home he went,
And lord, how glad he was of so much done.
Criseyde arose, and more or less content,
Went straightaway into her quiet room,
And there sat down as still as any stone,   600
And all the words he'd said began to wind
Round in her brain just as they came to mind,

87 Feeling somewhat surprised, disturbed and shaken
At what had happened, but with some reflection
And quiet thought, she felt that she had taken   605
Fright foolishly. A man may feel affection
Or love for any woman to distraction,
And think his heart within his breast may crack,
 Yet only if she wills need she love back!

88 But as she sat alone thinking this way,   610
A shout was heard, a sound of skirmishing,
Men in the street cried, "Troilus with dismay
Has filled the Greeks, their troops are trembling."
And all her servants shouted out, hurraying,
"Let's see, let's see, open the lattice wide,   615
For to the palace through the street he'll ride,

89 There is no other way back from the gate
Of Dardanus, where they took off the chain."
And as they shouted, there he rode in state
With all his men, jogging with easy rein,   620
And two by two, jostling in double lane.
This was his lucky day. Necessity
May not break into such serenity.

90 This Troilus sat there on his bright bay steed,
    In armour richly clad, but bare of head,   625
    His horse was wounded, and began to bleed
    Although he rode it gently with quiet tread.
    A knightly sight he made, or so they said,
    As if one saw the god of war go by,
    The mighty Mars himself armed cap-a-pie.   630

91 So soldierly he was, so true a knight
    To look at, and so skilled in high prowess,
    For he had brawn and body, strength and might
    To do all knighty acts with skilfulness,
    And so to see him in his battle dress,   635
    So fresh, so young, with such dexterity
    Was heaven itself and pure felicity.

92 His helmet had been hewn in twenty places,
    And hung behind his back held by a thread,
    His shield was dashed and marked with swords
                                          and maces,   640
    And many saw the arrows which had sped
    Piercing its sinews, horn and hide. They said,
    "Here comes our hero, see, here rides our joy,
    Next to his brother holder-up of Troy!"

93 At which he reddened, blushing modestly,   645
    Hearing the people shouting out his praise,
    And those who saw him smiled in joy to see
    How shy and serious was his downcast gaze,
    Criseyde saw how he looked, his modest ways,
    And let it in her heart so quietly sink,   650
    She thought, "Who gave me love potions to drink!"

94 For her own thoughts had made her blush quite red,
    And she remembered now, "Why, this is he
    Whom Uncle Pandar said will soon be dead

Unless for him I've mercy and pity—"   655
And with that thought in shame and modesty
She pulled her head in from the window fast,
Just as he and the crowd all jostled past.

95 And then she started rolling up and down
Within her mind his deeds, his great prowess,   660
His rank, position, also his renown,
His wit, his shape, also his gentleness.
But what she thought of most was the distress
Which she had made him feel, most wrong to do
A man to death whose love was right and true!   665

96 Now envious people might well grumble thus,
"Quick work, to love like this, how could it be
That she so lightly loved young Troilus
Right at first sight, and all so easily?"
Whoever thinks like that thinks stupidly!   670
For everything must somehow have beginning,
Before all's done, and the thread finished spinning.

97 And I don't say that she so suddenly
Gave him her love, merely that she inclined
To like him first, and I have told you why,   675
And then his manhood, and the way he pined
Made love go burrowing deeply in her mind.
And in this way, by time and true service
He gained her love, and in no other wise.

98 Delightful Venus, too, rightly disposed   680
Was in her seventh House in heaven that day,
Her aspect right, her favours ripe and poised
To help poor Troilus out of his dismay.
Truly she was by no means enemy
To Troilus in his horoscope at birth,   685
And so she helped him on to joy and mirth.

99   Now let us leave this Troilus for a space.
Let him ride on, and turn to fair Criseyde,
There, where she hangs her head and hides her face
Sitting alone, and trying to decide   690
How she will speak and act, and much beside.
For she knew well her uncle would not stop
From pressing Troilus' case both neck and crop!

100   And lord, over again she argued out
This case which I've explained to you and told,   695
What she should do, and what avoid or doubt.
She pleated all these thoughts in many a fold.
Now her poor heart was warm, now it was cold,
And all her thoughts, well, some of them I'll write,
Those that my author bothers to indite.   700

101   Firstly she thought that Troilus' person
She knew by sight, also his gentleness,
And to herself she said, "Though it's not done
To grant him love, yet for his worthiness
It would be right, light-hearted, with gladness   705
And honesty, placed as I am, to deal
With him in friendship, and his heart to heal.

102   For I know well that he is the King's son,
And since to see me he has such delight,
If altogether I his presence shun,   710
Maybe he'd view me with extreme despite,
Through which I'd quickly be in much worse plight.
Now, is it wise to make an enemy
Without need, when I might have amiety?

103   There is a middle way in everything,   715
For though a man may censure drunkenness,
He does not stop all other men from drinking,
And make a universal drought, I guess!

And though I know I caused his great distress,
For that, I should not one like him despise.   720
Since it is so, all for the best he tries.

104   And for a long time I have known quite well
He is well mannered, and he is no fool,
Nor is he boastful, or so others tell.
He is too sensible for such a school!   725
Not one who'd brag of those he'd made his tool,
Of how he loved and wooed, and won the day.
He'd never make me his in such a way!

105   Now, let me think. The worst thing might be this,
People to think he is in love with me!   730
Yet how could this dishonour or distress
Me? Can I stop it? No, no, certainly.
Why, I and everyone can hear and see
That men love women all through this city.
Are they the worse for this? No, certainly.   735

106   I'm thinking, too, how he is free to choose
From all the women here the very best
To be his love, provided she won't lose
Her reputation, for he's worthiest
Of men, save Hector, who is first and best.   740
Yet in my hand his life, his heart I hold.
But that's the way love, and my fate, unfold.

107   Nor is it strange that he should love me so,
For, to be honest, I myself know well,
(Although this thought I hope that none will know!) 745
That of the women who in this place dwell
I am among the fairest, truth to tell,
Or so men say throughout the town of Troy.
So then what wonder if I give him joy?

108   And I am my own mistress, well at ease,   750
       Thanks be to God, in rank and in estate.
       Youthful, I range untied through fresh green leas,
       With none to curb or rage in jealous state.
       No husband here to say to me 'Checkmate'.
       For men are either full of jealousy,   755
       Or masterful, or out for novelty.

109   What shall I do? And why do I live so?
       And if I wish to, why not fall in love?
       My goodness, I'm no nun, to lie so low!
       And even if love should my own heart move   760
       To find its rest in him, he'll worthy prove.
       And if I keep my honour and good name
       In fact, to love will bring no harm or shame."

110   But even as when the sun shines out most bright
       In March, when skies and seasons change their face, 765
       And clouds are flushed up by the wind in flight
       To overspread and veil the sun a space,
       A cloudy thought through her began to pace,
       And overspread the sunshine of her thinking,
       So that for fear she was in faintness sinking.   770

111   The thought was this—"Alas, since I am free,
       Should I now love, and put in jeopardy
       My safety, and start shackling liberty?
       How dare I think so very foolishly?
       May I not well in other women see   775
       Their anxious joy, constraint and constant pain?
       None love who do not also weep and plain.

112   For love is the most stormy sort of life
       Inherently, to choose, for anyone.
       For always some mistrust or foolish strife   780
       Crops up in love, some cloud will dim the sun.

And as for we poor women, nothing can
We do when love goes wrong, but weep and think
. Our lot is this, our cup of tears to drink.

113   Also so many spiteful tongues are ready   785
       To gossip of us. Also men aren't true.
       Their lust, their love fades quickly, burns unsteady.
       They soon fall out of love and look for new.
       But harm once done is done, though one may rue
       For though most men may seem with love
                                     deep pierced,   790
       The sharpest points are those which break the first.

114   How often, oh, how often have we known
       Such treason, woes that women must endure.
       I can't see why such seed of love is sown.
       Where does it go when dead and beyond cure?   795
       There's no one born who knows the place for sure
       Where dead love goes. None stumble on its grave.
       Nothing to nothing turns, we nothing have.

115   Besides, if I should love, I'll have to work
       So hard to hoodwink scandal-mongering folk,   800
       All those in whom back-biting spirits lurk,
       For even if there's no flame in the smoke
       They see a fire, and with their words they poke!
       And who can bridle every wicked tongue,
       Or hush the clamouring bells when they are rung!" 805

116   After all that, her thoughts began to clear.
       She said, "But he who nothing undertakes
       Gains nothing, be he bold, or full of fear."
       Then more ideas come. With fear she shakes,
       Her hopes all sleeping, now with dread she quakes, 810
       Now hot, now cold. So, putting thought away
       She rose and went out to relax and play.

117   Downstairs she went, and straightway out of doors
       Into the garden with her nieces three,
       And up and down the paths without a pause   815
       Went she, Flexippe, Tharbe, Antigone,
       So merrily that it was joy to see.
       And others of her women, crowding there
       Followed her through the garden everywhere.

118   Large was this garden, pleached and fenced
                                         the alleys,   820
       All shadowed by sweet blossomy branches green,
       With benches of fresh turf and sanded ways,
       Through which they all walked arm in arm between,
       And then Antigone, fair as a queen
       Began to sing a Trojan song, so clear   825
       It was like heaven her lovely voice to hear.

119   She sang, "O Love, to whom I am and shall
       Be humbly subject, true in my intent,
       As best I can, to you, Lord, I give all
       For ever more, my heart's desire to rent,   830
       For so much grace and mirth was never lent
       To anyone more freely than to me,
       For you have showered down joy so generously.

120   Yes, god of bliss, you have so choicely set
       Me in my love, that any creature living   835
       Could not be happier, or more joy have met.
       For, lord, with never a jealous word, nor chiding
       I love a man, attentive, ever striving
       To serve me well, unwearied and unfeigning,
       The best on earth, most true, most undesigning.   840

121   He is the very well of worthiness,
       The ground of truth, mirror of all that's good,
       In wit Apollo, stone of trustiness,

The root of virtue, joy his warm's heart's blood.
From me he's driven every sorrowing mood.   845
In truth I love him best, so he does me.
Now good luck be with him, where'er he be.

122   Whom should I thank but you, dear god of Love
For all this bliss in which I now begin
To bathe? And thank you, lord, because I love.   850
This is the true, the right life that I'm in,
Which banishes each kind of vice and sin.
Love makes me so much to all good things tend
That day by day my life and deeds amend.

123   Whatever man says love is wrong or sinful,   855
Or slav'ry, (though his words he may regret,)
Is either envious or a downright fool,
Or is too deep in selfish badness set
To love. Such people I have often met,
Who run down love, yet nothing of him know,   860
They talk a lot, yet never bent his bow!

124   Why, does the sun lose heat, or shine less bright
Because a man, through weakness of his eye
Cannot endure its brilliancy of light?
And is love wrong because of such outcry?   865
No joys are real that cannot sad tears dry.
Let him who has a head of glass look out
For showering stones, and fence himself about.

125   But I, with all my heart and all my might
As I have said, will love until I die   870
My dear heart, my true lover, my own knight
In whom my own heart's roots so deeply lie
And his in mine throughout eternity.
Though first I feared to love him was a sin,
I know well now, no perils are therein."   875

126 And with these loving words her song she ended,
     And as she did so, "Now, niece," said Criseyde,
     "Who wrote this song, with words and music blended?"
     Antigone replied at once, and said
     "Madam, my aunt, it was the worthiest maid   880
     Of birth and rank in all the town of Troy,
     Who led her life in honour, peace and joy."

127 "Truly it seems so by her happy song,"
     Criseyde then said, and she began to sigh.
     "Lord, is there really such real joy among   885
     Lovers, as poets sing in minstrelsy?"
     "Of course there is," said fair Antigone.
     "Although as yet no living man, I guess
     Has properly described love's happiness.

128 Yet do not think that every wretched man   890
     Knows the true bliss of love! No, of course not.
     Not all can touch true fire because one can!
     Not on your life! Most folks are never hot!
     People who want to hear of heaven, what
     Is lovely there must ask true saints to tell,   895
     And likewise devils what is done in Hell!

129 Criseyde made no comment, only said,
     "Well, well, and night will very soon be here."
     But she'd heard every word, and down it sped
     To be imprisoned in her heart. Now fear   900
     Of love began to lessen and appear
     Milder, more sweet. She felt her spirits glow
     With warmth. She'd changed. The seeds of love
                                          might grow.

130 The medal of the day, the heaven's eye
     The enemy of night, (I mean the sun,)   905
     Slid westwards, downward slipping crookedly
     F

Like one who had his daily errands run.
And white and shining things grew dim and dun
For lack of light, and stars shone in the sky.
Criseyde and all her folk went in quickly.   910

131   So, when she had grown tired and wished to rest,
And all had gone who ought by right to go,
She longed for sleep, and made her mild request
To all her maids to make her bed, and so
When all was hushed, and lights burned dim and low 915
She lay and thought of this, and that, *and* that—
You who are wise, do not need telling what!

132   A nightingale upon a cedar green
Under the bedroom wall in which she lay
Sang loud and clear against the bright
                                moon's sheen,   920
Perhaps, in his bird's wise, a lovely lay
Of love that made her heart feel fresh and gay.
She listened to his song gladly, wide-eyed,
Then at the last a deep sleep seized Criseyde.

133   And as she slept a dream she quickly met,   925
A mighty eagle, ivory white in plume
Under her breast his long, sharp talons set,
And then dragged out her heart, yet very soon
Put his own heart where there was space and room,
And she felt never a pang or pain or smart,   930
So off he flew, with heart exchanged for heart.

134   So let her sleep, and now our tale unfold
Of Troilus, as he to his palace rode
Away from skirmishings, of which I told,
And in his room he sat, and there abode   935
Till messengers he'd sent upon the road
For Pandarus, after long search was past
Found him and brought him to his friend at last.

135   This Pandar entered with one mighty bound
Into the room, and said, "Who has been beat   940
Today with sword and spear and slingstones round,
But Troilus, who's now in feverish heat!"
Teasing and mocking him, he said "You sweat!
But now get up and let us dine and rest."
And Troilus meekly answered, "You know best."   945

136   And so, as quickly as they could, they went
To supper, and from supper to their bed.
Out of the room were all the servants sent,
And quickly off to their own ploys they sped.
But Troilus felt as if his sad heart bled   950
With woe, until he heard some love tiding,
And said, "What news? Am I to weep or sing?"

137   Said Pandarus, "Lie still and let me sleep!
Be quiet! I've done your errand speedily.
Your choice now if you sing or dance or leap!   955
In short, and you need have no doubts of me,
My niece, Criseyde, will kind and courteous be,
And love you best, by God and by my word.
Only you lag behind, in sloth immured.

138   For so far I have all your love work done,   960
From day to day, till this day, that I vow.
And from her friendly love for you have won,
And she has pledged true faith. So your woes now
Have one leg less, are growing weak and slow."
But why do I repeat all this anew?   965
Pandar told Troilus just what I've told you.

139   But even as flowers, all through the chill of night
Close up, and on their stalks are bending low,
Yet shoot up briskly when the sun shines bright,
Opening, as is their nature, row on row,   970

So Troilus began to look up so,
And cried to Venus, "O my lady dear,
Your power, your grace, I praise and bless it here."

140   And then to Pandarus stretched out his hands
And said, "All that I have I give to you,   975
For I am whole, broken my fettering bands.
And if a thousand Trojans, two by two
Rendered me tribute, gave, and gave anew
They could not please me as you've done. My heart
Stretches with joy so it will come apart.   980

141   But lord, what shall I do, how shall I live?
When shall I next my dear, my sweet heart see?
How can I the lagging minutes drive
Until again you'll go to her from me?
Ah, you may answer, 'Patience, wait.' But he   985
That's in a noose and by the neckbone hangs
In great discomfort wriggles at the pangs."

142   "By Mars, be easy, don't you worry now,"
Said Pandarus, "For all there's time and place.
Stay here in bed till night and darkness go,   990
For just as surely as I see your face
Here at my side, will I at dawning race
And do your work for you. If I do not,
Commission someone else here on the dot!

143   By God, by God, I have been ever yet   995
Ready to help you, right up to this night
I've sweated, used up every grain of wit,
Done all you asked, and shall, with all my might.
So now obey me, and you'll do alright.
And if you will not, sing your own love song!   1000
You can't blame me if things are going wrong!

144 I know that you're a wiser man than I,
     Much wiser, but if I were in your shoes
     God help me, I would sit immediately
     And with my own hand write to her with news,   1005
     A letter telling her my woes, my blues
     All due to love, and beg her, pity me.
     Get on with it, don't slack so lazily.

145 And I will take it to her straightaway,
     Then, when you know that I am with her there,   1010
     Get on your finest horse, the splendid bay,
     Dress yourself up in all your smartest gear
     And ride past where she lives, as if it were
     By chance, and you shall find us in a seat
     Close by the window, staring at the street.   1015

146 Then, if you wish to, you can greet us there,
     And smile upon me with a pleasant face.
     But do not loiter, and take special care
     To be well on your guard. Go then with grace,
     Keeping your council, ride with steady pace,   1020
     And we will talk about you when you turn
     Your back, enough to make your two ears burn!

147 About your letter, you have wit enough,
     One suitable, I think you can indite.
     Don't show off, using phrases hard and tough.   1025
     Don't be too stiff, or like some dull clerk write.
     Blot it with tears, don't make the page too white,
     And if you write with good words, tenderly,
     Please don't repeat yourself too frequently.

148 For if the best of harpers yet alive   1030
     Should on the best-tuned and most cheerful harp
     That ever was, with all his fingers five
     Play one string only, then the tune would warp,

Even with skilful hand and nails made sharp,
All those who heard would want their ears to be   1035
Deaf to such dull and dreary minstrelsy.

149   Don't, to use terms of physic, mix or jumble
Drugs, or put in what will disagree.
Or, to use love's terms, see you do not fumble,
Keep to the point, and write with clarity.   1040
An artist painting fish within the sea
Won't give them heads of ape and hooves of moke.
That would be stupid and beyond a joke!"

150   All this advice seemed good to Troilus,
But as a nervous lover, he said this,   1045
"Alas, my dear friend, trusty Pandarus,
I dare not write to her, my joy and bliss
In case through foolishness I write amiss,
Or that in anger she will not receive it.   1050
And if I died, then nothing could retrieve it."

151   Pandar replied, "If this is what you wish,
Do as I say, and let me go straightway,
For by the gods who made flesh, fowl and fish,
I hope to get an answer back today
Straight from her hand. But if not, then I pray   1055
Let be. The man who tries to help a lad
Like you against your will will die quite mad!"

152   Said Troilus, "By the gods, I do assent,
And as you want me to, I'll go and write.
I pray that Cupid, with all good intent   1060
Will bless you, and the letter I'll indite,
And speed it on its way. Minerva white,
Give me the wit to write my letter well."
So he sat down and to composing fell.

153 First he addressed her as his lady dear,   1065
     His dear heart and his joy, healer of woe,
     His bliss, and all those words we always hear
     True lovers using as their passions grow,
     Then, writing as he spoke, humble and low
     He sought her love, her mercy and her grace.   1070
     To tell it all would take up too much space!

154 Then with humility he after prayed
     That she would not be angry though his folly
     Drove him to write so boldly. Then he said
     Love forced him on, and otherwise he'd die,   1075
     Then pitifully asked for her mercy,
     Then added, (but this was untrue,) that he
     Was worthless, and did nothing worthily.

155 She must excuse his lack of wit, for he
     Wrote haltingly because he feared her so.   1080
     Then of himself wrote most disparagingly,
     And afterwards, at length, told of his woe,
     Endless it was, no full stop to its flow,
     After assured her he would be most true.
     Then, before folding, read his letter through. 1085

156 And then he bathed with his salt flowing tears
     The ruby in his signet ring, and set
     It quickly on the wax despite his fears,
     And then a thousand times before he let
     The wrapper close, he kissed his letteret.   1090
     "My letter, what a blissful destiny,"
     He said, "Is yours, for you'll my lady see."

157 So Pandar took the letter. By that time
     It was the morning, and he reached the home
     Of Criseyde, swearing that it was past prime, 1095
     Then he began to joke, and said, "I've come

So early for my heart is gay, though some
Of love's own sorrow wakes me this spring morrow.
I have a jolly woe, a happy sorrow!"

158   Criseyde, when her uncle's voice she heard,   1100
      With quaking heart, yet longing much to hear
      The reason for his visit, then answered,
      "Now, tell me truly, uncle," said she, "Dear,
      What ever kind of wind now blows you here?
      Tell me your jolly woe, your gay penance,   1105
      How forward are you now in love's own dance?"

159   "By God," said he , "I always hop behind!"
      She laughed so much she thought her heart would burst.
      Said Pandar, 'Ah, I see you always find
      A joke beneath my hat! But listen first,   1110
      A visitor's in town, welcome, yet cursed,
      A Greecian spy, who says such startling things,
      Of which I'm bringing you the first tidings,

160   So come into the garden, and we'll hear
      In private of all this a long sermon."   1115
      So arm in arm downstairs they went, and there
      Down in the garden all had quiet grown,
      And Pandar found that they were quite alone,
      Well out of earshot and in privacy,
      So he pulled out the letter speedily,   1120

161   And said "Look, he that's wholly yours writes here
      In deep humility, craving your grace,
      Sending this letter by me, messenger,
      So read it when you have both time and space.
      Let him some favour or kind word purchase,   1125
      Or, by the gods, to speak out good and plain,
      He'll not live long, he's stricken with such pain."

162 Then terror-struck she tremblingly stood still
     And would not take the letter. Now in fear
     She was no longer humble. "Write no bill   1130
     For love of God about such things! I'll hear
     Nothing, nor take it! Also, uncle dear,
     Pay more regard to my position, pray
     Than to his pleasure! What more can I say?

163 Look, do you think this wise or reasonable?   1135
     Please speak your mind frankly and openly.
     Tell me the truth. Now, is it fit and seasonable
     In my position? Answer speedily.
     If I should read this letter, or pity
     Him, I would surely harm my reputation,   1140
     So take it back again. I prefer caution!"

164 At this Pandarus stared hard in her face
     And said, "This is most strange, the greatest wonder
     I ever knew. Stop thinking of disgrace!
     Why, may I be struck down by Jove's own thunder!   1145
     Even to gain that city standing yonder
     I would no letter to you take or bring
     That would cause harm to you in any thing!

165 How strangely you behave, you girls, each one,
     About the man who longs to serve you best   1150
     You care the least, or whether he become
     Demented, if he live or die! At least
     Whatever I deserve, hear my request,
     And don't refuse this letter." Then he pressed
     Her close, and thrust the letter down her breast, 1155

166 And said, "Now you can throw the thing away
     And all will see and stare at us two here."
     Said she, "I'll wait till they've gone off to play!"
     Then smiled and said, "I beg you, uncle dear,

Give him the answer you wish him to hear,　　1160
For truly, I'll no letter to him write."
"Oh, won't you! Then *I* must the thing indite."

167　At this she laughed and said, "Well, let's have dinner."
And he began to mock himself and say
In fun, "Dear niece, I'm getting so much thinner　1165
For love, and fast now every other day."
All his best jokes he rolled out light and gay,
And made her laugh so much with all his folly,
Criseyde thought with mirth she'd split and die.

168　And then, when they had come into the hall,　　1170
"Now, uncle," cried she, "We will dine quite soon."
Then of her women some began to call,
And went with them into her private room,
For amongst other things she wanted soon
To read her letter in fully privacy,　　1175
For she felt fear, yet curiosity.

169　Studying it word for word, and line for line,
She found nothing left out, all he'd done good,
Then putting it away, she went to dine,
And Pandar, who in a brown study stood　　1180
Before he knew, she'd pulled him by the hood,
Saying, "Ah, you were caught all unaware."
"That's true," he said, "Do with me . . . what you dare."

170　They washed their hands and then sat down to eat,
Then afterwards with cunning Pandarus　　1185
Edged right up to the window near the street,
Then said, "Niece, tell me, who has painted thus
The house which is directly facing us?"
"Which house?" she asked, and came near to behold,
And knew it well, and whose it was then told.　　1190

171   The two of them then with small talk and chat
Amused themselves there on the window seat,
Till Pandar thought it time to talk of what
Was on his mind. Her servants were at meat.
"Now, my dear niece, if I'm not indiscreet,   1195
How did you like that letter—which, you know!
Did Troilus write it well? Tell me if so."

172   At this she blushed, her face all rosy red,
And hummed and hawed and said, "Yes, pretty well."
"Then tell him so, for God's love," Pandar said,   1200
'I'll sow that letter where the seed will swell,"
Then his uplifted hands on his knees fell.
"Dear niece, let me do this, however slight
A task, to rear such seed to love and light."

173   "Yes, I could write to that effect," said she,   1205
"But I don't know what words, what thoughts to use?"
"My niece, don't speak quite so despairingly,
Thank him at least for his goodwill, and choose
Kind words so he will doom and death refuse.
Now if you love me, dear niece, don't deny   1210
My prayers and my requests so strenuously."

174   "Lord, lord," cried she, "I hope it will be well,
And may God help me, this is the first letter
I've written yet, and this is truth I tell."
Then she went in a little room, the better   1215
To write in private, and her heart unfetter
Out of the prison of her cold disdain.
So she sat down and wrote with might and main.

175   The substance of it I will tell you now
At least as far as I can understand.   1220
She thanked him for goodwill that seemed to grow
For her, but told him there could be no band,

No promises of love could he demand.
She'd love him like a sister if he pleased,
That with affection his heart might be eased.   1225

176   Then sealed it up and went to Pandarus,
There, as he sat and looked out at the street,
And pulled up near him, without any fuss
A stool of jaspar with a golden seat,
And said, "As God's my helper, never yet   1230
Did I perform a task with greater pain
Than this, to which you forced me 'gainst the grain."

177   She gave it him. He thanked her then, and said,
"God knows, things most unwillingly begun
Often turn out the best. My dear, indeed   1235
He should be glad that you're not easily won.
Indeed he should, by God and the bright sun.
Truly men say, "What's lightly come by, goes
As lightly, and no deep impression shows."

178   But you have played the tyrant much too long,   1240
And it was hard to cut into your heart.
Now throw away this mask, Disdain, that hung
About you, though you cherish a small part
Of it, but give him joy and end his smart.
Believe me, those who are too harsh too long   1245
Will end up scorned, immersed in sorrows strong."

179   Then, as they were debating more of this,
Troilus came riding there, at the street's end,
With all the troops about him that were his.
And at an easy pace began to bend   1250
His way towards them, for he used to wend
Homeward past Criseyde's house, and Pandar saw,
And cried, "Look, niece who's riding past the door!

180 Don't pull your head in, for he's seen us two,
And he will think that you're avoiding him!"   1255
"No, no," she said, and red as rosebud grew.
With that, he humbly bowed with graceful limb,
Saluting her, his colour waxing dim,
Then glancing up, a courteous look he cast,
Nodding at Pandarus as he rode past.   1260

181 God knows if he sat well upon his horse,
Or was admired as he rode by that day
God knows if he seemed knightly in his course!
Why should I bother telling his array?
Criseyde, who should be talking, well might say   1265
She liked all things about him, all his grace,
His person, clothes and armour, looks and face.

182 His well-bred actions and his gentleness
She liked so well, that, not since she was born
Had she so pitied any man's distress,   1270
However hard she'd tried before to warn
And shield herself, now she had such a thorn
Deep in her flesh that she'd not prise it out!
God send me no such thorns to fret about!

183 Pandar, who stood close to her, saw that now   1275
The iron was hot, so he began to smite,
Saying, "Now, niece, I hope that you'll allow
Your uncle here some questions! Is it right
A woman should condemn to death's deep night
A guiltless man, because she's pity none?   1280
Now, is this well?" She answered, "No, ill done!"

184 "Well, then, by God, you speak the truth," he said,
"And you know very well that I'm not lying.
Look, there he rides." "Why, so he does, indeed."

"Well, then," said Pandar, "Three times I've
　　　　　　　　　　　　been crying　　1285
For you to stop your foolish fuss, your trying
To put on airs, but speak and ease his heart,
Don't let your scruples make two people smart!"

185　But it was done, and up to heaven now!
　　And with all things considered, not to be.　　1290
　　Why, well, for modesty. She'd not allow
　　So early on, so great a liberty.
　　"For plainly my intention," so said she,
　　"Is love or like in secret, if I might,
　　Rewarding him with nothing more than—sight."　1295

186　But Pandar thought, "Oh no, it won't be so
　　If I have anything to do with it.
　　This sort of fuss won't last, but soon be through!"
　　But why should I on this wear out my wit!
　　It was agreed. So for a time did sit　　1300
　　The winds of love. And so, when it was eve
　　And all seemed well, he rose, and took his leave,

187　And on his homeward way he quickly sped
　　And for sheer joy he felt his gay heart dance,
　　And Troilus he found alone, in bed,　　1305
　　Lying, as lovers do, deep in a trance.
　　Half hopeful, half despairing was his glance.
　　But Pandar as he came was loudly singing
　　As if to say, "It's good news I am bringing."

188　He said, "Ah, who is in his bed so soon　　1310
　　Thus buried?" "It's me, Troilus," then said he.
　　"Who? Troilus? Now I swear, by love's own moon,"
　　Said Pandar, "You must now get up and see
　　A charm which has been sent right here by me,
　　One which can heal you of your feverishness,　1315
　　If you'll straightway get on with busyness."

189   "What! Why! My God!" cried Troilus, getting up,
      And Pandar made him then the letter take,
      And said, "Why, yes, God's helped us, filled our cup!
      Turn up the light, and look on all this black!"   1320
      But how his heart felt glad, and then did quake
      As Troilus scanned her words, and read, and read,
      And what she wrote made him first hope, then dread.

190   But at the last he took all for the best,
      The words she wrote, for through them he beheld   1325
      Some shreds of hope on which his heart might rest,
      Though what she meant was well beneath a shield!
      All that was best in it he grasped and held,
      So what with hope, and this encouragement,
      And Pandar's words, his worst woes waned and went. 1330

191   But as each one of us each day can see,
      More coal, more wood heaped on means much more fire,
      So hope increased, no matter what it be,
      In the same way increases, fans desire.
      Or as oaks spring from acorns in the mire,   1335
      So through this letter which she sent to him,
      Desire grew up, then raged and flamed within.

192   From this, I say, (and stress it) day and night
      Desire in Troilus now increased much more
      Than it did first, in hope. With main and might   1340
      He courted, Pandar helping as before.
      Daily he wrote her of his sorrows sore.
      There was no one day out of any week
      That by Pandar he did not write or speak.

193   He also did those rites and duties due   1345
      Which lovers must perform in such a case.
      And just as the dice fell, so luck fell, too,
      And he was happy, or in deep disgrace,

Adapting to the music step and pace.
According to the words from her he had   1350
His days were light or dark, sorry or glad!

194   But in the end to Pandarus he turned,
      And piteously to him moaned and complained,
      Asking advice and help, for love so burned,
      And Pandarus, who saw him so constrained,   1355
      With pity almost died, watching him pained,
      And tried by every means with might and main
      To find a speedy ending for that pain.

195   He said, "My lord, my friend, my brother dear,
      By God, your misery gives me such woe,   1360
      But put an end to all your gloom and fear,
      And by my soul, in just a day or so,
      With God's help I will plan, and strive, and do,
      And work so hard that in a certain place
      You'll meet and pray to her you love for grace.   1365

196   Though I'm not at all sure if you do know,
      But those who are expert in love all say
      One of the things that help affairs to grow
      Is for a man to have a chance to pray
      And plead his case on a fit time and day.   1370
      Pity is sure on gentle hearts to press
      When they both hear and see a man's distress.

197   Maybe you think that though it may be so
      That nature and her sex will soon begin
      To make her pity all your grief and woe,   1375
      Disdain will say, "No, me you'll never win!"
      With pride she rules her heart and soul within,
      So, though she'll bend, she'll stay inflexible,
      Rigid and rooted, and you'll suffer still.

198 But think again, just how the sturdy oak   1380
     Which men have hacked and hewn all day with groans,
     At last receives the joyful felling stroke,
     And down with sway and swish at once it comes
     Just like an avalanche of rocks and stones.
     Faster fall things that are of real weight   1385
     When they drop down, than those more light, less great.

199 As for the reed that bows to every blast,
     Easily, when the wind drops, it will rise.
     But not so a great oak, when it is cast.
     Now surely you don't need me to advise!   1390
     Men get most joy from a great enterprise
     Well carried out, and that without a doubt,
     Though long has been the toiling thereabout.

200 However, Troilus, tell me if you can
     What I am going to ask immediately.   1395
     Which is your favourite brother, which the man
     With whom you share your thoughts in secrecy?"
     "Of course with Deiphebus," then said he.
     "Well, then," said Pandar, "Quickly, too, I'll show it,
     He will have eased you though he will not know it. 1400

201 Leave me to get on in my own sweet way,"
     Said he, and went then to Deiphebus' door,
     Who'd been his lord and friend for many a day.
     Excepting Troilus, no man he loved more.
     In short, and may I not become a bore,   1405
     Pandarus said, "I beg you now to be
     Friend to a cause most close and dear to me."

202 "Of course," said Deiphebus, "Well you know
     I'll help you every way I can say and may.
     Except for Brother Troilus there is no   1410
     Man I love better. So speak up and say

G

What is the cause? For, since my earliest day
I've never disagreed or otherwise
Differed from you in thought or enterprise."

203   Pandarus thanked him warmly, and then said,   1415
"Look, sir, there is a lady in this town
Who is my niece, and she is called Criseyde.
But there are those who try to do her down,
And seek to cheat her of all she may own.
Because of this I ask you, sir, to be   1420
Our friend, like this, with informality."

204   Deiphebus then answered, "Is not this
Lady you speak about so distantly
Criseyde, my friend?" Pandar said, "Yes."
"Then there's no need," he cried immediately   1425
"To say another word, for certainly
I'll be her champion, yes, with spur and lance,
And I don't care if all her foes advance!

205   But you, who know the facts of this affair,
How can I help? Speak now and let me know."   1430
Said Pandar, "If you will, my lord most dear,
To my poor niece your helpful kindness show,
And courteously invite her here tomorrow
To unfold to you all her long complaint,
Her enemies will hear of this, and faint!   1435

206   And if I can ask more than this of you,
And burden you with even more travail,
Invite some of your other brothers, too,
Whose influence may in her cause prevail.
With help like this I'm sure she'll never fail,   1440
But conquer all, for what with your guidance,
And other friends' advice, she must advance."

207　Deiphebus, who was by nature kind,
　　　Most honourable and generous in intent
　　　Answered, "It shall be done, and I can find　　　1445
　　　Even more folk to help. Would you consent
　　　If I straightway some folk for Helen sent,
　　　And tell her of all this? It might be wise,
　　　For she'll win Paris over, I surmise.

208　Hector, who is my lord as well as brother　　　1450
　　　Needs no persuasion friend of hers to be,
　　　For I have heard him, one time and another
　　　Speak such good things of Criseyde, that he
　　　Could not say more, so well with him stands she.
　　　There is no need his help or aid to woo.　　　1455
　　　He'll act exactly as we'd have him do.

209　And you yourself must speak to Troilus
　　　On my behalf, invite him here to dine."
　　　"Sir, all this shall be done," said Pandarus,
　　　And took his leave. He did not peak or pine,
　　　But to his niece's home made a bee-line!　　　1460
　　　He came, and found her getting up from dinner,
　　　Sat down, and then he spoke like this to win her.

210　He said, "Oh, God, oh, God, how I've been running!
　　　Look, my dear niece, and see how much I sweat!　　　1465
　　　I don't know if you'll thank me for so coming,
　　　But don't you realise how false Poliphete
　　　Is making trouble, trying hard to get
　　　A case against you, and a law suit new?"
　　　"Why, no," cried she, and lost her rosy hue.　　　1470

211　"What, is he up to his old tricks, to make
　　　Me terrified, and wrong me? Oh, alas,
　　　What shall I do? Yet I'd not lie awake
　　　For him, but that Antenor and Aeneas

Will take his part in what law suits he has.   1475
So, for the love of God, my uncle dear
Give him what he is after, never fear,

212   Without it I've enough for all of us."
"No," Pandar said, "Of course it shan't be so.
For I've been talking with Deiphebus,   1480
And Hector, and another lord or two,
And made each one to Poliphete a foe.
So, through my careful planning he won't get
A thing from your estates, no, no, not yet."

213   So, as they were both thinking what to do,   1485
Deiphebus, in kindly courtesy
Came there in person, and on purpose too
Invite her with a friendly company
To dinner, which request she'd not deny,
Accepting with much sweetness. And so he   1490
Returned back to his home most speedily.

214   When this was done, Pandar, for it was noon,
To cut my tale short, quickly made his way
To Troilus, lying still as any stone,
And what had happened, word and deed that day   1495
Told him, and how his friends began to sway
To Cressid, saying, "Now the thing is done.
Act your part well tomorrow, and all's won.

215   Speak, beg, and then most piteously complain.
Don't let embarrassment, or fear, or sloth   1500
Hinder. Sometimes a man should tell his pain.
Believe me, and she'll pity you in truth.
Your faith will save you yet, be nothing loath.
But I can see that you're most nervous now.
The reason why I'm pretty sure I know!   1505

216   You're thinking now, "How can I do all this?
      For by the way I look folk will espy
      That all for love of her I'm out of bliss.
      I'd rather this stayed secret, and I die!"
      Now, don't think so, it's sheer stupidity.   1510
      For I have found a way for you to hide
      Your love-lorn state, the mood in which you're tied.

217   Before night you must go, in fact, straightway,
      And stay with Deiphebus, with the air
      Of one on pleasure bent, who drives away   1515
      His pains and woes, but see you're pale, and wear
      A sickly look, and say you're ill, and there
      Go soon to bed, say you cannot endure
      Longer your pain, then wait your adventure!

218   Tell them you're suffering from recurring fever,   1520
      Attacks of which come regularly, and will
      Last till the morrow. See your acting's clever.
      Truly a love-sick man is truly ill!
      Go now. Goodbye. May Venus bless you still
      I hope, and may you hold your purpose firm,   1525
      Then she with all her grace it will confirm."

219   Said Troilus, "Now in truth there is no need
      For you to counsel me sickness to feign.
      For I am ill in earnest and indeed,
      So that I'm almost dead from torturing pain."   1530
      So Pandar said, "Then better you'll complain,
      And have less need to act or counterfeit!
      Men think a man hot when they see him sweat!

220   Keep to that secret tryst of yours, and I
      Will drive the deer past so that you can shoot."   1535
      Then Pandar took his leave, left quietly,
      And Troilus to the palace went, hot foot.

He'd never been so happy. To the suit
And council of Pandar he gave consent,
And to Deiphebus's house that night he went.   1540

221   What need have I to tell you the good cheer
Which Deiphebus gave his brother then?
Of Troilus' feverish fit, his symptoms queer!
How blankets were heaped on by serving men
As he was put to bed, the efforts when   1545
He lay there sick, to cheer him. All in vain,
He acted just as Pandar had made plain!

222   But, before Troilus went up to his bed,
Deiphebus had begged him that same night
To be a friend and helper to Criseyde.   1550
God knows, he said he would do that alright!
He'd be her friend, and help with all his might,
For there was no more need to ask the lad,
Than for to tell a mad man to run mad!

223   The next day came, and it was soon the time   1555
For dinner, to which Helen, that fair queen
Had said she'd come, an hour after prime,
To Deiphebus, for she'd always been
Honest with him. And sisterly she'd deem   1560
It, cosy, homely, coming there to dine.
But God and Pandar knew the true design!

224   All innocent of this Criseyde also
Came with Antigone and Tharbe, too,
Yet we must not waste time, but quickly go
Straight to the point, with much more ado.   1565
No more circumlocution, telling who
The guests were, why they all came there that day.
So I'll leave out the things they do and say.

225 With etiquette, and form, and courtesy
     Deiphebus received and fed each one,   1570
     But kept on saying, "What a dreadful pity
     It is that Troilus' fever has begun,
     And he lies there so ill." He sighed, then done
     With gloom worked hard to entertain them all,
     And made all happy gathered in his hall.   1575

226 Helen said, too, how sad it was to find
     Troilus so ill, and spoke so pityingly
     That all grew most compassionate in their mind,
     Suggesting that he should a doctor see.
     They said, "That way you'll cure him speedily."   1580
     But there sat one, who, though she said no word,
     Thought, "I would be the healer he preferred!"

227 After complaining, they began to praise him
     As people do, when one man has begun
     To speak well of a friend, others will raise him   1585
     Higher and higher, up like the bright sun!
     "He's this, does that. Better than all he's done!"
     And as for Pandarus, well, he'd affirm
     All the good things they'd said he could confirm!

228 And as for Criseyde, she heard everything,   1590
     And noted all the words each person said.
     With quiet joy her heart began to sing.
     What woman's pride would not be rampant made
     By power to raise a knight, or strike him dead?
     But I'll press on, lest too long here you dwell.   1595
     One point, one ending has this tale I tell.

229 Then the time came from dinner to arise,
     And in the order due they left their seat.
     Of this, of that they talked in cheerful wise,
     But Pandar broke this up, rose to his feet,   1600

And said to Deiphebus, "May we meet,
If you agree, as yesterday I said
To talk about the troubles of Criseyde?"

230   Helen, who held Criseyde by the hand
Consented first, and said, "Let us begin,"   1605
And smiled at her with a sweet look, most bland,
Saying, "May Jove smite him who, deep in sin
Harms you, my dear, and may his griefs begin!
Even if it should hurt me, he will rue
If I can work it, and these friends be true!"   1610

231   "Outline your niece's case," said Deiphebus
To Pandarus, "For you can tell it well."
"My lords and ladies, now the case stands thus—
Why should I waste your time, even so it fell . . . "
With this he tolled the words out like a bell,   1615
Told them such things of wicked Poliphete,
So dreadful that to hear them made one sweat!

232   And each one hearing vied against the other
To damn him more severely with more blame.
"He well deserves to hang. Were he my brother   1620
I'd still say so, and censure him the same."
But why should I delay about this game!
In short, and all at once, they gladdened her
Promising help in all that might occur.

233   Then Helen spoke and said, "Now, Pandarus,   1625
Does my lord Prince, my brother, know of this,
Hector, I mean? And have you told Troilus?"
He said, "Yes, but now, if it's not amiss,
Since Troilus is now here, let him not miss
The chance to hear it all from her own lips,   1630
If you agree, before off home she slips.

234   It is more likely he will take to heart
      Her troubles, if her gracious self he sees,
      So, by your leave, I'll run and do my part,
      And let you know straightway just how he is,   1635
      And if he sleeps, or wants to hear of this."
      Then in he leapt, and yelled in Troilus' ear,
      "May God receive your soul! I've brought your bier!"

235   Troilus smiled at this, and Pandarus
      Not waiting and not worrying, went straightway   1640
      To look for Helen and Deiphebus,
      And said to them, "So that there's no delay,
      Yet no haste, neither, Troilus hopes today
      You'll bring my lady Criseyde whilst she's here,
      Then, whilst he's able, he'll her story hear.   1645

236   But, as you know, the room is very small,
      And a few people there will make it warm.
      So look here, I won't be responsible
      For bringing in a crowd that might do harm
      Or make his illness worse, not for my arm!   1650
      Should she not wait till afterwards, I know
      That you'll arrange what is the best to do.

237   But the best plan of all I think would be
      For no one else to go in but you two,
      Unless you let me go, for speedily   1655
      In fewer and conciser words than she
      I can tell him her case, then she can go
      To see him, beg his friendly help and say
      Goodbye. He won't be so disturbed that way.

238   Besides, since she's a stranger, he will lose   1660
      His rest in ways that he won't do with you,
      And he'll talk with me frankly of all those
      Matters—(no matter what) you know, you two—

Secrets, perhaps, or with the State to do—"
And they, who nothing guessed of his intent,   1665
Waiting no longer, in to Troilus went.

239   Helen, in her kindly, gentle wise
      Greeted him, and sweetly feminine
      Said, "You must get well soon, and quickly rise
      Sound, whole and fit, I beg you, brother mine."   1670
      She laid her arm across his shoulders fine,
      And tried in every way she could to cheer
      And comfort and console her friend so dear.

240   Soon afterwards she said, "We two beg you,
      Deiphebus, my brother dear, and I,   1675
      For love of God—and so does Pandar, too—
      To help Criseyde, and aid her heartily.
      She needs all your assistance certainly,
      For she is wronged, as Pandarus knows well,
      And he the facts better than I can tell."   1680

241   So Pandar made his tongue sharp as a file,
      And outlined everything of Criseyde's case.
      When he had told them all, after a while
      Troilus replied, "As soon as I can face
      The world and am restored, I'll try to trace   1685
      Her rights and wrongs, and help with all my might."
      "Good luck be with you," cried Helen, the white.

242   And Pandar said, "Now then, if you agree,
      May she come up and take her leave of you?"
      "I'd be put out if she did not," said he,   1690
      "If Criseyde is willing so to do."
      And with that Troilus added, "And you two,
      Deiphebus, and Helen, sister dear,
      I must discuss with you some more points here,

243 And get your good advice about this matter," 1695
   He took up from the table by his bed
   The copy of a document and letter
   Sent him by Hector, begging him to read
   And let him know straightway if there was need
   To execute or save a certain man, 1700
   And in most serious wise the papers scan.

244 Then Deiphebus, very earnestly
   Looked at the letter, so did Helen queen,
   Then took it, hoped to read it privately
   Downstairs, and both went to a garden green 1705
   Where they both scanned the documents between
   Them, and for full an hour or two, or more,
   Tried on the problem all their thoughts to pour.

245 Let them read on, and let us turn once more
   To Pandarus, who started to spy out 1710
   If all was well. Again on the ground floor
   He went to the great hall, where sat about
   The other guests, and hastening with a shout,
   "God save you all," he cried. "Come, my niece dear,
   Helen, awaits you with the princes, near. 1715

246 Come now, and bring with you Antigone,
   Or who you like, or if you wish it, none,
   The fewer come, the better, certainly.
   And see you thank them all for what they've done.
   Then, when it seems the time and place have come, 1720
   Take leave of them with every courtesy,
   Lest we should tire the invalid needlessly."

247 All innocent of Pandarus' intent
   Criseyde said, "Then let's go, uncle dear."
   And arm in arm with him upstairs she went. 1725
   Most serious were her words, and looks, and cheer,

And Pandar, with great earnestness of manner
Said to her followers, "Stay outside, and be
Discreet, amuse yourselves here quietly,

248   Remember who is lying feverish here,   1730
And what a state he's in. May God amend him!
So, niece, go in on tiptoe, walk in fear
Of harming Troilus. May the Lord defend him,
And let the Gods a happy issue send him.
Not even to gain two crowns please do not kill   1735
This man, your lover, who for you lies ill!

249   Think of the devil. Think just what he is,
And where he lies in wait! Come now, have done!
Think of all those who through delay lose bliss!
That's what you both will say, when you are one!   1740
Secondly, that as yet there's gossips none
Who know about you both. So, while you may,
While folk are blind like this, make hay, make hay!

250   With tittering, by following and delay
Gossips invent tales from a wagging straw,   1745
And though you two will long for mirth and play
In days to come, you'll dare not risk it, for
This one, that one might talk, this man deplore!
But I waste time with you like this to deal.
Come off it, niece, relax, bring him to heel!"   1750

251   But now, you lovers in my audience here,
Was not poor Troilus held on tenterhooks,
Who, as he lay, heard whispers loud and clear,
And thought, 'O Lord, am I in Luck's good books?
Will I get pain or comfort from her looks?'   1755
This was the first time he could speak or pray
To her of love! Great God, what should he say?   1757

Book Three

1   O blissful light, of which the beams so clear
    Drape the third part of heaven's mansion fair,
    Companion of the sun, Jove's daughter dear,
    Delight of love, goodly and debonaire,
    In gentle hearts most ready to repair,   5
    True cause of health and of glad happiness,
    Praised be your power and strength and your goodness.

2   In heaven and hell, in earth and the salt sea
    Your might is felt, (or so instruct my Muses,)
    As man, bird, beast and fish, plant and green tree   10
    Feel your hand's touch, which life and joy infuses.
    God, too, is love, he never love refuses,
    And in this world there is no living creature
    Which without love lives or fulfils its nature.

3   Love, you stung Jove himself, yet made him glad,   15
    Jove, through whom all things have life, and be.
    You drove him on till he with love was mad
    For mortal creatures, at your will, so he
    Had ease in love, or else adversity,
    And in a thousand shapes earthwards you sent   20
    Him seeking love, and where you willed, he went.

4   The anger of fierce Mars you lull and tame.
    To hearts, to souls you give nobility,
    And those in whom you wish to light love's flame

109

Fear to be shamed, and vice and evil flee.   25
You make them courteous, fresh, benign and free,
And to men high or low, who persevere
In love, you send the joys they joy in here.

5   Your unity binds realm, or family.
You are indeed the cause of friendship, too.   30
You know the secret, hidden quality
Of things, all those which puzzle people so
When they can't quite discover why things go,
Why he's in love with her, or she with him.
Why this fish and not that keeps in the swim!   35

6   Your subjects have a universal law.
I know this from all those who lovers be.
All those who fight you fall low to the floor!
So, lady bright, from your benignity,
And because lovers pray so faithfully,   40
(I am their clerk,) teach me, I beg, to teach
Some of that joy which those who serve you reach.

7   You've made my naked heart deep feeling's cage,
So help me show the world your true sweetness.
Calliope, I need your voice, your sage   45
Council. Ah, do you not see my distress,
How I must now reveal the great gladness
Of Troilus, all in Aphrodite's praise?
May Jove to bliss like his the needy raise!

———————

8   And all this long while there lay Troilus   50
Remembering his lessons in this way.
"Truly," thought he, "I'll speak just so, and thus—
Thus will I plead with her, my sweet lady.
Ah, that's the right word! This I'll do—or say—
I'll not forget all this, my place, my schemes."   55
Ah, may God let him do it as he dreams!

9   And lord, his heart, how it went pit-a-pat
    Hearing her come, her indrawn, quickened breath.
    Pandar, who led her by the sleeve, saw that,
    And coming near, peered round the curtain's wreath 60
    And said, "May God save all the sick from death!
    Look who is here to visit you, why, she
    Who is to blame for all your misery!"

10 With that it seemed as if he wept almost.
    "Ah, ha," said Troilus, very ruefully,   65
    "If I am wounded, mighty God, thou knowest!
    Who's there? Alas, I cannot clearly see."
    "Sir," said Criseyde, "It's Pandarus and me."
    "Ah, sweetheart, ah, alas, I cannot rise
    To kneel and do you honour in some wise."   70

11 Then he sat up, and she there straightaway
    Laid her two soft hands upon his breast,
    "For God's love, don't do that for me, I pray,"
    She cried, "Ah, sir, why are you so oppressed?
    I have come for two reasons, and the first   75
    To thank you, and to ask if you will still
    Grant me your help, protection, strength and skill."

12 This Troilus, who heard his lady pray
    Him for his help, sat like a thing of lead,
    Not one word in his shame could Troilus say,   80
    Even to save his skin or silly head!
    But lord, he blushed at once so crimson red,
    As for that lesson which he'd hoped to say
    To her, it seeped through all his wits away!

13 Criseyde saw all this happening well enough   85
    For she was wise, and loved him none the less
    Though he was shy. He did not make things tough,
    He was not bold as fools are to confess!

But when less grew his shame and his distress
I'll tell you how he reasoned, (if my rhymes   90
Hold out,) as legends tell in olden times.

14   In deepened voice, made so from fear and dread,
Quaking also, in voice and in manner,
Becoming abashed, with countenance red,
Then pale, he turned to Criseyde, his dear,   95
His eyes cast down, humble his look and cheer,
Why, the first words which from his mouth did start
Were, (twice in fact) "Mercy, mercy, sweetheart."

15   Then choked and stopped, and when he next could bring
The words out, they were, "God knows well I have 100
As faithfully as I have skill and cunning
Been true to you, and as God may me save,
Shall go on so, till I am in my grave.
And though I dare not, cannot now complain
To you, I suffer none the less deep pain.   105

16   So much as this, O sweet, sweet, gentle girl
I can speak now, and if this you displeases
I'll take it out upon myself, and whirl
Deathwards, and soon, if this your dear heart eases,
Glad if my death your heart, your soul appeases.   110
Yet, since you've heard me even these poor words say
I care not now if I should die today."

17   Now all his manly sorrow to behold
Might well have made a heart of stone to rue,
And Pandar wept as if he quickly would   115
To water melt, and poked his niece anew,
And said, "Ah, woebegone are two hearts true.
For God's sake, end this thing that you've begun,
Or you'll kill both of us before you've done!"

18 "I? What?" said she, "By God, and by my faith,   120
    I don't know what it is you'd have me say."
    "I? What?" said he, "Why, pity him, in faith,
    For God's love, do not let him die away!"
    "Why then," said Criseyde, "I will him pray
    To tell me what's the point of his intent.   125
    I have not understood quite what he meant."

19 "What it is that I mean! O, sweetheart dear,"
    Troilus exclaimed, "Sweet girl, so fresh, so free,
    Only that with the beams from your eyes clear
    You'll sometimes look in friendly wise on me,   130
    And then agree that I perhaps may be
    Without a vein of vice in any wise,
    And fit to do you honour and service

20 Such as is due to you, my dear lady,
    With all my wit and all my diligence,   135
    And grant me as you please all comfort truly
    Under your yoke, or what fits my offence,
    Just punishment, if I break your defence.
    And of your grace grant me the honour great
    Of serving you, obeying long and late.   140

21 And let me be your very humble, true
    And secret servant, patient in my pain,
    And may I ever long, afresh, anew
    To serve you, and be diligent again,
    And cheerfully all you have given maintain,   145
    Keeping your talent well, even though I smart.
    I mean all this, my own, my dear sweetheart."

22 Said Pandar, "Well, that *is* a hard request,
    Reasoned well, too, for ladies to refuse!
    Now, my dear niece, by Jove's own birthday feast,   150
    Were I a god, you'd get your proper dues

H

For hearing how this man will nothing choose
But your honour, and yet you'd let him die,
Suffering his service so unwillingly!"

23 At this she looked directly at Troilus,   155
With pleasure and with gracious courtesy,
Reflecting without hurry or much fuss,
In silence first, then said to him softly,
"Honour permitting, I will truthfully,
In such a way as he can now devise   160
Take him as lover into my service,

24 Beseeching him for God's own love, that he
Will with all honour, truth and gentleness,
As I to him, will act as well to me,
And my honour, with skill and carefulness   165
Keep bright, and so, if I may give him gladness,
Henceforth, indeed, I never will refrain.
Be whole, be healed, my love, no more complain.

25 Nevertheless, I warn you," then said she,
"Though you may be a King's son, born to bliss,   170
You shall no more have utter sovreignty
Of me in love than good and rightful is.
Nor will I hold back if you do amiss
To scold you, but whilst you correctly serve
Me, I will cherish you as you deserve.   175

26 In short, my dear heart and my own true knight,
Be glad, look forward now to happiness.
And I will truthfully, with all my might
Your bitter woe turn into honied sweetness.
If I am she who gives you joyfulness,   180
For every pain you shall make up with blisses."
Then took him in her arms with tender kisses.

27   Pandar fell on his knees, upcast his eyes
      To heaven, and held his thankful hands on high.
      "Immortal god," said he, "Who never dies,   185
      Cupid, I mean, glory to you I cry.
      Venus, you now may well make melody!
      I seem to hear in joy from every steeple
      Bells ringing out, untouched by hand or people.

28   But ho, my friends, no more now of this matter,   190
      For they who read the letter will soon come.
      I hear their footsteps clattering on the stair.
      Criseyde, I urge you first of all, for one,
      And two, you Troilus, both of you to run
      To my house at my pressing invitation.   195
      I'll so arrange it for your delectation,

29   And there you both shall ease your hearts indeed,
      And see which of you two will bear the bell
      In speaking well of love," he chuckling said.
      "There you shall have full leisure all to tell!"   200
      Said Troilus, "Now then, how long shall I dwell
      Here, ere you do all this?" "When you arise
      I'll have it pat, and just as you'd devise."

30   Helen, at this time, with Deiphebus
      Was on the landing, and, their hearts to grieve,   205
      Lord, lord, how hard, how deep groaned Troilus
      His brother and his sister to deceive.
      Said Pandar, "It is time we took our leave.
      Now, niece mine, say goodbye to all these three,
      Hear what they say, and then come home with me."   210

31   She took her leave of them most charmingly,
      As well she could, and they with all politeness
      And well-bred manners answered courteously.
      And when she'd gone spoke well of her, her rightness,

Her excellence, good manners, lovely brightness,   215
And all there was about her, loud and clear,
Commending so that it was joy to hear.

32   Now let her go back into her own home,
And turn to Troilus lying there alone.
Ah, quickly with that letter he had done,   220
The one his brother read with so much pain.
Of Helen and Deiphebus he'd fain
Be rid, so he said he much wanted rest,
For sick men, sleep after much talk was best!

33   So Helen kissed him and soon took her leave,   225
Deiphebus also. Home went each knight.
But Pandar just as fast as he could drive
Came back to Troilus, straight as line ruled right,
And by him on a camp bed lay that night.
Merry they were together, talking, glad   230
That they were friends and much in common had.

34   When every man had gone except those two,
And all the doors were bolted and shut fast,
To tell, in short, without much words, or few,
This Pandarus rose up straightway, and cast   235
About, and sat on Troilus' bed at last,
Starting to speak in solemn, serious wise
To Troilus, just as I will devise.

35   "My dearest lord, my friend and brother dear,
God knows, and you know, too, it hurts me sore   240
When I saw you so languishing, so spare
For love, from which your grief grew more and more,
That I, with all my skill and craft and lore
Have made it ever since my sole business
To bring you into joy from your distress.   245

36 And, as you know, have worked so things now stand
    That all through me you're now well on the way
    To prosper. I don't boast, you understand.
    Do you know why? Much shame it is to say
    For you I've started such a game to play   250
    Which I shall never do again for other,
    Not if he were a thousand times my brother!

37 That is to say, for you I have become
    Half jesting, half in earnest, means or mean
    Through whose wiles women unto men will come,   255
    I say no more, you well know what I mean!
    For you I have my niece, of sin quite clean
    So fully made to trust your gentleness
    That all will be just as you wish, doubtless.

38 But God, who knows all, be my true witness,   260
    I never planned this thing for greed or gain,
    But only for a cure of your distress,
    From which you almost died in grief and pain.
    But brother dear, act as you should, for shame,
    And for God's love, keep her from blame or hurt, 265
    As you are wise, shield her good name from dirt.

39 For you know well, her name as yet shines bright
    Among the people, like that of a saint.
    For no man has been born, and I am right,
    Who can see sin in her, or blame or taint.   270
    But woe is me, that I may her attaint,
    Remembering she is my niece most dear,
    And I her uncle, yet a traitor clear!

40 And were it known that I, through all my scheming
    Had put this fancy in my niece's head,   275
    To do your will, and to be yours, then deeming
    Me to be villain, worthy to be dead,

They'd call me traitor, fit to lose my head,
For doing the worst day's work yet begun,
And call her lost, and you, my lad, undone!   280

41   Wherefore, before I stir another foot
I beg of you, and at length also say,
Be most discreet, private and hushed to boot,
That is, you must in nothing us betray,
And don't be angry if I often pray   285
You to hold secret such a serious matter.
(Note that I pray with skill, and don't words scatter.)

42   And think what grief has struck men before this
Through bragging and through boasting, (so they say)
And of mischance that in this sad world is   290
Even for such wicked boasts, day after day,
And for this reason wisest scholars grey
Include among their proverbs for us young,
"The leading virtue is—to hold your tongue."

43   And were it not that I must now abridge   295
And cut down on my words, I could almost
A thousand ancient tales from memory dredge,
Telling of women lost through a fool's boast.
Many such saws you know, and for the most
Part speaking against boasting, for a blabber   300
Is one with him who is a gift-of-the-gabber.

44   O Tongue, alas, so often through your scorn
You've made so many a lady bright of hue
Say "Woe is me, the day that I was born!"
And many a maiden all her griefs to rue.   305
And for the most part, everything's untrue
That mankind yelps about, proof there is none.
The boastful have no leg to stand upon!

45 A man who's boastful is a liar, too.
    For an example, say a woman grant me   310
    Her love, and says to me that she'll be true,
    And that I promise every secrecy,
    Yet after boast of this to two or three,
    Well, then I am, at least, a bragging crook,
    And liar, also, for my word I broke.   315

46 Now, look then, if such men are not to blame.
    I don't know what to call rascals like that,
    Who talk familiarly of girls by name,
    Girls who never granted—you know what—
    Or knew them, any more than my old hat.   320
    It is no wonder, (may God say Amen,)
    Women are scared to mix too much with men!

47 I do not say this through mistrust of you
    Or other wise folk, but because of fools,
    And all the troubles that are common now,   325
    Due less to malice than to dolts and mules.
    For I know well that folk who keep the rules
    Don't scare a woman if she's sane and wise.
    Yet wise folk are by deeds of fools chastised.

48 Now, to the point. My well-loved brother dear,   330
    Have all these things that I have said in mind
    And keep your council, but be of good cheer,
    For when your chance comes, faith in me you'll find.
    I'll set your matter going in such kind,
    With the gods' help, that it will make you glad, 335
    For it shall turn out as you'd wish, my lad.

49 I know quite well that you mean well, that's true,
    And so I'm ready this to undertake.
    You know all that your lady granted you.
    Now the hour's come for us the plans to make.   340

But now, goodnight. I cannot keep awake,
So pray for me, since you are now in bliss,
God sends me death, or joy through my girl's kiss!"

50   Now who can tell half of the happiness
     Which like the sunshine Troilus' soul then felt,   345
     Hearing Pandarus' promises, no less.
     Pains which had scored his heart with many a welt
     Were healed, his miseries began to melt,
     And all the luxury of his sighings sore
     Faded, he languished in their folds no more.   350

51   But even as the spinneys, woods and hedges
     That all through winter have been dead and dry
     Are once more dressed in green when May time fledges
     The twigs with leaves, and blood runs lustily,
     Even so, in this same wise, most truthfully   355
     The heart of Troilus felt the sap of joy
     Race, and there was no happier man in Troy.

52   And now his look on Pandarus he cast
     Serious, intent, and yet most like a friend,
     And said, "Pandar, my friend, in April last   360
     As you well know, if you your memory bend
     How near to death you found me, and did mend
     Me, making it indeed your business
     To find out all the cause of my distress.

53   You also know how long that I delayed   365
     To tell my love, though you're the friend I trust.
     I knew there was no peril when I said
     What ailed me, but now tell me, friend, you must,
     Since I was so reluctant at the first
     To speak, how could I boast now of this matter,   370
     I, who shake, though not a soul is here?

54 Nevertheless, by that same god I swear,
    The god of love, who rules both poor and great,
    (And if I lie to you, may Achilles' spear
    Cleave through my heart, or death be my just fate),   375
    If I today, tomorrow, early, late,
    Betray, reveal or boast of this, may I
    Know no good here, or in eternity.

55 I'd rather die than do such wrong, and lie,
    (Or so I think) in stocks or prison cell,   380
    In wretchedness, with vermin, filthily
    Infested, bound by Agamemnon, dwell,
    And I'll swear this by every sacred bell,
    By every temple, every god in town,
    Whatever you demand or may lay down.   385

56 And all the things that you have done for me,
    All that I know I never could deserve,
    I now admit, and for you certainly
    I'd die a thousand times, if this preserve
    Or please you. I can do no more. I'll serve   390
    You as a slave, and come as you command
    For ever more, and do as you demand.

57 I beg you from the bottom of my heart
    Not to think me so sunk in foolery
    As to believe your own words for a start,   395
    And take all this, done free and friendlily
    For a bawd's work, performed in villany.
    I'm not quite mad, though I am ignorant.
    I know quite well what you my good friend, meant.

58 As for the man, who all for gold or money   400
    Acts as a go-between, well, call him names.
    But what you've done, I call it courtesy,
    Compassion, friendship, keeping faith, the claims

Of love. Distinguish them, the very same's
Not true of both, for things may share a skin,   405
Twins on the surface, yet divide within.

59   And so that you may know I do not deem
     What you have done shameful, twisted, black,
     I'd give you my fair sister, Polixene,
     Cassandra, Helen, any of the pack,   410
     However lovely, rounded, straight of back,
     Tell me which one you'd like, short, plump or tall,
     Then say no more, let me arrange it all.

60   But since you've done this service all for me,
     To save my life, and not at all for gain,   415
     For God's love, see it through, and speedily
     Bring to an end this business, for my pain
     Goes on, I need you yet, again, again,
     And all you ask I'll do, your council keep.
     So now, goodnight, let us both go to sleep."   420

61   So each was with the other so well pleased
     That nothing more could make them happier,
     And on the morrow, dressed and washed, much eased
     By sleep, each turned to his own tasks, the stir
     Of life. But Troilus, though he burned like fire   425
     With his desire, with hope and love's pleasance,
     Did not forget control and temperance.

62   And in himself with manly self-control
     Restrained all rash deeds, each impetuous glance,
     So that nobody living, not a soul   430
     Should know from word or action in what dance
     He trod, nor how he planned now to advance.
     Distant he was to all as clouds, unbending,
     Yet fooled them so by acting and pretending.

63   And all the while, as I'm now telling you,   435
     This was his life, with all his main and might
     By day he worshipped Mars, and gave him due
     Service, that is, as soldier and armed knight,
     And for the most part, all through the long night
     He lay and thought how ever he might serve   440
     His lady best, and all her thanks deserve.

64   And I won't swear, though he was comfortable,
     That in his thoughts he was quite well at ease!
     He tossed upon his pillows, most unstable,   445
     And wanted what was missing, felt it tease,
     His lack, his loss. Nothing can ever please
     A man love-lorn as he was. Certainly
     This seems a likely possibility.

65   But, to make progress, it is certain, though,
     That at this time, (so the romances say,)   450
     He saw his lady sometimes, and also
     She spoke with him, when bold enough, or gay,
     And both of them planned very cautiously
     How, when and where they'd meet, and how proceed,
     As far as they both dared, in this their need.   455

66   But all their meetings, all their talk together
     Was secret, stolen, hurried, and in fear
     Lest anyone should see them, and should gather
     They were in love, or might uprick an ear
     Of gossip. Nothing would have been more dear   460
     To them than Cupid's help, a place to walk
     Unseen, and there, poor things, unharassed, talk.

67   But in that little time they spent together
     Wisely he took such special care and heed
     Of all, she felt he read her thoughts, and whether   465
     Or what she wished, and so there was no need

To speak or tell him what to do. Indeed
She thought that love, though it had come so late,
To every joy had opened wide the gate.

68   And, to press onward at a cracking pace,   470
     So well he used his deeds, his words, that he
     Was so advanced, and in his lady's grace,
     That twenty thousand times, and joyfully
     She thanked the gods she'd met him. Cleverly
     He organised and planned all that he did   475
     To serve her, and yet kept it all well hid.

69   Because she found him so discreet in all,
     So secret, yet so kind, compliant, warm,
     She felt he was to her a sheltering wall
     Of steel, a shield from all distress and harm,   480
     That under his protection she grew calm,
     He was so wise, and so she felt no fright
     At loving, in so far as it was right.

70   But Pandarus, who still to stoke the fire
     Was likewise busy, active, diligent,   485
     Helping his friend was now his sole desire.
     He shoved, he pushed, and to and fro was sent,
     Played postman, save when Troilus was absent.
     Never did man so help a friend in need,
     Or do it better than he did, indeed.   490

71   But now, perhaps, some of you audience
     Would like me to describe the words, the cheer,
     The very voice of Troilus, and his stance
     Talking or walking with his lady dear.
     Believe me, it would take an age to hear!   495
     How can one draw from life a man whose love
     Is in the balance, so that all approve?

72 Truly, no one has done this thing as yet
    In story or in poem, that I do know.
    And though I'd like to, I'm sure I can't set   500
    My words aright, or such things clearly show.
    My author, from whose works all my rhymes grow
    Says plainly that he cannot such things write,
    So how can I a line of it endite?

73 But to be plain, and to be brief, then, thus—   505
    Both in accord, calm, happy and discreet
    Were these same two, Criseyde and Troilus,
    Just as I've told you, in this time, so sweet,
    Sweet, save that often they could never meet,
    Nor leisure have for talk or love to grow,   510
    That it fell out just as I'll tell you now,

74 That Pandarus, who worked with main and might
    Towards that object that I'll write of here,
    To get together at his house one night
    Troilus and fair Criseyde, his niece so dear,   515
    Where, at their leisure, he might talk, she hear,
    And there, with her, at the right time and place
    Unlock his love, find happiness and grace.

75 And Pandar, with much grave deliberation
    Had thought out everything that might avail   520
    To help, and put it into execution,
    And omit nothing that might well prevail.   ·
    If they both came, nothing, he thought, could fail.
    And as for being seen or found out there
    It was impossible, the coast was clear!   525

76 Gossiping magpies, spoilsports of each kind
    Might well have got wind of this love affair.
    But all is safe, and the world now seems blind,
    And every man oblivious where they are.

All waits as these two for the task prepare.   530
Nothing is needed now, but the right hour
When she, the bird, will flit into the bower.

77 Troilus, who knew about this preparation,
And all the plans, waited impatiently,
And made arrangements that his reputation   535
And hers might be safeguarded, carefully.
If he was missed at all he said he'd be—
(The while he did his lady all service—)
Within the temple making sacrifice.

78 Mostly, he said, at one shrine, wide awake   540
He'd wait Apollo's answer eagerly,
To be the first to see the laurel quake
Before the Sun God's voice came from the tree,
Telling him when the Greecian hosts would flee.
No one must hinder him, but let him pray,   545
And join their prayers to his, for victory.

79 Now there was little more left to be done,
And to cut short this somewhat lengthy tale,
Pandar arose just as the fickle moon
Changed, and the nights grew dark, starless, a veil   550
Of rainclouds blowing up, all grey and pale.
And straightaway round to his niece he went.
You all have heard just what he planned and meant.

80 And when he'd come, he straightway started teasing
As was his wont, and of himself made fun,   555
And finally he said, with smile most pleasing,
"Criseyde, my dear, you'll not escape, I've won.
Don't keep me dangling, tease, or make me run.
I've caught you now, and you must come and eat
At my house, now, tonight, my niece most sweet."   560

81 At which she laughed and quickly made excuse,
    Saying, "Look how it rains. How can I come?"
    "Don't put me off," he cried, "You can't refuse.
    You must, you can't deny me, it's not done."
    So at the last they both agreed, were one.   565
    If she had not, he whispered in her ear,
    "Never again would you have seen me here!"

82 Soon afterwards she asked suspiciously
    In a low voice if Troilus was there.
    "No, no," he cried, "He's out of town today."   570
    And added, "Even now suppose he were,
    You would not need to have the leastest fear.
    For rather than that men might him espy
    I'd rather twice ten thousand times to die."

83 Now I'm afraid my author does not say   575
    What Criseyde thought when Pandar answered so
    That Troilus had left the town that day,
    If she believed he told the truth, or no.
    But anyway, as he wished her to go
    She straightaway agreed, and as she ought,   580
    Obedient niece, did all her uncle sought.

84 Yet all the same she begged him earnestly,
    Although it was correct to go with him,
    To be most careful, gossips stupidly
    Could misconstrue things, innocence make dim.   585
    "Uncle, take care just whom you ask within,
    And since I now trust most of all in you,
    Make sure all's well, and then, as you wish, do."

85 He promised her, "My dear, my stock and stones,
    By all the gods who in the heavens dwell,   590
    I'd rather lose myself, both flesh and bones,
    And with dark Pluto plunge deep into Hell

Like Tantalus." Why should I further tell?
When she was pacified, he took his leave,
And she came there to supper that same eve,   595

86 Bringing with her some of her serving men,
And also her fair niece, Antigone,
And of her waiting women, nine or ten.
But who was glad at this? You know, surely!
Why, Troilus, who stood, and all could see   600
Out through a little pantry window, where
He'd been, since midnight stuffed, sans light, sans air,

87 Unseen, unknown, except by Pandarus.
But, to the point. Now, when Criseyde had come
With friends and servants, happy now and joyous,   605
Her uncle hugged her, then, when he had done,
They went to supper, gaily, everyone,
Where it was served, in comfort, and, no fable,
There were no dainties lacking at that table.

88 After the meal, full fed, they all arise   610
Contented, and with hearts all fresh and glad.
Happy was he who then could best devise
Something to please her, make her laugh with mad
Jests. He sang. She played. He told a sad
Old tale of war. But as all things have ending,   615
She said goodbye. "My ways I must be wending."

89 But O, Fortune, the weaver of our fates,
O influence that rules the heavens on high.
You are the shepherdess, you guide our gaits
Aright even when they seem to twist awry,   620
And Criseyde, who thought homeward to hie,
Had all her plans upset, without consent
At goddess Fortune's will, and must assent.

90 The bent and sickle moon, with her horns pale,
    Saturn and Jove, in Cancer joined together,   625
    So that from heaven such a rainstorm fell
    That every single woman that was there
    Feared that smoky rain, that whirling weather,
    At which Pandarus laughed and said straightway,
    "Now it's high time a lady went away!   630

91 But seriously, good niece, to please me, please
    I beg you now," he cried most earnestly,
    "If you would like to put me well at ease,
    Stay here in my house, quiet and comfortably.
    Everything here is yours, look round and see,   635
    For by my soul, and I'm in earnest now,
    To go home in this storm I can't allow."

92 Criseyde, who always liked to please, was glad
    To please him then, and listened to his prayer,
    And since it rained, and all was splash and flood,   640
    She thought, "I may as well stay dry shod here,
    And give way gracefully and with good cheer,
    Smile, not grumble, with good grace, not moan,
    Stop with my uncle, for I can't go home."

93 And so she said, "I'll stay, my uncle dear,   645
    Since you ask me, its reasonable also,
    I'm glad and happy to be with you here.
    I only joked when I said I must go."
    "Thank you, my dear," cried Pandarus, "Although
    I wasn't sure if you made fun, or were   650
    In earnest, I'm most glad you're staying here."

94 So all was well, and they began once more
    To jest, to dance, and feast over again.
    But Pandar to this did not cry "Encore."
    He wanted her to go to bed, quite plain,   655

I

And said, "Oh, lord, this is a mighty rain.
This sort of weather is for sleeping in,
And I propose we very soon begin.

95   Now do you know, niece, where your room's prepared?
You will sleep well, we lie not far asunder,   660
And where you rest I know you'll not be scared
Or roused by noise of rainstorms or of thunder.
I've put you in the little room just yonder,
And I will in the big room there alone
Keep watch over your women, every one.   665

96   And in this middle room, this one you see,
Your maids shall slumber comfortable and right,
And in the centre room there you will be.
So come again if you sleep sound and tight.
You won't care what the weather is tonight.   670
They'll bring a cup of wine when you require
To drink, and so, let us now both retire."

97   They said no more, but after this quite soon
They drunk their nightcaps, and the curtains drew,
And every one whose task or job was done   675
Went from the bedroom, leaving but a few
And ever more it poured with rain and blew
With roaring winds so hideously loud
That words were drowned as the fierce tempests rowed.

98   Then Pandarus, her uncle, as he ought,   680
With her chief waiting women courteously
Criseyde, most willing, to her bedside brought,
And took his leave, and bowed, and bent his knee,
And said, "Outside this door, in privacy,
Sleeping in comfort are your women all,
And if you want them, they are within call."

99   So when she was in the small bedroom laid,
     And all her women had in turn gone out,
     And were in bed themselves, as I have said,
     No soul was stirring then to dance about,   690
     All were asleep, excepting those, no doubt,
     Who restlessly disturbed the ones who slept,
     And by their noise others from slumbering kept.

100 But Pandarus, who knew each step, each pace
     In the old dance of love, each point therein,   695
     When he saw everything was in its place,
     He thought he would upon his work begin.
     Firstly that pantry door he did unpin,
     And still as any stone, without delay
     By Troilus' side he sat down straightaway,   700

101 And quickly, shortly to the point he went,
     Telling him everything he'd planned that day.
     "Make yourself ready now, for joy is sent,
     You soon shall bask in bliss most heavenly."
     "Now, joyful Venus, send me grace, I pray,"   705
     Said Troilus, "So great never was my need
     As now it is, nor yet my fear indeed."

102 Said Pandar, "Do not worry, never a deal,
     For it will be just as you shall desire.
     As I may thrive, this night your pain I'll heal,   710
     Or toss the stew and stewpot in the fire!"
     "All the same, Venus, help I do require,"
     Cried Troilus. "I'm your servant, and will serve
     You better yet, as you, goddess, deserve.

103 And if I'm ruled, O Venus, full of mirth,   715
     By fateful signs of Mars, or of Saturn,
     Or if your light was quenched in me at birth,
     Pray that your father will annul the harm

Through grace, and from me all such ill luck turn,
Lady, for love of him you loved so well,   720
Adonis, slain by wild boar in the dell.

104   And Jove, also, who fair Europa's love
Captured within bull's shape, I pray to you.
Help me, O Mars, with blood-stained cloak, the dove
Of Venus think of, speed my loving, too.   725
Phoebus, remember Daphne, you did woo
Her, and a laurel she became through fear,
Aid me, who love also, for that love dear.

105   Mercury, for love of Herse, too,
Which made Minerva with Agraulos wroth,   730
Now help me, and Diana pure, also,
May you both to my journey be not loath.
O fatal sisters, who cut out my cloth
And spun my life, my destiny, my fate,
Speed on this work before it is too late."   735

106   Said Pandarus, "You wretched mouse's heart,
Are you so scared that Criseyde will bite?
Come, put on this furred cloak above your shirt,
And follow me, I've courage and foresight,
No, wait, let me go on ahead, with light."   740
And as he spoke, unlocking a trap door
Hauled Troilus by the scruff to the next floor.

107   The stern wind then so loud began to roar
That any other noise no one could hear,
And those who lay before Criseyde's door   745
Slept sound, and deep in drowsy dreaming were,
And Pandar, very quiet, as if with fear,
Crept through the doorway without stumbling
Where they all lay, shut it, and was within.

108   And as he came on tiptoe secretly,   750
      His niece awoke and cried out, "Who goes there?"
      "Dear niece," said Pandar, "It is only me,"
      Don't be surprised, and also don't let fear
      Alarm you." Then he whispered in her ear,
      "Psst, not a word, for God's love, I beseech,   755
      Don't let a soul wake up and hear our speech."

109   "Why, how did you get in? By our lady,"
      She cried, "And where, unknown, unseen by all?"
      "Here, through this secret trap door," then said he,
      And Criseyde begged, "Let me some servants call." 760
      "No, God forbid, the thought does quite appal,"
      Cried Pandarus, "That you should be so mad!
      They might well think us up to something bad!

110   It's never good a sleeping dog to wake,
      Nor to give men something to guess about.   765
      Your women are asleep, I undertake,
      For all they know, the house could fall, no doubt.
      They'll sleep until the midday sun is out.
      And when I've brought my tale to its true ending,
      Unseen, just as I came, I will be wending.   770

111   Now, my dear niece, you've got to understand,
      That if you go on, as do women all,
      And grasp a man's love, so, in your small hand,
      And if you 'darling' and 'dear heart' him call,
      Yet, at the same time, hoodwink him, and fall   775
      In love with someone else, you would disgrace
      Yourself, hurt him, and shame the human race.

112   Now, you may ask, why do I tell you this?
      You know yourself, as well as any might,
      How that your love now fully granted is   780
      To Troilus, the best and worthiest knight

In all the world. You swore to him outright
That you'd be true to him, unless he'd give
You leave to leave him, so long as you live.

113 Now it has happened, since I left you here,   785
     That Troilus, to be direct and plain,
     Up by the guttering, through a private stair
     Climbed to my bedroom, here, in all this rain.
     Nobody saw him come here, that is plain.
     I alone know he's here, and if I lie   790
     May I, without more joy, fall down and die.

114 And he's come here, in such pain and distress,
     That if he isn't quite insane by this,
     He'll certainly soon fall into real madness,
     Unless God helps, and the real cause now is   795
     He tells me that a certain friend of his
     Told him you love a person called Horaste,
     And the shock almost made this night his last."

115 Criseyde, who all the while this story heard,
     Felt all at once her heart grow icy cold,   800
     And Pandar, with a deep, sad sigh answered,
     "Alas, I'm sure whoever such tales told,
     My dear heart wouldn't credit them or hold
     Me false so easily. Alas, what wrong
     Mistakes can do! I've lived too long, too long!   805

116 Horaste! For him betray dear Troilus!
     Why, I don't know him, God help me," cried she
     "What wicked creature lied and told him this?"
     Tomorrow, uncle, when I go and see
     Him, I'll explain it all most carefully,   810
     And he'll believe me, he'll excuse me, sure,"
     And with these words the poor girl sighed most sore.

117 "O God," she said, "So worldly happiness
     Which scholars know as false felicity,
     Is mixed with many strains of bitterness.   815
     Nothing more full of anguish is," said she
     "Than life, that's full of vain prosperity,
     For either joys come altogether never,
     Or else men are bereft of them forever.

118 O bitter web of happiness unstable,   820
     Whoever owns you, or where you are found,
     Either he knows your joys are mutable,
     Or thinks he'll always have your light around.
     Now, if he thinks this, he may well confound
     Himself. How can he be in happiness,   825
     When he's a fool, and sunk in stupidness?

119 And if he thinks that happiness is fleeting,
     And knows that every earthly joy must fly,
     Then every recollection is completing
     That pain of loss, making him certainly   830
     Most sure there is no real felicity.
     And if he sets no store on loss of joy,
     It has no value, it's a hollow toy!

120 Therefore it's my conclusion in this matter,
     That truly, and so far as I can see,
     There is no real joy in this sad world here.
     But O, you wicked serpent, Jealousy,
     Envious and suspicious foolery,
     Why have you made Troilus mistrust me,
     I never was untrue nor yet guilty."   840

121 Said Pandar, "Well it's happened, even so!"
     "Oh, my dear uncle, who has told him this?
     Why does my dear heart so suspicious grow?"
     "My dear, you know quite well the way it is,

And yet I hope to right what's gone amiss.   845
For you, my niece, can quench this burning fire,
And do it straightaway, if you desire."

122   "That I will do tomorrow," then said she,
"With God's help I will make the thing alright."
"Tomorrow? What a fine thing that would be!   850
"No, no," he cried, "he's in too bad a plight.
My niece, wise scholars with discretion write,
That there is danger in too much delay.
Such tarrying won't carry home the hay!

123   Niece, all things have their own appointed times,   855
And when a bedroom's burning, or a hall,
Greater the need to put it out betimes
Than to dispute, and argue one and all
How came the candle in the straw to fall!
Oh, benedicite, while arguing   860
The harm is done, the brisk bird's on the wing!

124   And, my dear niece, I beg, don't get me wrong,
But if you let him stay all night in woe
I'll swear yon never loved him much or long.
I'm speaking frankly, since we are but two.   865
But I know well that you will not do so.
You are too wise for stupidness outright,
Which might well risk his precious life this night."

125   "Never loved him! By my God, I say
You never loved a thing so well," said she   870
"Now, by my soul," said he, "We'll see today,
For since, as an example, you take me,
I couldn't lie, as you do there, and see
Sorrow like his for all the gold in Troy,
And if I could, may God take from me joy!   875

126 Now, look then, if you, niece, that are his love,
    Risk his life like this the whole long night,
    And all for nothing, now, by heaven above
    I swear it's only due to stupid fright,
    And also to sheer malice, and I'm right!   880
    Why, plainly, if you suffer his distress
    Like this, you've neither warmth nor gentleness."

127 Then Criseyde said, "Then will you do one thing,
    And by it end his sadness and disease?
    Hold out your hand, here, take him this blue ring,   885
    For there is nothing that will better please
    Him, save myself, nor more his heart appease.
    And say to my dear heart that all his sorrow
    Is groundless, and I'll tell him so tomorrow."

128 "A ring! That is quite useless, all my eye,   890
    Why my dear niece, that ring would need a stone
    With enough magic to make dead men cry!
    And jewels such as that I'm sure you've none.
    Discretion, wit out of your head are gone,
    Of that I'm sure! A shame, that's what I say,   895
    All this time wasted, soon you'll rue delay.

129 Don't you know that noble, lofty natures
    Do not give way to grief, neither hold back.
    But if fools rage, that suits the stupid creatures,
    And little notice of their griefs I take,   900
    Placating them with empty, soothing quack,
    And put them off, and make them wait my pleasure.
    But this, it is more like neglecting treasure.

130 This man is gentle, and so tender of heart
    That only death will cure his sorrow great.   905
    Believe me, girl, however deep his smart,
    He'll never speak a jealous word in hate.

As for you, niece, before his heart you break
Speak to him yourself about this thing,
For with one word you well may healing bring.   910

131   Now I have told you what peril he's in,
And how nobody knows that he is here.
I swear to you that there's no harm or sin.
I'll be with you myself, keep you from fear.
You know he is your knight, your love, your dear, 915
And that by love's own law him you must trust,
And when you wish, fetch him to you I must."

132   This incident so piteous was to hear,
And on the face of it seemed likewise true,
And Troilus, her knight, to her so dear,   920
His coming secret, and the place so, too,
That though her favours maybe were undue,
Considering all things as they then stood
It is not strange. She did it all for good.

133   Criseyde then answered, "May the gods bring rest 925
Unto my soul, I feel for him such woe,
And truly I would like to do the best
For him, if I have grace to do just so.
But whether you stay here, or for him go,
I'm fixed on a dilemma's horns, about   930
At my wit's end, till God shows the way out!"

134   Said Pandarus, "Now, listen, niece, look here,
To be so fixed, well, it's the fool's way out
And that seems hard. Hard heads won't persevere
Because they're lazy, or have faults, no doubt.   935
They say this to excuse themselves. Don't pout.
You're sensible, and what we have on hand
Does neither skill nor logic much demand."

135 "Then, uncle," said she, "Do just what you must.
     Only, before he comes, let me arise,   940
     And for the love of God, since all my trust
     Is in you two, and both of you are wise,
     Manage with all the skill you can devise,
     So that my good name and his happiness
     May be preserved. So do your best, no less."   945

136 "That is well said," he cried, "My niece most dear,
     May good luck bless your wise and gentle heart.
     But don't get up, let him come to you here.
     No need to fuss or make him go apart,
     But talk quite frankly, ease each other's smart.   950
     For God's love, Venus, now I pray to you
     In hope that joy to us will soon ensue."

137 Then Troilus came, and knelt down as he should
     Most soberly, and there, by her bed's head
     Greeted his lady the best way he could.   955
     But lord, she blushed at once so very red
     That, had men come to strike the poor girl dead
     She would not, could not one short word out bring
     For all the shock of his sudden coming.

138 And Pandarus, sensitive, quick to feel   960
     In everything, to jest and joke began,
     And said, "Look, niece, just how this lord can kneel,
     Now, by my soul, look at this gentleman!"
     And with that word he for a cushion ran
     And said, "Kneel now, as long as you desire,   965
     May God as quickly quench, abate your fire."

139 I can't say if she failed to bid him rise
     Because grief put it from rememberance,
     Or if she merely took it in the wise
     Of duty, that he did this observance.   970

But I *do* know she did him so pleasance,
She kissed him, though she deeply sighed, and sore,
Then told him, "Sit, and kneel down there no more."

140   Said Pandarus, "Now will you both begin.
       Make him sit down there, Criseyde, my dear,   975
       At your bed's side, just there, and well within,
       So each of you the other well may hear."
       So saying, to the fireside he went near,
       And held a light, pretending that he took
       A tale of old romance at which to look.   980

141   Criseyde, Troilus' lady now by right,
       Clearly was so in all security,
       And thought that he, her servant and her knight
       Should find in her no infidelity,
       Yet knew his loss of calm felicity,   985
       Also that love could cause such deep distress,
       And so spoke of his jealous foolishness.

142   "Why, my dear heart, as one who values well
       Love's goodness, against which no creature may
       Or can defend himself, so deep the spell,   990
       Also because I feel, and likewise say,
       I know your trust, your service every day,
       And that your heart is mine, this will explain
       Just how it made me pity all your pain.

143   And of your goodness I have found no end,   995
       Of which, my dear heart and my own true knight,
       I thank you for, and will make you amend,
       Though I can't do as much as would be right.
       And I, as far as skill or strength or might
       Can do, and will do, though it makes me smart,   1000
       Be true to you with my whole steadfast heart.

144 And doubtless that will soon be put to proof.
     But, my dear heart, all that there is to say
     Shall now be told, so that you'll have no grief.
     Though I blame you for all this grief, I say   1005
     Soon enough now I'll all your grieving stay.
     This grief that weights your heart, and my heart, too,
     I'll end it, and set right each wrong also.

145 My darling and my own, I don't know how
     Jealousy, alas, that wicked snake,   1010
     So without cause spewed poison seeds in you,
     The harm of which from you I now will take.
     Alas, that he, entire or part, may make
     His bolt hole in so very noble a place
     May Jove soon make him from your heart to race. 1015

146 But Jove, O Jove, creator of all things,
     Is it an honour to your deity
     That here the innocent bear sufferings,
     And that the guilty creatures go scot free?
     If only our complaints could lawfully   1020
     Be sent to you, of unjust jealousy,
     Inflicted so, then soon, and so, I'd cry!

147 Also my trouble's this, that people all
     Say this, "Why, jealousy is born of love."
     A load of poison's sweetened, so they bawl,   1025
     When on it one small grain of love they shove!
     God knows the truth of that, sitting above,
     And whether it's like love, or grief, or hate!
     It ought to bear its rightful name and state!

148 But certainly, some kinds of jealousy   1030
     Are more excusable than others, true.
     For instance, such where cause is, certainly.
     Yet that can be repressed by pity, too,

So that it does or says no thing undue,
But holds itself in check, swallows distress,   1035
And that kind I forgive, for gentleness.

149   And there is jealousy so full of fury
That rage and malice may not be repressed.
But, my dear heart, that's not your plight. Be sure I
Thank God for it. The trouble in your breast   1040
Is only an illusion, caused and stressed
By overflowing love, worry and stress
Which makes your heart feel all this fierce distress.

150   For which I feel much sorrow, yet no wrath.
But, for my duty, and for your heart's ease,   1045
Whenever you desire, by trial or oath,
By lottery, or in that way you please,
For God's love, test me, see I don't deceive,
And if I'm guilty, let me die straightway.
Alas, what more now can I do or say?"   1050

151   With that a few bright, sparkling tears anew
Fell from her eyes, and then she sighed and said,
"Now, God, you know, in thought or deed, untrue
To Troilus was never yet Criseyde."
With that her head down on her bed she laid,   1055
Covered it with the sheet, and sighed so sore,
And held her peace. Not a word spoke she more.

152   Now may God help to quench all this deep sorrow.
I hope he will do so, for he best may,
For I have said, from many a misty morrow   1060
Shines out many a merry summer's day,
And after winter comes the green, fresh May.
Men see each day, and also read in stories
Sharp struggles lead to shining victories.

153   This Troilus, when he her words had heard,   1065
      Don't worry—he had then no wish to sleep—
      With quite a deal of pain his heart was stirred,
      To see or hear Criseyde, his lady, weep.
      Indeed, he felt about his sad heart creep
      For every tear that started from her eye   1070
      Such cramping pains that almost made him die.

154   And inwardly he cursed the very hour
      That he came there, and that he had been born,
      For bad was turned to worse, and his labour
      All done in vain, and held in utter scorn.   1075
      He thought all lost, and he quite, quite forlorn.
      "O Pandarus," he thought, "Your subtlety
      Is all in vain, alas and woe is me."

155   And as he said these words, he hung his head,
      Fell on his knees, and sorrowfully sighed.   1080
      What could he say? He felt as if half dead,
      For she was angry, who should smile with pride.
      Nevertheless, when he could speak, he cried
      "God knows, indeed, that in this present game
      When everything is known, I'm not to blame."   1085

156   And then his sorrow so closed up his heart
      That from his eyes came never one healing tear.
      And all the vital forces in each part
      With shock quite quenched and stunned and dampened
         were.
      The pangs of sorrow, or else thrilling fear,   1090
      In fact, every sensation, fled away,
      And in a swoon, he dropped down rapidly.

157   This was most terrible and sad to see.
      But all was quiet. Pandar sprang up fast.
      "Be quiet, niece, or we are lost," said he.   1095

"Do not be frightened." Then, right at the last,
For this reason or that, in bed he cast
The lad, and said, "Rogue, have you a man's heart?"
And speaking, stripped him right down to his shirt,

158   And said, "Niece, if you do not help us now,   1100
Alas, your own dear Troilus is lost!"
"I want to help you, if you tell me how.
Oh dear, alas, woe's me, I'm torn and tossed."
"Why, then, pull out the thorn, you can and must,
The thorn stuck in his heart," said Pandarus,   1105
"Say all's forgiven, and be done with fuss."

159   "Yes," said she, "I'd rather do that thing
Than have the kindling goodness of the sun."
And with these words, in his ear whispering
Said, "Listen, dear heart, anger have I none.   1110
I swear to you I'm true, my dearest one.
"Now speak to me, to me, your love, Criseyde."
But all in vain to pierce his swoon they tried.

160   So that they rubbed his wrists, also the palms
Of both his hands, and bathed his temples, too,   1115
And to deliver him from bitter harms
She kissed him often, and to make words few,
Did all she could his numbed sense to renew,
And at the last a long breath from him broke.
Soon after that from his deep swoon he woke,   1120

161   And was more sensible and sound in mind,
Yet puzzled at his half-stunned misery,
And with a sigh, when he new strength could find
Said, "Mercy, God, what has become of me?"
"Why do you treat yourself so cruelly?"   1125
Criseyde asked. "Is this a manly game?
Troilus, why do you so, for shame, for shame!"

162   And as she spoke, across him her arm laid
       Forgiving all, and gave him many a kiss.
       He thanked her then, and spoke to her, and said   1130
       Words which made calm his heart, and gave him bliss.
       And she replied, with talk as sweet as his,
       With kindly words comforting his distress,
       Healing his sorrow with warm happiness.

163   Said Pandarus, "For all that I can see   1135
       This light and I serve no good purpose here.
       Light is not good for sick folks' eyes, truly!
       But, for the love of God, since now you are
       In such a happy state, let no thought mar
       With heaviness your hearts, but both be gay."   1140
       And then he took his candle to the chimney.

164   Soon afterwards, although no real need were
       For reassurance, she begged him to swear
       No harm was meant, yet felt no pang of fear,
       Nor bade him rise for fear of harm, but there   1145
       Was no occasion for such oaths, the care
       He had for her sufficed. Each man, I guess
       Who is in love acts with true gentleness.

165   But then she wanted to be told straightway
       From whom, and where, and when, and also why   1150
       With no good reason he felt jealousy,
       Also the sign and cause he took it by
       She wanted him to tell her busily,
       Or else, so she accused him, she'd believe
       It had been done maliciously to grieve.   1155

166   Without more words, in short, he must obey
       His lady's firm request, so, not to hurt,
       And to prevent suspicion, told a lie,
       Telling her she had cut him and looked curt

J

When at some feast, and treated him as dirt!   1160
Who needs must fish will catch at straws indeed,
So Troilus snatched and pulled up—this poor weed!

167   And Criseyde answered, "Sweet, if it was so,
        What was then wrong? No ill or harm I meant.
        I swear to you by God who made us two,   1165
        I never did so, I am innocent,
        It is not worth one bean, such argument.
        Why, you are like a jealous child, my sweeting,
        And really you deserve a proper beating!"

168   Then Troilus began in sorrow to sigh   1170
        Thinking if she was angry, that his heart
        Would die, and said, "Have pity, O, have pity
        Upon my woe, my darling, for a start.
        And if in what I've said there's any part
        That grieves, be reassured, I'll sin no more,   1175
        I'm in your power, do as you wish therefore."

169   She answered then, "Your guilt indeed I pity.
        That is to say, I do forgive all this.
        Remember it, this night, this house, this city,
        And then resolve to do no more amiss."   1180
        "Dear heart," he said, "I've noted, so it is!"
        "And now," she added, "That I've made you smart,
        Forgive me this also, my own sweetheart."

170   This Troilus, with so much bliss surprised,
        Put all in the gods' hands, as one who meant   1185
        Nothing but good, and mind made up, he seized
        Her fast within his arms. Pandarus went
        Towards his bed, and with much good intent
        Lay down to sleep, saying, "If you are wise
        Don't swoon now, or maybe more folk will rise!" 1190

171   The innocent lark, what can or could it say
      When grasped within the sparrowhawk's clawed foot?
      I can't tell, but of their love make a lay,
      A story, first sweet sugar, then sour soot.
      Though I delay a year, yet I will do it,   1195
      And following my author, tell their gladness
      As well as I've described their previous sadness.

172   Criseyde, who, when she felt him so take
      Her, just as wise men in their wise books told,
      Right as an aspen leaf began to quake,   1200
      When she felt how his arms began to fold.
      But Troilus, now cured from cares so cold
      Gave thanks to all the joyful gods, the seven
      Powers who raise suffering men from woe to heaven.

173   This Troilus in his arms began to strain   1205
      His love, and said, "O sweet, as I'm alive,
      Now you are caught, now there is but we twain,
      Yield, love, there is no point to fight or strive."
      And to him gentle answer gave Criseyde.
      "If I had not ere now, my sweetheart dear   1210
      Yielded to you, I would not now be here."

174   O, it is true indeed that healed to be
      From fever, or from any grave sickness
      Men must drink down, as you can often see
      A bitter draught, and to have happiness   1215
      People must gulp down pain and great distress,
      By this I mean that Troilus in his life
      Before he found such joy endured much strife.

175   And now, indeed, the sweetness seemed more sweet
      Because they'd tasted bitterness before,   1220
      From woe into such bliss they rose, so fleet,
      Nor had they felt such joy could be in store.

Better like this, than both be lost and sore!
For God's love, let each woman take good heed
To act just so, if ever she's such need!   1225

176   Criseyde, free now from every fear and grief,
      And with good reason to trust Troilus well,
      Cherished him so, it was beyond belief,
      When she had heard him of his true love tell,
      And as around a tree, with its sweet smell   1230
      Circling and binding twists the soft woodbind,
      Each in their arms the other one did wind.

177   And as the newly fledged shy nightingale
      Hesitates when first she starts to sing
      Whenever she hears any herdman's tale,   1235
      Or in the hedgerows any foot stirring,
      Yet after will her song in silence ring,
      Even so Criseyde, when her fear was over
      Opened her heart, and told all to her lover.

178   And even as one who waits for execution   1240
      Daily expecting death, as he may guess,
      Yet rescue brings him sudden absolution,
      And out of death he's brought to happiness,
      For all the world, into just such gladness
      Was Troilus, and had his lady sweet.   1245
      May all of us with no worse mishap meet!

179   Her slender arms, her back so straight and soft,
      Her thighs so long, plump, smooth and very white
      He stroked, and blessed and praised often and oft
      Her snowy throat, her round, small breasts
                                           so bright,   1250
      And so in all this heaven he did delight,
      And many thousand times he kissed her, too,
      So that for joy he scarce knew what to do?

180   Then he said, "O love, O charity,
        Your mother also, Cytherea sweet,   1255
        After yourself may she all praised be,
        Venus, I mean, planet of bliss complete,
        And next to that Hymenaeus I greet.
        Never did man owe gods such thanks, such praise
        As I, whom you from cares so cold did raise.   1260

181   Love so benign, most holy bond of things
        Whoever will not honour, heed you, praise,
        Lo, his desire will flee, losing its wings,
        But from your bounty you will help and raise
        Your labourers who have served you all their days, 1265
        And yet without your grace, where would we be?
        We'd all be lost without your charity.

182   And as for me, who least deserve your aid
        Out of all those to whom you grant your grace,
        You've helped me when in deadly pain I laid,   1270
        And now have raised me to so high a place
        That there are no bounds set to joy and praise.
        My heart is full, and I can only pray
        Extol and laud your bounty reverently."

183   And with these words he straightaway kissed
                                                  Criseyde.   1275
        That kissing truly gave her no disease!
        "Oh, would to God I knew," then Troilus cried,
        "How you, my darling sweetheart I could please!
        What man," he said, "Was ever thus at ease
        As I, on whom the fairest and the best   1280
        That ever I saw, deigns her dear heart to rest.

184   In this men see the mightiness of mercy.
        I know this well, I know how great is she.
        I, all unworthy to possess such beauty.

But, dear heart, of your generosity   1285
Believe, although I all unworthy be,
That I'll amend, improving in some wise
Through the great virtue of your high service.

185   And, for the love of God, my lady dear,
Since God has shaped me to serve you indeed,   1290
This is my meaning, be my star so clear,
Lead me to life, if you will so, or lead
Me deathwards, teach me to deserve indeed
Your thanks, that I, through folly and ill breeding
May never do what is to you displeasing.   1295

186   For truly, my fresh, womanly, sweet girl,
This I dare say, that truth and diligence
You'll lifelong find in me. And I'll not hurl
Stones at your stainlessness, break your defence.
And if I do, present, or in absence   1300
For God's love, kill me with my own bad deed
If you, so tender hearted, can indeed."

187   "Truly," said she, "Sweetheart, my own heart's pleasure,
My ground of ease, my dear heart, O, most dear,
Be kind. I trust you. Trust is now my treasure.   1305
Words, what use are they? For love's true matter
Lies in our actions, in that we are here.
So, with one word, I pause not, nor repent.
Welcome, my knight, my peace and my content."

188   Of their delight, even of joys the least   1310
Is quite impossible for me to write.
You judge, if ever you've been at such feast
Of gladness, of their happiness that night.
All I can say is that these lovers bright
Felt in that time of peace, love's joy freely,   1315
Half fearful, yet half in security.

189 O blissful night, of them so long besought,
     How happy then to both of them you were!
     Another such I wish I could have bought.
     I'd give my soul for the least pleasure there!   1320
     Make off, imperious disdain and fear,
     And let them in this heavenly pleasure dwell,
     So great that all of it I'll never tell!

190 Pleasure that's true, though I dare not tell all
     As does my author, of that excellence,   1325
     Yet I've told something, and with God's help, shall
     Echo in everything sense and sentence,
     And if I have, respecting love, been dense,
     And failed or spoiled the sense most stupidly,
     Fill out yourselves, correct or amplify.   1330

191 For all my words, in this and every part,
     I write them always subject to correction
     By you, my audience, skilful in love's art.
     I put it to you all, in your discretion,
     Add, or subtract, alter, or change the diction,   1335
     Vary the language, that I do beseech,
     But now to get on quickly with my speech.

192 These two, that in each other's arms I left,
     Were both so loath to tear themselves apart,   1340
     That each without the other felt bereft,
     Or else, and this dread niggled at their heart,
     They thought their joys were but of dreams a part,
     And often each to each would say, "O sweet,
     Do I hold you, or only dream we meet?"

193 And lord, he stared with so much joy at her,   1345
     That his look never wavered from her face,
     And he said, "Dear heart, is it true you are
     Beside me? Are you here, now, in this place?"

"Yet, my own heart, I thank God for his grace,"
Criseyde said, and gave him many a kiss,   1350
He knew not where his spirit was, for bliss!

194   Then Troilus kissed her eyes again, again,
And said aloud, "O eyes, so bright and clear,
You were the villains who caused me such pain,
You were the baits laid by my lady dear!   1355
Though there is mercy written in your cheer,
God knows that message there is hard to find
With no bonds how could you trap me and bind?"

195   And with those words he took her in his arms,
And many a hundred times or more he sighed,   1360
Not sighs like those men give when pains or harms
Wring them, or those whom sickness tired and tried,
But sighs of ease that from a full heart glide,
Showing the deep affection in his breast.
Such sighs, such joys, they could not be repressed.   1365

196   Soon after this they spoke of many things
Which had a bearing on their love affair,
And in their joyfulness exchanged their rings.
I cannot tell what the inscriptions were,
But I do know, a brooch, gold and azure   1370
In which was set a ruby like a heart
Criseyde gave him, and pinned it on his shirt.

197   Surely you know a covetous, wretched man
Who runs down love, and holds it in despite,
Though he may hoard and grab the coins he can,   1375
Never finds gold can give him such delight
As there is found in love, man's bliss, man's light,
But without doubt, and I am saying so,
Such perfect joys a man's heart cannot know.

198 Such may say they know love, but lord, they lie,   1380
     Such busybodies, rogues, fearful and dour
     Look upon love as madness or folly,
     But they'll be treated as befits such sour
     Creatures. For them Love will no fine wines pour.
     He'll serve them with the dregs, and with mischance! 1385
     But lovers who are true, these he'll advance.

199 I would to God the wretches who profess
     To scorn Love's service all grew ears as long
     As those of Midas, with his covetousness,
     And also drunk a draught as hot and strong   1390
     As Crassus did for his opinions wrong,
     To teach them that the lovers they despise
     Are in the right, and they quite otherwise!

200 These two of whom I told you recently,
     When well relaxed, at heart contented there,   1395
     Began to talk together happily,
     And to remember how and when and where
     They met at first, and every doubt and fear
     That now had passed, but all such heaviness
     Thanks be to God, had turned to happiness.   1400

201 And evermore, when they began to speak
     At all of times like that, so long ago,
     Their kisses into such sad tales did break,
     And out of this new joys, new hopes did flow.
     All that they could they did, made one, to grow   1405
     In happiness, and to relax, at ease,
     And present joys made these past woes to cease.

202 It is not reasonable to speak of sleep,
     For that won't fit with what I have to write.
     God knows they did not so night's watches keep! 1410
     But lest the happiness of all that night

Vainly should slip them by, with main and might
They filled it full of joy and business,
And everything to do with happiness.

203   But when the cock, to all astrologer,   1415
Beat upon his breast, and after crowed,
And Lucifer, the new day's messenger
Began to rise, and out her bright beams glowed,
And in the east, to those who knew it, showed
Jupiter's planet, then quite soon Criseyde   1420
With a sad heart to Troilus turned and said,

204   "Life of my heart, in whom is joy and trust,
Alas, that I was born, and woe is me,
This day will part us, ah, alas, it must,
It's time to rise and go hence speedily,   1425
Or else I'm lost forever certainly.
O night, alas, why won't you linger here
As long as when Jove lay with Alcmena?

205   O black, black night, as all in books may read,
God shaped you so that you this world should hide 1430
At the appointed hour with your dark weed,
So that mankind might in sweet rest abide.
Indeed beasts may complain and people chide,
For day loads us with labour, yet you flee,
And will not grant us rest perpetually!   1435

206   You finish off your work with too much greediness,
O hasty night, may God, maker of all
Chain you for your most wicked speediness,
So from our hemisphere you'll never fall,
Nor underground wind your black weeds and pall. 1440
For now, because you're hurrying out of Troy,
I've had to do without my fill of joy."

207 And Troilus, who with all her words agreed
    So well he might have said them, through distress
    Felt just as if his heart blood tears did bleed,   1445
    He'd never yet felt quite such heaviness
    Arise so quickly from such great gladness,
    And thereupon Criseyde, his lady dear
    He closely hugged and spoke in this manner.

208 "O cruel day, revealer of the joy   1450
    That night and love both hid and covered deep,
    Accursed be your coming into Troy,
    Your bright eyes peer through every hole, and peep!
    Envious day, why do you spy and creep?
    What have you lost, what seek you in this place?   1455
    May God quench your light here, we pray his grace!

209 Alas, how have we lovers done you harm,
    Pitiless day? You bring the pains of hell!
    For unto many a lover you've brought shame.
    Your streaming light won't let them quietly dwell.   1460
    What, are you trying now your light to sell?
    Hawk it to those who hack out trinkets gay.
    We don't want light, we have no need for day."

210 And then the god who drives the sun he scolded,
    And said, "Oh fool, men may well you despise,   1465
    Because night long in your arms Dawn's been folded,
    Yet you so early let the goddess rise
    To tease and torture lovers in this wise.
    Keep to your bed, you god, and your mistress
    Hold with you there, else may you feel distress!"   1470

211 And then he deeply sighed, and thus he said,
    "My lady true, of all my weal and woe
    The source and well, my darling, my Criseyde,
    Must I arise, alas, and must I go?

Ah, now I feel my heart will break in two.   1475
How can I live at all without you, love,
Since now with you is all the life I have?

212   What shall I do? In truth I do not know.
Nor when, alas, I shall that good time see
When I shall be again, as now, with you,   1480
And as things are, God knows when that will be,
Since longing and desire so gnaw at me
Till I'm half dead, and will, till I come back,
How can I then endure your loss, your lack?

213   Nevertheless, my own dear lady bright,   1485
If only I was sure with certainty
That I, your humble servant and your knight
Was in your heart and love set utterly
As you are set in mine, which thing, truly,
I'd rather have than all the wide world gain,   1490
Then better I'd endure my loss and pain."

214   To which Criseyde answered straightaway,
And with a sigh she said, "Dear heart, my dear,
The love game's gone so far, this game we play,
That Phoebus first shall fall down from his sphere,   1495
And eagles for the gentle doves feel fear,
And the fixed mountains from their stations start
Before you, Troilus, leave Criseyde's heart.

215   You are so deeply in that heart engraved
That even if I wished to wipe away   1500
The thought of you, as I hope to be saved,
I could no do so, nor could I betray
You even if torturers threatened me today,
So don't let any other fantasy
Invade your brain, and scare me so I die!   1505

216 And that you'll hold me fast within your mind
As I hold you, that is what I beseech,
And if I could believe that I would find
This true, I could no greater pleasure reach.
But, my dear heart, now, with no further speech,   1510
Be true to me, or sad, sad will I be,
For I am yours and will be so, truly.

217 Be glad at this, live in security.
I've not said this before, nor again will,
And if for you to come back here would be   1515
Happiness, that same return would fill
Me with an equal joy. To have you still
Would give me greater joy than heaven's bliss."
Then she embraced him, too, with many a kiss.

218 Against his will, since it had got to be,   1520
Troilus got up from bed, and quickly dressed,
Then in his arms he hugged his dear lady
A hundred times, then on his way he pressed,
With words wrung from his heart he then addressed
His love and said, "Farewell, dear heart, my sweet, 1525
God grant that soon we, safe and sound, may meet."

219 To which no word from sorrow she answered,
So much did parting from him wring her heart,
And Troilus back to his own palace fared,
And miserable as she was, for his part.   1530
So much desire and pain tore him apart.
To be with her again was his longing,
And in his mind was always this one thing.

220 Back in his princely palace, Troilus soon
Softly and quietly slunk into his bed,   1535
Hoping to sleep there late, well into noon,
But all in vain. He blinked and sunk his head

Vainly into his pillow; sleep had fled,
Thinking how she more precious was by far
Than he had guessed, he burned with hot desire.   1540

221   And in his memory began to wind
All of her words, and every look and glance,
Firmly fixing in his thoughts and mind
Each detail which could make his pleasure dance,
And truly, every point and rememberance   1545
Made hot desire flare up. Lust to make love
Was stronger now, and yet he could not move.

222   Criseyde also, just in the same way
Pictures of Troilus in her memory set,
His wisdom, worthiness, the pleasures gay   1550
He gave, his gentleness, how they had met,
And she thanked Love she was with love beset,
Yet longed to have with her once more her dear,
So she could make him happy without fear.

223   Then Pandarus, who with the morning came   1555
To greet his niece, spoke to her cheerfully,
And said, "All night it poured so hard with rain
My darling niece, I ask this fearfully,
I think you had few dreams, slept direfully!
In fact, all night the storm kept me awake.   1560
Some of our heads this morning well may ache!"

224   Then he came near and said, "How goes it now
This merry morning, niece, how do you fare?"
Criseyde said, "Never the better for you,
Ah, you old fox, may you feel bitter care!   1565
God help me, you caused all this whole affair,
For all your bland words and your innocent smile!
Ah, those who meet you little know your guile!"

225   And with these words her face she covered over
      With bed clothes, and in deepest shame blushed red, 1570
      And Pandar peeped beneath the sheltering cover
      And said, "Niece, if you think I should be dead,
      Take out a sword, and then cut off my head."
      With that he suddenly thrust out his arm
      Beneath her neck, then kissed her with much charm. 1575

226   I'll skip all that which there's no point in saying.
      In short, as God forgives, Criseyde too
      Forgave her uncle, jested, laughing, playing,
      It was the only thing that she could do.
      But to the point I'll now directly go.   1580
      At the appointed time homeward she went,
      And Pandarus had done all that he meant.

227   Now we must turn again to Troilus
      Who restlessly lay a long while in bed,
      And then sent privately for Pandarus   1585
      To come in haste, and so good Pandar sped
      With no delay, straightway, and no nays said,
      And greeted Troilus very solemnly,
      And sat down by his bedside soberly.

228   Then Troilus, with deep and warm affection   1590
      And friendly love, all that you can devise
      Upon his knees to Pandarus fell down,
      And before Pandar made his friend arise
      Troilus gave thanks to him in his best wise
      And then a hundred times he said, "I bless   1595
      You, Pandarus, who saved me from distress.

229   Oh, friend, of all my friends the very best
      That ever I had, and this is truth I tell,
      You've brought my soul to heaven, into sweet rest,
      Out of the fiery floods of burning Hell,   1600
      That though a thousand times I might well sell

In one day my poor life to serve you, friend,
It would not for your goodness make amend.

230   The sun, whose shining all the world can see
Never beheld, on this my life I lay,   1605
A creature who's more fair and good than she
Whose love I am, and shall be so for aye.
And that I'm her love also, I dare say,
Thanks to the grace and the great worthiness
Of love, and also all your busyness.   1610

231   Indeed, you've given me no little thing,
For which I'm in your debt for ever and aye,
For my whole life. Life came by your helping,
Without you I'd have died this many a day."
And with these words down in his bed he lay.   1615
Pandarus heard him with solemnity,
Till all was said, then answered quietly.

232   "Dear friend, if I've done any courtesy
To you, it was what I desired to do,
And I'm as glad as any man could be,   1620
God help me. But don't take offence, or grow
Angry at what I say, be wary now
That you are prosperous, and in such bliss,
That through your own fault things may go amiss.

233   For, out of Fortune's sharp adversity,   1625
The worst of evils that could fall is this,
For man to tumble from prosperity,
Yet to remember happier days of bliss.
You are a wise lad, so don't go amiss.
Don't tempt fate now, though you sit snug
                                    and warm,   1630
For if you do, then sure, you'll come to harm.

234 You're now at ease, and think yourself dug in,
    Yet sure as red burns up the well-stoked fire,
    It takes more skill to keep and hold, than win!
    Bridle your conversation and desire.   1635
    Joys of the world hang from a fragile wire!
    Every day you'll see them fall and break,
    So do not test or twist the threads of fate."

235 Said Troilus, "I hope, God helping me,
    Dear friend, that in all things I'll bravely bear   1640
    Myself so that I'll not be lost or guilty.
    I'll not be rash, making you grieve or fear.
    You need not sermonise so smugly here!
    Pandar, if you could look into my heart
    You'd find no cause to play a preacher's part."   1645

235 Then he told him of his joyful night,
    And why he'd first felt fear, and when, and how,
    And then said, "Friend, as I am a true knight,
    And by the faith I owe to God and you,
    I never had it half so hot as now!   1650
    And all the time, the more desire so bites me
    For making love, so it the more delights me!

237 Truly I do not know just why this is,
    Yet now my love has a new quality
    Quite different from the way I felt ere this."   1655
    Pandar replied and said to him, that he
    Who once in heaven finds true felicity
    Can feel his bliss in other ways, I guess
    Than the first time he knew such happiness.

238 To sum up all, this joyful Troilus   1660
    Could never say enough of this matter,
    Nor cease from praising so to Pandarus
    The bounty of Criseyde, his lady dear,

K

Nor thank his friend enough with word or cheer, 1655
And spoke this tale, span new, straight from his heart
Until the black night made his two friends part.

239 Soon afterwards, when Fortune willed it so,
 At last there dawned that blissful day so sweet
 When Troilus was told that he should go
 To Pandar's house, and there his lady meet, 1670
 At which he felt his heart with pleasure beat,
 And prayed to all the gods most faithfully.
 Now let us see if he will merry be!

240 They kept to the same plan, just the same wise
 Of her coming, likewise of his also 1675
 As at the first. This I need not devise.
 Plainly and to the point I meant to go.
 In happiness, and safe, Pandar those two
 Put into bed, where they both wished to be,
 And there they are in quiet security. 1680

241 I need not tell you, now these two have met
 If they were happy and in blissful bliss.
 For if it first was good, now better yet
 It was a thousand fold, I'll tell you this!
 To sorrows and to fears they gave a miss, 1685
 And both of them had now, and felt it grow
 As much of joy as any heart can know.

242 This is not easy to describe or measure.
 This is a thing no wit can clearly tell.
 Each lover tried to give the other pleasure. 1690
 Happiness, which scholars outline well
 And praise, is still not large enough. The spell
 Of their great joy can't be pinned down by ink.
 This passes all that hearts can dream or think.

243 But cruel day, ah me, that evil hour,   1695
    Now it draws near, as they by all signs know,
    For which they thought death's darting pangs must lour
    So much oppressed they were, lost joy, lost hue,
    And once again cursed morning all anew,
    Calling it traitor, jealous wretch, and worse,   1700
    And bitterly the fresh day's light they curse!

244 Said Troilus, "Alas, I'm now aware
    That Phoebus and those swift, bright steeds all three
    Which draw out into day the sun god's chair,
    Have galloped on apace in spite of me,   1705
    And that will make it soon the daytime be,
    And as Apollo's in such haste to rise
    I'll never more make him a sacrifice!"

245 But with the day the lovers had to part,
    And when their talk, embrace and looks were done, 1710
    As once before they tore themselves apart,
    Arranging first a time to meet quite soon,
    And so spent many a night as this sweet one.
    So Fortune for a time led into joy
    Criseyde, and also Troilus, prince of Troy.   1715

246 In great contentment, bliss, with pleasure singing
    This happy Troilus now began to live.
    He spent his money, jousted, went out feasting,
    He bought and wore new clothes, would freely give,
    And had around him, so secure in love,   1720
    A world of well-born people, gay and free,
    The best and merriest in the whole city.

247 So that his fame and good report was spread
    Throughout the world, of honour and largesse,
    And up to heaven's gate it rung indeed,   1725
    And through his love he was in such gladness,

That in his heart he felt, (this is my guess)
There was no lover in this world at ease
Quite so completely, so much did love please.

248   The beauty and the loveliness which nature   1730
      Had given other women could not make
      The least impression on his heart. For sure
      Criseyde's net was close, he could not break
      Free of the toils and meshes, nor could take
      Hold of the knot that tied him and go free,   1735
      For all that he could try, that could not be.

249   And by the hand quite often he would take
      Pandar, and lead him to the garden green,
      And such a fuss and such a long tale make
      About Criseyde, her goodness feminine,   1740
      And all her beauty, that to cut it fine,
      It was a heaven his happy words to hear.
      And then he'd sing of love in this manner.

250   "Love, who of earth and sea has governance,
      Love, who in his power holds heaven high,   1745
      Love, who in wholesome, healing alliance
      Keeps people linked and joined delightfully,
      Who spins our strong desire for company,
      Makes mankind long in couples knit to dwell,
      Bind, bless our union, which I've told, and tell.   1750

251   Love, which gives the world stability,
      Making all hours and seasons move in time,
      And elements which seem to disagree
      Be linked and made harmonious and to chime,
      So Phoebus leads out rosy Day at prime,   1755
      And the Moon rules in turn over the night.
      Love does all this, all praise then to his might.

252 Love constrains the sea, greedy to flow,
     Confines to proper limit all its flooding
     Waves, in fierceness that they do not grow
     To drench the earth and all within it budding.
     And if, unbridled, Love's bright steeds go scudding,
     All that he binds will break, scatter, be tossed
     Asunder, and the things he saves be lost.

253 For God, who rules all things has willed it so   1765
     That with his quickening power Love binds all fast
     Within his cincture, making each heart go
     Through his warm maze, where safe and held at last
     They can't escape. May he the cold hearts twist
     To make them love, and may he pity, too,   1770
     Sad hearts, and keep them safe, whose hearts are true."

254 And after this, most ready for the war
     Troilus was, the first to arm for fight,
     And (unless the books I've looked at err,)
     Save Hector, the most feared of any knight.   1775
     And this increase of bravery and might
     Came all through love, his lady's praise to win.
     This changed and fired his spirit so within.

255 In times of truce out hawking he would ride,
     Or else to hunt the boar or bear or lion,   1780
     From smaller game that he turned aside.
     And when he came back riding through the town
     His lady from her window looking down
     Peeped like falcon sleek from perch or mew,
     Ready to smile upon him, fresh of hue.   1785

256 And all of love and goodness was his speech.
     He scorned all evil things and wretchedness,
     And there was no need, doubtless, to beseech
     Troilus to honour men of worthiness,

Nor to give alms to people in distress.   1790
And most of all he liked to hear men tell
Of lovers prospering and doing well.

257   For truth to tell, he held that any man
Was good as dead, unless he was a lover,
(People, that is, of the right age, who can   1795
Love, or who should.) And then he would go over
Love's symptoms, and such sentiments uncover,
That everyone in love who listened, knew
All that he did was right, what he said, true.

258   And though he came of blue and royal blood,   1800
He had no arrogance, no pride of race.
To all he was most courteous and good,
And men of every rank, in every place
Praised him. For love (all honoured be his grace,)
Made Troilus anger, pride and avarice   1805
Abjure, and with them every other vice.

259   O lady bright, daughter of Dione,
Also your son, Dan Cupid, winged and blind,
You Muses nine, who live on Helicon,
Or who upon Parnarssus men may find,   1810
Through your help so far I my thread can wind,
But fear I'll break it now. Yet since you will
Now leave me, I must praise you for your skill.

260   Through you I have told all, here, in this song,
Of Troilus' love, and its effects and joys,   1815
Although there was distress and pain among
The happiness, or so my author says,
My third book ends now, in these latter days,
And Troilus in calm and joy complete
Is with Criseyde, his own dear heart most sweet.   1820

Book Four

1   But all too little, woe betide the while,
    Such joy can last, thanks be to harsh Fortune,
    Who seems most true when she will most beguile,
    And can to foolish men sing such a tune
    That thus she'll trap and blind them all too soon,   5
    And when a man is thrown down from her wheel,
    She mocks and laughs, and can no pity feel.

2   From Troilus she turned her shining face
    Away, and took of him no care or heed,
    But cast him clean out of his lady's grace,   10
    And on her wheel aloft set Diomede.
    In pity still this thing makes my heart bleed.
    Alas, my pen here, this, with which I write
    Shivers with dread of what I must indite.

3   For how Criseyde Troilus forsook,   15
    Or, at the very least, became unkind,
    Must henceforth be the matter of my book.
    The source I follow this sad thing enshrined.
    Alas, that it should ever reasons find
    To say ill of her. If my source should lie,   20
    Well, he that wrote it bears that villany!

4   O you dire Furies, Night's dark daughters three
    Who mourn without an end, in pain, on fire,
    Megaera, Electo, Tisiphone;

Cruel god Mars, of cruel Quirinus sire,   25
Help me to write this my fourth book so dire,
And loss of life and love, (both things so dear,)
By Troilus, may I now reveal them here.

5   Lying in hosts, as I have said ere now,
Was all the Grecian strength about Troy town,   30
And so it fell, when the sun's beams sloped low
Upon the sign of Hercules' lion,
That Hector, and full many a bold baron
Cast lots to find which day was best to fight
Against the Greeks, and hurt them with their might.   35

6   I do not know how long the time between
The lottery day, and when to fight they meant,
But on a certain day, bright, and with sheen
Of armour, Hector, with his vanguard, went
With spear in hand, and warlike long-bows bent,   40
And by the beard, (so, with no more delay,)
He took the foemen in the field that day.

7   All that long day, with spears to points well ground,
With arrows, darts, swords and with maces fell
They fought and brought both man and horse
                            to ground,   45
And with their axes split their skulls as well.
But in the last affray, sad truth to tell,
The men of Troy were double-crossed, and led
So far astray that home at last they fled.

8   On this one day was taken Antenor,   50
In spite of Polydamus, Menoetus,
Antiphus, Sarpedon, Polymnester,
Polites, or the Trojan, Dan Rhesus,
And folk of less account, like Phebusus.
So, for this mishap, all the folk of Troy   55
Lost through his capture nearly all their joy.

9   And Priam granted at the Greek's request
    A time of truce, in which they both might treat,
    Exchange their prisoners of high rank or least,
    And for them mostly pay out ransoms great.   60
    This news was talked about in every street
    By Greeks, and by the Trojans everywhere,
    And first of all it came to Calchas' ear.

10 When Calchas knew this truce was to be made,
    He forced his way to where in council sat   65
    The Greeks, with all the elders there arrayed,
    And from his usual seat, with strange looks that
    Showed his distress, asked their indulgence, flat,
    For love of God, show manners and good sense,
    Be quiet, shut up, and give *him* audience!   70

11 Then he said, "Now, good lords, in truth I was
    A Trojan once. My face you know indeed.
    Call then the rest to mind. I'm that Calchas
    Who preached and gave you comfort in your need,
    Told you the future, how in war you'd speed.   75
    Indeed I know at the appointed hour
    Troy shall be burned by you, tower by bright tower.

12 And in what form and manner, in what wise
    You'll take this town, and your desire achieve
    You've heard me often to you all devise.   80
    My lords, you know this well, so I believe!
    And, as I wished you well, loved you, indeed,
    I came myself, leaving the Trojan town,
    To teach you how your victory could be won,

13 Not troubling over wealth, savings or rent,   85
    For your welfare I had in mind, your ease,
    And so I lost my goods, to you I went
    Thinking through this, my lords, all you to please.

Yet all my loss is not to me dis-ease,
Because through you and yours I have much joy,   90
I don't care what I left behind in Troy,

14   Except my daughter, whom I left, alas,
Sleeping at home when out of Troy I fled.
Hard-hearted, cruel father that I was!
How could I be so cold? Why not instead   95
Have brought her with me, night-gowned, fresh from bed?
Grieving about this thing, I'll die tomorrow
If you, my lords, won't pity my great sorrow!

15   Because there was no opportunity
Nor a fit time to get her out of Troy   100
I've held my peace, but now, if you agree
I'll have her here, and soon, my girl, my joy.
Your help, your grace I crave, lest grief destroy.
May I find those to pity my distress,
I, who for you have suffered heaviness !   105

16   You captured and have fettered in prison
Trojans enough, and if you, lords, agree,
Through one of them my child may have redemption.
Now, for God's love, and from your great bounty
Give one of those same Trojan lads to me.   110
Do not refuse to grant my prayer, you'll have
The city soon, and all its folk enslave!

17   I swear upon my life I do not lie.
Apollo told it to me faithfully.
I've also found it through astronomy,   115
By lottery and augury, truly,
And tell you now that soon and speedily
Both fire and flame through all that town will spread,
And so Troy shall turn into ashes dead.

18 For certainly Phoebus and Neptune both   120
    The gods who built the walls of the same town
    Are with the folk of Troy enraged and wroth,
    That they will bring the city tumbling down
    To spite the wicked King Laomedon
    Who would not pay those gods their due and hire.   125
    For this the town of Troy shall burn in fire."

19 And as he told his tale this old, grey man,
    Humble in looks and speech, lowly and meek,
    Wept, and the salt tears from his two eyes ran
    Fast down the furrows of his grizzled cheek,
    So long he begged and prayed, mercy to seek,
    That without more ado, to heal his woe
    They gave him Antenor, his captive foe.

20 Then who was glad but Calchas, and he turned
    The matter to his profit, begged the men   135
    Who made the treaty terms, as they returned
    To take Antenor, offering him again
    In an exchange for Criseyde. And when
    King Priam sent his safeguards, the Greeks sent
    Ambassadors, who into Troy's town went.   140

21 The reason for their coming soon was told
    To Priam, and straightaway in general
    To all his parliament he did unfold
    The matter, and the gist of it I shall
    Tell you. In fact the Trojans liked it all,   145
    The terms suggested, the exchange proposed
    Of prisoners. So the first moves were closed.

22 Poor Troilus was present in that place
    When for Antenor they asked for Criseyde,
    And when he heard, ash grey became his face,   150
    As though, struck by these words, he'd almost died,

And yet he spoke no word, groaned not, nor cried,
Lest those who watched should his affection spy.
With manly heart he kept his deep grief dry,

23   And full of anguish and most bitter dread   155
Waited to hear what Parliament would say,
And if they would agree, (which God forbid,)
To her exchange. Two things racked him that day,
First, how to guard her honour, and what way
He could prevent the planned exchange, and how   160
This could be done he puzzled high and low.

24   Love made him want her still in Troy to bide,
And rather die than to be made to go,
But reason added on the other side,
"Without your girl's assent do not do so   165
Lest through your interference she turn foe,
Saying that all the world, through your meddling
Knows of the love that was a secret thing."

25   And so he thought perhaps it would be best
That, should the lords decree Criseyde went,   170
Unhindered he would grant them their request,
Explaining to his lady what they meant,
And when she'd told him truly her intent,
He'd do the thing she wanted, quickly, too,
Though all the world tried otherwise to do.   176

26   Hector, who the Greek proposals heard,
How for Antenor they would have Criseyde,
Spoke out against them, seriously answered,
"Sirs, she is no prisoner," he said,
"I don't know who demands like these had made,   180
But, for my part, to him you now can tell,
Women are not among the goods we sell!"

27   The shouts of people then blew up straightaway
    Furious as flames in straw all set on fire.
    Ill luck would have it that the mob that day   185
    Had made Criseyde's downfall their desire.
    "Hector," they cried, "You're mad. What can inspire
    You so, to shield the woman, make us lose
    Lord Antenor? Mistakenly you choose.

28   Antenor is wise, a bold baron,   190
    And we need men like him, as all can see.
    He is a man indeed, the best in town.
    Hector, be done with all this fantasy!
    King Priam," then they said, "It's our decree
    To let the woman go, release Criseyde.
    We want Antenor," so they screamed and cried,

29   Juvenal, master, true your adage is,
    The people little know what they desire,
    And in their own desire they find no bliss.
    The mists of error hide truth's shining fire,   200
    They can't see what is best. For instance, here,
    These folk of Troy now want deliverance
    For Antenor, who'll bring them to mischance,

30   For soon he will be traitor to the town
    Of Troy. Alas, they ransomed him too soon.   205
    Oh, foolish folk, so much for your discretion!
    Criseyde, who never harmed them, now they doom
    To bathe no more in bliss for many a moon.
    But as for Antenor, he shall come home,
    And she must go—that is the mob's moan!   210

31   And this decree was made by Parliament,
    Antenor should be yielded for Criseyde,
    And it was ruled so by the president,
    In spite of Hector's 'No', so loudly cried,

And in the end whoever this denied   215
Was shouted down. It must be, and should stand,
For most of Parliament did this demand.

32   When all had from the place of meeting gone,
     This Troilus, without another word
     Up to his own room hastened, all alone,   220
     Excepting for a valet or a guard,
     And these he sent away with curt, brisk word,
     Because he wished to sleep, or so he said.
     Then flung himself in haste upon his bed.

33   And as in winter leaves are tossed and torn   225
     One after other till the tree stands bare,
     And bark and branch alone are left forlorn,
     So Troilus lay, bereft of all that's fair,
     Bound fast within the coal-black bark of care,
     Half mad, and with wits turning, loudly cried,   230
     For he felt so the changing of Criseyde.

34   Then he got up, and every door he shut,
     Also the windows, then this sorrowful man
     Sat down forlornly at his couch's foot
     Like a dead creature, bloodless, pale and wan,   235
     And in his heart the heaped up woe began
     To break out, and he acted in this wise
     In crazy sorrow, just as I devise.

35   Exactly as a maddened wild bull lunges
     Now here, now there, with darts plunged to its heart, 240
     And gives a bellowing death cry as it plunges,
     So round the room Troilus, with many a start,
     With beating, flailing fists made his chest smart,
     Knocked his head on the wall, his body threw
     Upon the ground, to punish and subdue.   245

36   And his two eyes, in pity of his heart
     Streamed out with tears like two swift flowing springs.
     The sobs wrung from him by his sorrow's smart
     Robbed him of speech, and so he scarcely brings
     Himself to say, "Why feel I not Death's stings?   250
     Accursed be that birthday in which Nature
     Shaped me and made me into a live creature!"

37   But after, when the fury and the rage
     With which his heart was twisted and pulled fast
     By length of time began then to assuage,   255
     Upon his bed to rest he himself cast,
     But then his tears began to pour in haste,
     That it was wonderful that so much woe
     Could be contained in his one body so!

38   And then he said, "Fortune, alas the while,   260
     What have I done, of what am I guilty?
     Why did you not feel pity, nor beguile
     Me? Have you then no grace, in cruelty
     To take my Cressida away from me?
     Alas, how can you find it in your heart   265
     To be so cruel, and cause such bitter smart?

39   Have I not honoured you throughout my life?
     You know I have indeed, more than gods all.
     Why will you plunge me out of joy to strife?
     Oh, Troilus, what will the people call   270
     You, but a wretch of wretches, who must fall
     From his high place to misery, to wail
     "Criseyde, Criseyde," till the breath in me fail.

40   Alas, Fortune, if my life lived in joy
     Displeased you, foully eaten by envy,   275
     Why did you not my father, King of Troy
     Bereave of life, or make my brothers die,

Or slaughter me, who so complain and cry?
I, who outlive my use, a lump like lead,
In pain forever dying, yet not dead.   280

41   If only Criseyda to me was left,
What way you blew my boat I would not care!
But her you've taken from me, I'm bereft
For ever, too. You plot in this manner,
You rob a man of what to him is dear,   285
To show through this your veering and violence,
And so I'm lost, I now have no defence.

42   O god of love most true, O god, alas,
You who best know my heart and all my thought,
What shall I do, and how my sad life pass,   290
If I must lose the love so dearly bought?
Since you Criseyde and me have fully brought
Into your grace, our hearts as yours you sealed,
How can you let this bond then be repealed?

43   My life henceforth I'll lead, while live I may,   295
In torment and also in cruel pain,
And my ill luck and misadventures may
Bewail alone, as I was born. Again
I'll look no more on sunshine nor on rain,
But end my days, like Oedipus, in darkness,
Bearing my pain, and dying in distress.

44   O weary spirit, flitting to and fro,
Why do you not fly from this woefulest
Of bodies that can on this poor earth go?
O soul that lurks in grief here, leave your nest,   305
Fly from my heart, let it within my breast
Break. Follow her, Criseyde, your lady dear,
Your rightful place is now no longer here.

45   O you two woeful eyes, since all your pleasure
      Was to look into Criseyde's eyes so bright,   310
      What will you two do now that all my treasure
      Is lost, but weep until you've lost your sight?
      Since she is quenched who once gave you your light,
      From this time forth in vain I have two eyes,
      Since what gave them their value fades and dies.   315

46   O my Criseyde, O lady, sovereign
      Of my poor suffering soul that weeps and cries,
      Who will now give me comfort, ease my pain?
      No one, alas, but when my sad heart dies
      My spirit, which toward you hastes and hies,   320
      Receive with kindness, it will always love
      You, though the body rot within a grave.

47   O lovers who are high upon the wheel
      Of fortune, in good luck and happiness,
      God grant you find your love as true as steel,   325
      And lead your life in joy, not in distress,
      But when you pass my grave, pause there to bless
      He who was your fellow, now at rest,
      Who, though unworthy, lived, loved and was blest.

48   O old, unwholesome and wrong-living man,   330
      Calchas, I mean, alas, what's wrong with you
      To turn a Greek when you were born Trojan?
      Calchas, you'll bring me to my death day, too,
      Unlucky was your birth for me also!
      I would to God in Troy I had you now,   335
      To give you your deserts, and my wrath show!"

49   A thousand sighs, hotter than embers glowing,
      Out from his chest, one after other went,
      Mixed up with new complaints, his sorrow showing,
      For which in woeful tears his streams he sent,   340

L

And soon, his troubles tore him so, and rent
Him that in crazy grief he felt no thing,
Sorrow nor joy, but lay there, half fainting.

50 Pandar, who standing in the Parliament,
Had heard what every lord and burgess said,   345
And how they all agreed, with one assent
For Antenor so to give up Criseyde,
In maddened grief was almost crazed and dead,
So that for woe he scarce knew what he did,
But half stunned, ran to Troilus with all speed.   350

51 The knight, whose turn it was to keep the door
Of Troilus' room unbarred it straightaway,
And Pandarus, in tears, and more and more
Distraught, into the room where Troilus lay
Tiptoed, and to the bedside crept, but say   355
A word he could not, he was so confused
With sorrow that he found himself bemused.

52 And with his looks and usual cheerful face
Twisted by grief, with folded arms he stood
There, in front of Troilus; with amaze   360
He saw that pitiful face in pitying mood,
And then his heart grew cold and dead as wood
To see his friend in woe, whose heaviness
Choked his own breast, it seemed, with deep distress.

53 This woeful man, this Troilus, who felt   365
His friend, Pandarus, creeping him to see
Began like snow in sunshine then to melt,
Because of which Pandarus, in pity,
Began to weep as bitterly as he,
And each looked at the other silently,   370
For grief choked words, and they could nothing say.

54 Yet at the last this woeful Troilus
    Near death for sorrow, groaned and gave a roar
    Of grief, and choking with his sobs, spoke thus,
    Half strangled by his tears and sighs so sore.   375
    "Oh, Pandar, I am dead, so say no more.
    Have you not heard in Parliament," he said
    "How for Antenor they'll exchange Criseyde?"

55 Then Pandarus, like death, so pale of hue,
    With pity answered him, and said, "Ah, yes   380
    I hoped it might be false yet it is true
    That I have heard, I know just how it is.
    O mercy, God, who would have thought of this?
    Who would have guessed that with one throw of dice
    Fortune would lose our joy, and in a trice?   385

56 For in the whole wide world there is no creature
    That I can see, who ever ruin faced
    Stranger than this, through chance, or like misfeature.
    But who can foretell all, or his fate taste
    Ahead? Such is the world, if trust is placed   390
    In Fortune, men will find her prove untrue,
    She spreads her favours widely, yields to few.

57 But tell me this, why are you now so mad
    As to give way to grief? Why in this wise
    Lie here, since you your full desires have had,   395
    So that, by right, it ought well to suffice?
    But I, who in my love and long service
    Have never had one friendly look or smile,
    Might well give way to tears, and grieve a while!

58 And also think of this, you yourself know   400
    This town is full of ladies everywhere,
    And I can tell you, any place can show
    Twelve lovely girls or more, each quite as fair

As Criseyde ever was, they're everywhere!
So then be glad, my own dear friend and brother,   405
If one sweetheart is lost we'll get another!

59   Why God forbid that every form of pleasure
Be centred in one thing, and in one creature!
If one girl sings well, others tread a measure,
If this one's handsome, that one's gay of nature,   410
This one is kind, that one perfect in feature.
There's the right hawk for every kind of game,
For river, field or wood, the wild, the tame.

60   Also as Zanzis wrote, and he was wise,
"New love will often chase away the old,"   415
And new affairs need different advice.
So then consider, save yourself, be bold.
Such fires of love in time die down, grow cold,
And since they are but monetary pleasures,
Another moment will bring other treasures!   420

61   For quite as sure as day will follow night,
The new love, the new work, or the new woe,
Or else seldom to see one's girl, or knight,
Will make the old affection flee or go.
And for your part, one of these things must grow   425
In you to shorten all your pain and smart.
Her absence may well drive her from your heart."

62   These words he said all for the very best,
To help his friend, lest he for sorrow died.
For without doubt, to put his grief to rest,   430
He did not know what wickedness he cried.
But Troilus, who almost for sorrow died,
Took little heed of what Pandarus meant,
All in at one ear, out the other went!

63 But at the last he answered and said, "Friend,   435
    This sort of medicine and this doctoring
    Would suit me if I were an evil fiend,
    And ready to betray my true sweeting.
    I pray God may your counsel come to nothing,
    I'd rather die, be killed right here, than do   440
    The things you want, these evils taught by you!

64 She that I serve, whatever you may say,
    To whom I dedicate my heart by right,
    Shall have me wholly hers until I die,
    For Pandarus, to her my troth is plight,   445
    And I'll not be untrue for any knight,
    But as her servant, though deprived, will live,
    And to no other lady service give.

65 And though you say girls quite as fair as she
    I'll find, let be, make no comparison   450
    To any creature born here naturally.
    O Pandar, friend, this then is my conclusion,
    I would not be of your opinion
    About all this, and so I do beseech
    You to be quiet, you kill me by your speech.   455

66 You say to me that I should love another
    And start anew and let Criseyde go.
    It lies not in my power, dear friend and brother,
    And if I could, then I would not do so.
    Can a man play at rackets, to and fro,   460
    First nettles, and then docks, now this, now that!
    Bad luck to your girl, then, for tit, then tat!

67 Just so you treat me, wretched Pandarus,
    As he, who when a man is woebegone
    Comes up to him and smugly speaks, even thus,   465
    "Don't think about your pains, and you'll have none!"

First of all you must turn me to a stone
And take from me passions and feelings all
Before you'll make my sorrow's load to fall.

68   Death may well drive my life out long before   470
My body ceases from its grief and pain,
But from my heart the dart goes never more
With which Criseyde struck me. In the train
Of Prosepine I'll walk, in death's domain,
Sadly complaining of my sorrows sore,   475
Telling we two are parted evermore.

69   You've argued up a case whose point is this,
That it will be less agony to me
To let Criseyde go. We had our bliss
You say, so live in pure felicity,   480
Why did you lie and speak so idly,
Saying "He's worse off when from bliss thrown down
Than he who never had such pleasures known"?

70   But tell me, since you think it all so easy
To change in love and flutter to and fro,   485
Why have you not done so, been light and breezy,
And left the lass who causes you such woe?
Why don't you let your heart from that girl go?
Why don't you love another lady fair,
And give your heart a holiday from care?   490

71   If you have had in love so much mischance,
And yet can't drive love out of your own heart,
I, who lived in joy, bliss and pleasance
With her so happily right from the start,
How can I then forget so good a part   495
Of life? Where have you been, stuffed and made dense
To argue with apt words, yet little sense?

72 No, no, God knows all your advice is wrong,
And now because of it, what e'er befall,
With no more talk I will be dead ere long.   500
Oh death, the ender of our sorrows all,
Come now, for I so often on you call,
For blissful is the death, I say again,
Which comes when called upon, and ends all pain.

73 I know quite well when life was fair and sunny,   505
To evade Death I would have paid much gold,
But now his coming is as sweet as honey,
More than all else I want him to enfold
Me. Death, since I'm in burning sorrows rolled,
With my own tears let me then drown and drench, 510
Or with cold hands hot coals of sorrow quench.

74 Since you kill many men in many a wise,
And all against their will, both day and night,
Do me, at my request, this last service,
Free me from this sad world, and you'll do right   515
By me, who am the most sad, weary knight
That ever was. It is high time I died.
I'm no more use here, in this world so wide."

75 Then in his tears poor Troilus was distilled,
As liquor from an alembeck, so fast,   520
And Pandar then his tongue so chattering stilled,
And to the ground his eyes abashed he cast,
Nevertheless he thought, right to the last,
"Why God, rather than that my friend should die
I'll say some more to him, and speedily."   525

76 So added, "Friend, since you're in such distress,
And since you hold my arguments to blame,
Why don't you help yourself to some redress,
And through your manhood end this foolish game?

Go on, take her by force, why not, for shame!   530
And either out of town together go,
Or keep her here. Stop shilly-shallying so!

77   Are you a Trojan, and yet haven't guts
Enough to take a woman who loves you
And will be willing, butting you no buts?   535
This is more fuss, to make so much ado,
Get up straightway, and leave off weeping so,
And show you are a man. For I will kill
Myself this hour, or she will be ours still!"

78   To all this Troilus made an answer soft,   540
And said, "In truth, my friend and brother dear,
I've thought all these things out often and oft,
And much more, too, than you have dwelt on here.
But why I've left this thing undone, you'll hear,
And when you've given me an audience,   545
You can go on and finish your sentence.

79   First, since you know our town is plunged in war
All through the rape of women, snatched by might,
I should not then do likewise, and the more,
Or so I see it, nor do what's not right.   550
I should be blamed by every worthy knight
If what my father granted I withstood,
For she's exchanged all for our city's good.

80   I've also thought, if Criseyde gave consent,
To ask her of my father, of his grace,   555
Then I've thought, she'd be blamed if I thus went,
For I know now I can't my love purchase,
Since he, my father, in so high a place
As Parliament, put his own royal seal
To the exchange, so can't, for me, repeal.   560

81   And most of all I dread to harm her heart
     By violence if I start such a game,
     If openly I did this, for a start,
     People would talk and slander her good name.
     I'd rather die than bring her to such shame.   565
     By God, I'd rather her fair honour have
     Unsmirched and bright than my poor life to save.

82   So all is lost for all that I can see.
     One thing is certain, since I am her knight,
     I honour her above myself, truly,   570
     In everything, as lovers should by right.
     And so desire and reason twist me tight.
     Desire tells me to take her, drives me mad.
     Reason says no, and so my heart is sad."

83   So, weeping as if he would never cease,   575
     He said, "Alas, what ever shall I do?
     I feel my love is still on the increase,
     And hope grows less and less. I never knew
     The causes of my grief I'd so much rue.
     Alas, alas, why won't my poor heart break?   580
     No rest, like love, pain pricks me wide awake."

84   Then Pandar answered, "Friend, most certainly
     Do as you want. If I had it so hot
     And had your fortune, she should go with me,
     Though all the town cried out, said she should not,   585
     I'd take no notice of them, not a jot.
     When men have raised their voice, they soon pipe down.
     Nine days alone a wonder lasts in town!

85   Don't worry about rights or wrongs, nor let
     Good manners hinder. Help yourself, my friend,   590
     Let others weep and into trouble get!
     Since you two are of one mind, then defend

The girl, for my soul, they shall not send
Her off. Why, better let them blame you much,
Than die here like a gnat without a scratch!   595

86   It is not shameful nor a vice at all
To keep her here in Troy whom you love so.
She might well think you stupid and a fool
To let her thus to the Greek army go.
Realise that Fortune, as you quite well know,   600
Helps a bold man in every enterprise,
Forsaking those who skulk in cowardice.

87   And though your lady may a little grieve,
You can make up to her when all is over.
But as for me, indeed I can't believe   605
That she will blame for love her own dear lover.
Why do you quake for fear, then? Quick, recover,
Think how your brother, Paris, has his girl.
Why not the same for you, an equal pearl?

88   And Troilus, one thing to you I swear,   610
That if Criseyde, who is your darling dear
Loves you as well as you, I know, love her,
God help me, she'll not be upset, I swear,
If you get help through taking her from here.
And if she wants to leave you in distress,   615
Then she is false and you must love her less!

89   Therefore take heart, and think, like a true knight
That all for love each day some break each law.
Show that you've courage, act with strength and might.
Have mercy on yourself, and don't show awe.   620
Don't let this grievous woe your sad heart gnaw,
But man-like, set the world at six and seven,
And if you die love's martyr, go to heaven!

90   I will myself be with you in this deed,
     Though I and all my kinsmen shall this day   625
     Like dogs in Troy's streets here lie stiff and dead,
     Stabbed with great wounds and stricken with dismay.
     You'll find I am a friend whatever may
     Befall, but if you wish a cowardly wretch
     To die here, may your soul the Devil fetch!   630

91   Troilus began to quicken at these words,
     And said, "Thanks, friend, indeed I do assent.
     But it's no good to prick with words like swords.
     Nor will pain drive me to it, nor torment.
     Whatever happens it's not my intent,   635
     To put it in few words, to forcibly
     Take Criseyde, unless she first agree!"

92   "Why, that's what I've been saying all this day!"
     Said Pandarus, "But have you asked her, man?
     You seem so gloomy." Troilus answered, "Nay."   640
     "Then why are you in such a state? How can
     You tell that she won't like the plot, your plan
     To take her off, since you have not been there?
     Or did some god come whispering in your ear?

93   Get up and look as if nothing is wrong.   645
     Wash your face, and go straight to the King.
     Or he may wonder where you are so long.
     Be clever, he and all the rest deceiving.
     Or if in need, for you he'll soon be sending
     When you're not ready. So, my brother dear,   650
     Be cheerful, let me handle this matter.

94   For I will work things so that speedily
     This very night, some time, and in some way
     You can talk with your lady privately,
     And from her looks and all that she may say   655

> You'll soon find out how far the girl will play.
> And I am sure all will be for the best.
> Goodbye for now. Leave me to do the rest."

95 Swift-footed Rumour, who all untrue things
  Alike reports with things that are quite true, 660
  Flew all through Troy with prompt and eager wings,
  From man to man, and told the tale anew,
  How Calchas' daughter, lovely, fresh of hue,
  By Parliament, with no word to deplore,
  Was granted in exchange for Antenor. 665

96 Which story, soon as Criseyde had heard,
  She, who now felt nothing for her father,
  Did not know even if he lived, nor cared,
  Knelt and besought great Jupiter that rather
  Evil should fall on him who'd made this bother, 670
  She hoped the tales were false, but lest they were
  True after all, dared not enquire, for fear.

97 For she had all her heart and all her mind
  Bound up in Troilus so deep, so fast
  That nothing could loose love, nor yet unbind 675
  It, nor Troilus from her heart to cast.
  She would be his while life and breath could last.
  So she was burned in turn by love and dread,
  Not knowing what to think, or hear, or heed.

98 But as you'll often see, in town or out, 680
  Women enjoy to call on friends, and visit,
  So to Criseyde came a female rout,
  Half pleased, half pitying, thinking to delight
  Her with their gossip, stuff not worth a mite!
  So all those dames who in the city dwell 685
  Sat down and said all that I'm going to tell.

99   The first one said, "Oh, I'm so glad, truly,
     For you, that soon you'll your dear father see."
     Another said, "My goodness, no, not I,
     Too short a time she's lived in our city."   690
     The third said, "I sincerely hope that she
     Will bring us peace, alike to Greece and Troy,
     So may the gods guide her, and give us joy."

100 These words and all their female chatterings
     She heard as if she was not there at all.   695
     God knows her mind now dwelt on other things,
     Although her body sat there in the hall
     All her attention was elsewhere. Her soul
     For Troilus, Troilus always searched and sought,
     Silently always of her love she thought.   700

101 These women, who were hoping her to please
     All about nothing idle words were turning.
     Such emptiness could do Criseyde no ease,
     For she all this long while in pain was burning,
     With passion about which they knew nothing,   705
     So that she almost felt her sad heart die
     With woe and weariness of company.

102 And so no longer could the girl constrain
     Her tears, and up they soon began to well,
     To give a sign of all that bitter pain   710
     In which her spirit was, and now must dwell,
     As she remembered how from heaven to hell
     She now had fallen, since she must forgo,
     Her lover, and she sighed with bitter woe.

103 And all these foolish women round about   715
     Thought that all her tears and sighing sore
     Was just because she'd got to leave that rout
     Of sillies, and have fun with them no more.

And they, who'd known her all that time before
Thought that she wept from friendly kindliness.   720
And each wept also for the girl's distress.

104   And then to comfort her they tried so hard
For what, God knows, was never in her mind,
Told tales and stories, sought with many a word
To cheer her with intentions very kind,   725
And ways to ease her sorrows tried to find,
Like one who tries to cure an aching head
By clawing madly at his foot instead!

105   But after all this foolishness in vain
They took their leave, and home went one and all,   730
And Criseyde, sad, self-pitying, again
Up to her own room went from the great hall,
And fainting on her bed straightaway did fall
As if she never thought from there to rise,
And there she acted as I will devise.   735

106   Her wavy mass of sungold coloured hair
She tore, also her fingers long, yet small
She wrung, and prayed the gods would pity her,
And send down death to ease her without fail.
Her cheeks, which had been rosy, now were pale,   740
And showed the depth of woe and sore constraint.
And thus she spoke, with sobs, this sad complaint.

107   "Alas," she said, "From this dear town and place
I, wretched creature, touched by doom and blight,
Born under the wrong stars, cursed by disgrace   745
Must go, and leave my love, my dear, my knight.
I now bewail the day, the hour, the light
In which I first saw him with these two eyes
From which arose our sorrows, tears and cries."

108   And as she spoke, from both her eyes the tears   750
      Fell down as swift and free as April rain.
      She beat her white breast, and in woe and fears
      Begged, prayed for death to take her for her pain,
      Since he who'd lighted life and made woes wane
      Was to be taken from her, and for this   755
      She thought herself forlorn and robbed of bliss.

109   She said, "What will become of him? Of me?
      How shall I live if I am torn from him?
      Oh, my dear heart, whom I love desperately,
      Who'll cure the pains that now you're burning in?   760
      O Calchas, father, yours is the great sin.
      And O, my mother, Argyre, Calchas' wife,
      Sad was the day when you brought me to life.

110   To what end should I live and sorrow thus?
      How can a fish out of its stream endure?   765
      And can Cressid live without Troilus?
      How can a plant or any living creature
      Live without the food to suit its nature?
      This proverb I remember will apply,
      "Without a root the greenest plant will die."   770

111   And so will I, for sword or pointed dart
      I dare not handle, being cowardly,
      That on the day when from my love I part,
      If sorrow does not kill me speedily,
      No meat nor drink shall by me taken be   775
      Till I unsheathe my soul out of my breast,
      And bring myself to everlasting rest.

112   And Troilus, love, my garments every one
      Shall be coal black in token, my heart sweet
      That I am from this wicked world now gone,   780
      I, who once gave you love and peace and quiet,

And my religious Rule, till death I meet,
Shall be observance, love, in your absence
Of sorrow, mourning, fasting, abstinence.

113   My heart, and the sad spirit held there in   785
I do bequeath with yours to grieve and mourn
Eternally, for they'll not part our twin
Souls, though on earth we're pulled apart and torn
Asunder, in Elysium, not forlorn
But joined at last we shall embrace and kiss   790
As Orpheus and Eurydice, in bliss.

114   So, my dear heart, for Antenor, alas
I soon shall be exchanged, I know this well.
What will you do then, if this comes to pass?
How will your loving heart endure this hell?   795
Dear heart, forget this sorrow dire and fell,
Forget me, too, for, love, if you're content
And well, I'll care not if my life be spent."

115   How could it ever be read of, or sung,
This plaint she made out of such deep distress   800
I know not? As for me, my little tongue,
If without cuts it tells her heaviness,
It well might make her sorrows seem much less
Than in real life they were, and, like a child
I'll have her tragic woe spoiled and defiled.   805

116   Pandar, who had been sent from Troilus
To Criseyde, as you've just heard me devise,
All for the best they had arranged it thus,
And he was glad to do him this service,
And go to Criseyde in such secret wise,   810
And where she lay in grief and great torment
Came to bring the message Troilus sent,

117 And found how she'd begun herself to treat
     Most grievously, for with her salty tears
     Her breast, her face were bathed and wringing wet. 815
     The flowing tresses of her sunbright hairs
     Unbraided hung in tangles round her ears,
     Which made her look a martyr with desire
     For death for which her sad heart was on fire.

118 When she saw him, in sorrow straightaway   820
     She hid her tear-stained face between her arms,
     And Pandar felt so sad he scarce could stay
     There in that house of woe. Now his heart warms
     With pity for his niece, in grief's dark storms.
     For if she'd at the first complained most sore,   825
     Now mourning seemed a thousand times the more.

119 And in her bitterness she turned and said,
     "Pandar, the joy you brought me carried two
     Meanings. It was Logic's first cause, that led
     Me into bliss, then changed to bitter woe.   830
     I don't know if I'll 'welcome' say, or no
     To you, who brought me first into service
     Of Love, which ends so cruelly in this wise!

120 Does love end always so, in grief? Why, yes,
     And all life's bliss ends so, it seems to me.   835
     Sorrow is the true tail to happiness.
     And he's a fool who thinks this will not be.
     Let him, for an example, my state see,
     Who hate myself, my birth and being curse,
     And feeling so, from one ill sink to worse.   840

121 At one time whosoever looks on me
     Sorrow mixed up with torments, woe, distress,
     In my one wretched body there will see,
     With anguish, languor, cruel bitterness,

M

Anger and fear and smarting grief and sickness.   845
Why, even from heaven tears like mine must rain
In pity of my bitterness and pain!"

122   "My dear, dear niece, so full of misery,"
Said Pandarus, "What do you mean to do?
Why not behave more self-respectingly?   850
Why make yourself in such a state through woe?
Stop working up your grief and listen to
What I shall say, hearkening with good intent
These words which your own Troilus to you sent."

123   Criseyde turned round, such lamentation making   855
It almost killed poor Pandarus to see.
"Alas," she said, "What message can you bring?
What will my dear, my darling say to me,
He whom I fear I'm never more to see?
Will he complain or rage or weep before   860
I go? I've tears enough. I need no more!"

124   Her look, her face was ghastly then to see,
Just like a man in graveclothes on his bier.
Her face, once like an angel's, heavenly,
Was changed, transformed in nature now by fear.   865
The gaiety and laughter which were there
In her, and all her charms and joys, each one
Had fled, and now Criseyde lay alone.

125   And now around both eyes a purple ring
Was traced, and told most truthfully of pain.   870
Even to see it was a deadly thing.
And so Pandarus now could not restrain
The tears that from his eyes poured down like rain.
Yet all the same, as best he could, he said
These words, which came from Troilus to Criseyde.   875

126   "Look, niece, I well expect you've heard just how
       The King and all his lords, all for the best
       Agreed the exchange of Antenor for you,
       And this has caused your sorrow and unrest.
       But how all this does Troilus' heart molest   880
       No tongue on earth could ever truly say.
       Indeed for woe his wits have gone astray!

127   We grieved so at these tidings, he and I,
       That almost our great sorrow us both slew.
       But through my good advice he finally   885
       Out of this well of weeping soon withdrew,
       And now above all things he wants with you
       To be all night, that you may both devise
       What's to be done in this sad enterprise.

128   This, short and plain's the matter of my message,   890
       As far as my poor wit can comprehend.
       And you, who've been in torment such an age
       Must terminate your grief, and make an end,
       And answer to your sweetheart straightway send.
       And, for the love of God, my niece most dear,   895
       Dry all those tears before the lad comes here."

129   "My woe's so great," she said, and sighed so sore,
       Like one who feels the pangs of sharp distress,
       "But yet to me his grief is so much more.
       I love him better than himself, I guess.   900
       Alas, for me has he such heaviness?
       Can he so piteously for me complain?
       If so, this sorrow doubles all my pain.

130   It hurts and grieves me so, God knows, to part,"
       Said she, "Yet it will harder be for me   905
       To see the grief which strikes him to the heart,
       For I know well that will my death pang be.

And die I will most certainly," cried she.
"But bid him come before Death, that cruel guest
Drives out the spirit trembling in my breast." 910

131 And as she spoke these words, on her two arms
Fell grovelling and weeping piteously.
Said Pandar, "Why act so, and spoil your charms,
Since you know well the time is speeding by
And he'll come soon. So get up hastily, 915
So that he won't a tearful mistress find,
Or you will send him mad, out of his mind!

132 For if he knew you were behaving so
He'd kill himself. If I had ever thought
You'd make a fuss like this, I'd have you know 920
I'd not, for all King Priam's gold, have brought
Troilus to see you, to new grief be wrought.
I know well what he'd do, and so I say
Stop grieving, or your man himself will slay!

133 Behave so that you make his sorrow cease, 925
And don't augment it, my dear niece most sweet,
Temper his sharpness, don't let it increase,
With wisdom and good sense his sorrows beat.
What will it help to weep and drown the street,
Or drench you both in floods of salty tears? 930
A cure is worth more than complaints and fears.

134 I mean, when I your lover hither bring,
Since you are sensible, both of one mind,
Arrange some way to stop yourself from going,
Or ways to come back once you've gone please find. 935
Women are wise in matters of this kind.
So see how well your wits can now avail.
And I'll help if I can. I will not fail."

135   "Go," said Criseyde. "And uncle, now, truly,
      I promise I'll try harder to restrain   940
      My tears in front of him. Obediently
      I'll try to bring him happiness again,
      Using all that's within my heart and brain,
      If for his sore there can be found a cure
      And I can help, he shall not lack it, sure."   945

136   So Pandar went, and Troilus he sought,
      Till in a temple he found him alone,
      Like one who hates his life. There, all distraught,
      He to the gods for pity made his moan,
      And with great feeling prayed to every one   950
      To take him from this weary world of pain,
      Thinking he'd not feel happiness again.

137   And so, in short, if I tell truth to you,
      He'd fallen in such deep despair that day
      That he'd prepared to die, and quickly, too,   955
      For so he argued, to himself he'd say
      All now was lost, and crying, "Welaway,"
      He added, "All that happens is ordained,
      My fate it is to be forlorn and doomed.

138   For certainly this I know well," he said,   960
      "That the divine foresight of Providence
      Always foretold that I would lose Criseyde,
      Since God doubtless sees everything, each chance,
      And he disposes through his ordinance
      In ways that suit his order and decree   965
      As right for them, and through predestiny.

139   But oh, alas, what, which shall I believe?
      For there are mighty scholars, many a one
      Who destiny by arguments can prove.
      And others quite as great who say there's none, 970

But that free will is given each man's son.
Alas, so cunning wise men are today,
That I don't know quite what to think or say!

140   For some men say, if God sees what will come,
And God can't be deceived, no, no, truly,   975
It will fall out just so, fate, chance or doom,
Providence knows just how all things will be.
If so, I say that from eternity
God can foretell the way we'll act or think
Freewill can't be, and scholars waste their ink!   980

141   For other thoughts and other deeds than these
Could never be, except if Providence
Which cannot be deceived, otherwise please,
Or can perceive through its wise ordinance.
For if there could be chance or variance,   985
If we could wriggle out of what God plans,
There could be no foretelling, God's, or man's.

142   Foreseeing would be only guesswork, then,
Uncertain, not foretelling what's to be.
And truly it would be absurd for men   990
To say God can't into the future see
Further than sinful folk like you and me.
To make God capable of error so
Is false and foul and wicked, that I know!

143   And then, indeed, there are the views of some   995
Very high Highbrows, shiny egghead men
Who speak like this, "Things never merely come
When Providence ordains. They happen when
The time is ripe. Things only happen then.
And so, quite plain, Providence only sees   1000
What will take place through Nature's wise decrees."

144   And so what seems was bound to be may well
       Turn out quite opposite than was expected,
       For there's no need to think necessity
       Will make things fall out just as was directed   1005
       Or else foretold. But it may be predicted
       That things which happen must have been foreseen,
       How otherwise could they be, or have been?

145   I'm acting as if labouring at this,
       Worrying out what causes things to be,   1010
       Whether God's foreknowledge truly is
       The certain cause of what's necessity,
       And if all things take place with certainty,
       Or if necessity of what must come
       Is cause of what Fate will do, or has done.   1015

146   But now I don't insist on showing forth
       The ordering of why things happen so.
       I know that what's to be, the future birth
       Of things must be foreseen, and foretold, too.
       Though that it is so is not always due   1020
       To Province, nor does necessity
       That things will come ensure such things will be.

147   For if a man sits down upon a seat
       As fate, and his necessity require,
       And if you think he's sitting there, complete   1025
       And right you are, your judgment's quite entire!
       And furthermore, to take the matter higher,
       I can turn round this argument and say,
       (Listen, O listeners, I will not delay,)

148   I say, if what you think he does is true,   1030
       To wit, sits sitting, I say furthermore
       He sits there. Fate, Necessity, these two
       Compel him to do this, and nothing more.

He needs to sit. To speak just three or four
True and straightforward words you need. And so 1035
Necessity has both of you in tow!

149   But you may say he does not sit because
You say he sits, not even though that's true.
He sits because to sit his habit was
Of yore. Yet your opinion's valid, too,   1040
And though the reason for your thought is due
To the plain fact that on that seat he sits,
The need is different for you both, yet fits!

150   So, from this one example, and from doubt
I can make out, as seems quite plain to me   1045
A reasoned case of God's foresight, about
All things that are to come, futurity,
Because of this men can quite plainly see
That everything which happens upon earth
Happens because it must come so to birth.   1050

151   So, although things which are to come I'm sure
Can be foreseen ahead most certainly,
This that they're preordained does not ensure.
Nevertheless it's needful, fittingly
That things should be foreseen that are to be, 1055
Or else that what good Providence decrees
Needs must be so, and happen so, to please.

152   And this itself is quite enough, plainly
To put an end to freewill for us all.
Yet it is wrong, absurd indeed to say   1060
The way things happen here on earth, and temporal
Fall so because of God who is eternal.
Truly it's false to reason so, and say
That what's to be makes God see things that way.

153   I'd think, if I thought philosophically   1065
      God only foresees things that are to come
      Because they *are* to come, quite certainly.
      And I might also guess that all and some
      Things that have come to pass, or have been done
      Were root and cause of mighty Providence,   1070
      And its all-seeing power, foresight and sense.

154   And then, on top of this, I might say, too,
      That just as when I know there is a thing,
      That thing must needfully exist just so,
      And when I know that such a thing is coming   1075
      It will and must come. And so the foretelling
      Of what things happen, well before they do
      We can't escape, nor dodge what will ensue."

155   Then he said, "Mighty Jove upon your throne,
      O God who knows the way things will turn out,   1080
      Pity my grief, or kill me very soon,
      Or save Criseyde and me from pain and doubt."
      And while he was by sorrow wrapped about,
      Disputing with himself in this matter,
      Pandar came in, and spoke as you shall hear.   1085

156   "O mighty God," said Pandar, "On your throne,
      Alas, who saw a wise man acting so?
      Why, Troilus, now whatever's to be done!
      Are you so keen to be your own worst foe?
      Why, lad, your Criseyde has not yet to go!   1090
      Why sentence your poor self to death from dread
      So that your eyes roll dully in your head?

157   Haven't you lived for many a year before
      Without her, and were yet quite well at ease?
      Are you born just for her, and for no more?   1095
      Did nature make you this one girl to please?

Stop, think now, carefully in your dis-ease,
That as in games of dice come loss and gains,
So in the game of love come joys and pains.

158 And, then, this is most curious of all,   1100
That you make such a fuss, since you don't know
As yet whether she'll go, what will befall,
Or if she can refuse, demur, say no.
You've given her no chance at all to show
Her cleverness. No need for you to mourn   1105
Your death before the execution dawn.

159 So therefore take good heed of what I'll say.
I've spoken with her, been with her, agree
So well with her, we've talked so much today
That I've a shrewd suspicion now that she   1110
Has made a secret plan most cleverly
With which she can, if I read things aright,
Change all these matters that now cause you fright.

160 So my advice is this, when it is night
Go to her, Troilus, make of this an end,   1115
And joyous Juno, through her power and might
Will, as I hope, her grace to us all send.
"My heart says, "Why, they won't your Criseyde send,"
So don't torment yourself, let your heart rest.
Cheer up, be resolute, for that is best."   1120

161 This Troilus answered then, sighing most sore,
"What you say's true, and I will do just so."
All that he wished he said, and even more,
And when it was the time for him to go
In secrecy to Criseyde, quick, not slow   1125
He went, as he had done so hitherto,
And what they did and said I'll tell to you.

162   The truth is, when these lovers came to meet,
       So deeply pain their hearts did wring and twist
       That neither of them could the other greet,   1130
       But each fell in the other's arms, and kissed.
       And neither of them spoke, or else confessed
       Their pain, but stood in silence, and could bring
       No word out plainly for their sad sobbing.

163   The sorrowful tears that both of them let fall   1135
       Were the most bitter tears which ever were,
       Like bark of aloes or the sourest gall,
       Tears bitterer by far than those which myrrh
       Sheds when pierced through bark and rind. And there
       Is not in all this world so hard a heart   1140
       As would refuse to pity all their smart.

164   But when their woeful weary souls returned
       Back to the bodies wherein they must dwell,
       And when their fires of woe less strongly burned
       Because they'd wept so long, and when the well   1145
       Of tears began to dry, the heart's sad swell
       Grew less, with breaking voice, hoarse with her tears
       Criseyde to Troilus spoke of all her fears.

165   "O Jove, I die, your mercy I beseech,
       Help, Troilus!" With these words her face   1150
       She hid upon her breast, and lost her speech,
       And as she spoke, there from its rightful place
       Her spirit, crushed with grief, with fluttering pace
       Fled. With face now ghastly, pale and grey
       She lay there, who had once been fresh and gay.   1155

166   And Troilus as he saw here fainting there
       Called her by name, (she lay there like one dead
       Not answering; her limbs quite icy were,
       Her eyes upcast and staring in her head,)

The grief-struck man was now half dazed
                        with dread.   1160
All he could do was her cold mouth to kiss.
God knows, and he, how far he'd come from bliss.

167   Then he got up and laid his darling down,
       Yet signs of life, however hard he tried
       He could not find. Criseyde in death-like swoon   1165
       Lay there, and bitterly her lover cried.
       Speechless she was, and lay like one who's died.
       And so with sorrowing voice and joyless heart
       He cried that death had torn Criseyde apart.

168   And after he had mourned her and lamented,   1170
       Wrung his hands, and no more words could say,
       Had bathed her breast with salt tears, and, demented,
       Dried them, and as they fell, wiped them away,
       He knelt, and for her soul began to pray.
       "Lord, almighty God upon your throne,   1175
       Have mercy on me, I shall follow soon!"

169   She lay there, cold, no movement, warmth nor feeling
       For aught he knew, and he could feel no breath,
       So this to him was proof, indeed revealing
       That his Criseyde lay in the arms of death.   1180
       And when he saw no hope was left, most loath,
       He laid her out, in just such a manner
       As men do those they place upon a bier.

170   And after this, with resolute, bitter heart
       He pulled his sword straightway out of its sheath,   1185
       Meaning to kill himself, so great the smart
       Of agony, resign his life and breath,
       And lie in Hades' realms, the place of death,
       Since love and cruel Fate would not allow
       Him to live longer in this world below.   1190

171 Then he spoke thus, driven by deep despair,
    "O cruel Jove, and you, Fortune, my foe,
    You wretches all, who killed my Criseyde fair,
    Betraying love, since you can't further go
    In harming me, damn you to Hell below!   1195
    You cowards, you'll never get me in your power!
    Death cannot part me from my love one hour.

172 For from this world, since you have slain her thus,
    I'll go, following her soul below, or high,
    No fellow lover can say Troilus   1200
    Dared not for fear with his dear love to die,
    For certainly I'll bear her company.
    And since you will not let us live together,
    At least let our two souls be joined for ever.

173 And Troy, my city, which I leave in woe,   1205
    My father, Priam, and my brothers all,
    Mother, farewell, farewell, for now I go,
    Atropos, set my bier out with its pall.
    Criseyde, my dearest sweetheart, now I call
    On you, receive my soul." This was his cry,   1210
    Sharp sword blade at his heart, ready to die.

174 But as God willed she woke, her long faint over,
    And sighed, and softly, "Troilus," she cried,
    And he replied, "Criseyde, why you recover,
    You're still alive" and down let the sword glide.   1215
    "Oh, my dear heart, thanks Venus now indeed,"
    She said, and deeply, sadly, sorely sighed,
    Whilst Troilus to comfort her now tried.

175 He took her in his arms and kissed her hard,
    An tried to make her happy, soothe her smart,   1220
    And her sad spirit, fluttering like a bird
    Came back into its cage, her human heart,

But suddenly her glance fell, with a start
Upon his unsheathed sword, gleaming and bare,
And she cried out in fear to see it there.   1225

176   She asked him why he'd drawn it violently,
      And Troilus at once the reason told,
      How he had almost killed himself that day,
      And Criseyde stared at him, aghast and cold,
      Then fiercely clutched him in her warm arms' fold, 1230
      And cried, "Lord, lord, this almost stops my breath!
      Alas, how near both of us were to death!

177   Then, if I had not spoken, and thank God
      I did so, you'd have killed yourself?" said she.
      "Yes. that I would." And she replied, "Ah, lord,   1235
      For by the gods that made both you and me,
      I would not have lived on, sad and lonely,
      Not even if they'd wished to crown me queen
      Of every land on which the sun's rays stream,

178   But with this very sword which now here is   1240
      I would have killed myself at once," she said.
      "Dear heart, we've spoken quite enough of this,
      Let us get up and straightway go to bed,
      And there we'll talk about our grief instead,
      For by that guttering candle burning low   1245
      Morning is near, love's long night soon will go."

179   When in their bed and in each other's arms
      It was not like those other blissful nights.
      Despairingly each looked at each, the storms
      Of fate had wrecked their joy, put out their lights. 1250
      They now bewailed their sad and wretched plights,
      Till at the last, unhappy, lost Criseyde
      Spoke thus to Troilus as they lay in bed.

180   "Oh, my dear heart, this you know well," said she,
      "If a man always talks about his woe,   1255
      But never tries to find a remedy,
      It's only stupidness and adds to sorrow.
      And since we're both of us together now
      To find a cure for this grief that we're in,
      Then it's high time for thinking to begin.   1260

181   I am a woman, as you know quite well,
      And my impulsive thoughts, intuitive, free,
      I'll tell you now, while they are hot as Hell.
      I think that neither you nor I should be
      So cast down, nor so sad continually,   1265
      For there are ways in which we can redress
      All that's gone wrong, and end our heaviness.

182   It's true now, is it not, that all our woe
      Is due to one thing only, which is this,
      That you and I will part, when I must go.   1270
      And this is all, there's nothing else amiss.
      But there's a ready remedy, which is
      For us to plan straightway a future meeting.
      This is the whole of it, my darling sweeting.

183   Now, I will work it so it comes about   1275
      That when I've gone, I'll soon come back again.
      Of this I have not any shred of doubt.
      Don't worry, in a week or two, quite plain
      I'll be back here. I'll try with might and main
      To make quite sure. And now, with words quite few 1280
      I'll tell you how, and ways and means both show.

184   I'll not make a long sermon of all this,
      For time once lost may not recovered be,
      But will come to the point, and this it is,
      All's for the best as far as I can see,   1285

And for the love of God, forgive it me
If I speak anything which spoils your rest,
For truly, love, I say it for the best.

185 Yet still protesting, with much fuss and fret
That all the words which I am going to say   1290
Are but to show you how I'm trying yet
To help us both, and what is the best way,
So do not take it otherwise, I pray.
To sum it up, whatever you command
I'll do, and I'll obey you out of hand.   1295

186 Now listen, dearest, you have understood
That Parliament has voted I must go,
So we can't gainsay what they think is good,
Not for the whole wide world, as they've said so,
And since there's no way out, this I must do,   1300
We cannot stop the plan, we've got to find
Some way to make it easier and more kind.

187 For truly, parting us, who love, will be
So deep a sorrow and so great a pain,
Yet there are times when bitter agony   1305
Lovers must feel before joy comes again.
And since I'll ride no further on the plain
Of Troy than can be crossed in half a day,
Remembering this should make you almost gay!

188 And after all I'll not be mewed up close,   1310
So day by day, my own sweetheart so dear,
Since it is now a truce, as the world knows,
You'll surely news, and how I'm faring hear,
And ere the truce is over, I'll be here,
And then Antenor you will well have won,   1315
And me also, so be glad if you can!

189 And think like this, "Criseyde has gone away.
     What of it? She will soon be back again.
     And when, ah, when? Why, soon enough, I say,
     Before ten days are up we shall regain   1320
     All our lost happiness, forgetting pain.
     Than we in true love will together dwell,
     In bliss so great none can its real joys tell.

190 Why, often, situated as we both are now,
     All for the best, our love affair to hide,   1325
     You do not speak with me, nor I with you
     For two weeks sometimes, neither meet beside,
     So surely we can ten short days abide.
     For my good name, in such an adventure
     You'd gladly greater, harder things endure!   1330

191 You know how all my family live in Troy,
     Excepting for my father, they are here.
     And here's my house, and all that gives me joy,
     And greatest of all these, you, my best dear,
     Whom I would not forsake and go elsewhere   1335
     For all the world, with its broad lands and space,
     And if I lie may I not see God's face!

192 Why do you think my father in this wise
     Pines so to see me, but for dread indeed,
     Lest in this town the people me despise   1340
     Because of him and his base, treacherous deed.
     How does he know what sort of life I lead?
     For if he knew how happy I am here
     We would not now be in such pain and fear.

193 You've noticed how each day more and yet more   1345
     Men talk of making peace. And now they say
     Our leaders may Helen, the queen, restore,
     And the Greeks, too, make up what's gone astray.

N

So, though our two hearts are in much dismay,
That peace is talked of now on every side   1350
May make you more in ease of heart abide.

194   For if we do have peace, my sweetheart dear,
      Negotiations, treaties, these must drive
      Men to ride back and forth, from there to here,
      Pass to and fro quite freely, swarm and weave   1355
      All day as thick as bees do from a hive.
      Unchallenged every man will come and go
      Just as he wills, and just as the winds blow.

195   And although in the end peace may not come
      I will come back, even if there's still war   1360
      I must return, for this place is my home.
      Why should I stay unhappy over there
      Among those foreign soldiers, sick with fear?
      So, darling, I can't see why you should dread
      This thing so much. Look forward, love, instead.   1365

196   If you are not convinced by what I've said
      I have another plan. Listen to me,
      My father, as you know quite well indeed
      Is old. Old age is often miserly,
      Greedy and covetous, so, cleverly   1370
      I've thought just how my cunning net I'll cast,
      If you agree. Hear how I'll hold him fast.

197   Troilus, my dear, men say that hard it is
      To feed the wolf, yet the sheep whole still have.
      In other words, folk find the truth of this,   1375
      One got's to spend before one hopes to save.
      Gold is the stuff with which to make or pave
      A pathway right into a miser's heart.
      And this I mean to do. Here's how I'll start.

198 The goods and furniture that I have here   1380
     I'll pack and to my father take, and say
     It's sent him by some friends to keep secure,
     Safe from war's perils and out of harm's way.
     And those friends also beg of him and pray
     He'll send for more goods, and that speedily   1385
     While there's a truce and some security.

199 And I will tell him what a quantity
     Of goods they have, but lest folk see the game
     He's up to, he must give the task to me
     Of carrying the stuff. I'll say my name   1390
     Is praised in Troy, I've friends at Court, my fame
     Is wide, and so I'll say I can assuage
     Anger against him, and cool Priam's rage.

200 So, what with one thing and another, sweet,
     I shall enchant him with my words and saws,   1395
     He'll think that he's in bliss, in heaven complete,
     For all Apollo's or his priesthood's laws
     And all their prophecies don't rate two straws!
     Desire for gold his seeing eyes will blind,
     And where I wish I'll lead him, that you'll find! 1400

201 And if by crystal, lottery or trance
     He tries to find if I tell truth or no,
     I'll interrupt, upset the cards by chance,
     Disturb his fortune telling, let him know
     He hasn't understood all the gods show,   1405
     For the gods speak with ambiguity,
     You'll find one half truth in a peck of lie!

202 Our fears made our first gods. I'll tell him that,
     Adding that out of terror he misread
     The oracles at Delphi, what was what   1410
     Getting mixed up and muddled, till instead

He does just what I tell him, will be led
Whatever way I will. If I do not
My love, put me to death upon the spot!"

203   And truly, as I find it written, too,
All this was said to him with good intent,
And I believe her heart was kind and true
Towards him, and she spoke just as she meant,
And almost died with grieving when she went.
And she intended to be true for ever,   1420
Or so they wrote who knew her and her lover.

204   This Troilus, with open heart and ears
Heard her explain all she would say and do.
It seemed to him he must forget his fears
And think as she did, yet to let her go   1425
He felt such deep misgivings to do so.
But finally he made his sad heart trust
In her, and to accept it since he must.

205   And so his bitter sorrow and penance
Was now shot through with hope, and now between 1430
Them all for joy began the amorous dance,
And as the birds in the sun's golden beam
Delight in song between the leaves so green,
Even so the words they spoke when love making
Delighted them and made their sad hearts sing.   1435

206   Nevertheless, her going out of Troy
For all the world, stayed still in Troilus' mind,
And piteously he prayed, between love's joy,
That true to all her vows he would her find,
And said, "Oh, darling, if you are unkind,   1440
And if you don't return again to Troy
I'll not know honour, health, or hope, or joy.

207   For surely as the sun will rise tomorrow,
        (And God, wretch that I am, as surely bring me
        To rest out of this cruel pain and sorrow,)   1445
        I'll kill myself if you're not back promptly.
        And though my death won't matter so greatly,
        All the same, rather than make me so smart,
        Stay here in Troy with us, my own sweetheart.

208   For truthfully, my own lady so dear,   1450
        The plans which you've outlined to me, alas,
        Are doomed to failure, this I greatly fear.
        Men say, "One onlooker may think all was
        The bear's skill, others think his leader has
        The mastery." Your father's very wise.   1455
        You can outrun, but not outwit his eyes!

209   It's hard pretending lameness when you're watched
        By a real cripple, for he knows that skill.
        Your father's eagle eye cannot be matched,
        Although he's lost his wealth and goods, he's still 1460
        Cunning and clever and does nothing ill.
        You will not blind him with your womanly wiles,
        Nor baffle him, I fear, with all your smiles.

210   I do not know if peace treaties will last,
        But peace or no, in earnest or in game,   1465
        I think, since Calchas with the Greeks has cast
        His lot, and dragged in mud and filth his name,
        He'll not dare show his face in Troy for shame.
        And otherwise to think, for ought I see,
        Can't be depended on, is fantasy!   1470

211   You will soon see, your father will persuade
        You to remarry, and as he speaks well
        He'll praise some Greek so much, he will have made
        You listen, and be lost, through his fine spell,

Or else by force he'll make you do his will,   1475
And you'll forget poor Troilus, who will die
Still faithful to his love eternally.

212   And what is more, your father will pour scorn
Upon us all, and say this city's lost,
The siege will not be raised, the Greeks have sworn   1480
To kill us all, tear down our walls, they boast
They'll make each Trojan man a wailing ghost,
And with his dark threats he'll make you afraid
Till you believe them all, and this I dread.

213   You'll also meet so many bold, strong knights   1485
Among the Greeks, so full of worthiness,
And each of them with wit and heart and might
Will seek to please, make it his business
To try and make our wit seem stupidness,
Us foolish Trojans, unless you in pity   1490
Remember us, your promise, this fair city.

214   And it hurts me so much to think like this
That from my breast my very soul seems rent.
No good will come of it, I think it is
Bound to bring sorrow if to them you're sent,   1495
Because your father's tricks are clearly meant
To ruin us. So if you go from Troy
As I have said, my life I'll lose with joy.

215   So, my Criseyde, with true and humble heart
A thousand times for mercy I now pray,   1500
Pity my bitter pangs, my pains, my smart,
And listen to me, do as I will say,
Let us now both together steal away,
Thinking it stupid, when a man can choose
For him, through choice, all worldly goods to lose. 1505

216   I mean, that since we can, before its day
      Steal away and be together so,
      What sense then, to make trial of or assay
      What might befall if to the Greeks you go,
      To find if you can come back here, or no?   1510
      It would be foolish to test what is sure.
      Better to hold it fast whilst it's secure.

217   And, to be down to earth, both goods and gold
      We can take with us, quite enough to be
      Comfortably off, and honoured, too, till cold   1515
      And dead within our peaceful graves we lie,
      So we'll escape all this anxiety.
      But all those other plans which you suggest,
      They scare the very heart out of my breast!

218   In any case, do not fear poverty,   1520
      For I have friends and relatives elsewhere,
      And even if we came in nudity,
      We'd soon be given gold and gifts and gear,
      And live in honour there throughout the year.
      So let us go at once, for I can see   1525
      This is the best plan, if you will agree."

219   Criseyde, with a sigh, just in this wise
      Answered, "That's so, my love, my own dear heart,
      We can creep away as you desire,
      And find at first this gave us a new start,   1530
      But soon enough we'd taste the bitter part!
      And anyway, as sure as God's above,
      So sure am I your fears are groundless, love.

220   For on that day when I, for praise or love,
      Or fear of father, or of any other,   1535
      Or for ambition, pleasure, marriage, prove
      False to you, Troilus, love, and more than brother,

May Saturn's daughter, Juno, mighty mother,
Maddened against me, cast me down to dwell
Eternally in Styx, the pit of Hell.   1540

221 And this by all the gods celestial
     I swear to you, by every goddess, too,
     By every nymph and spirit infernal,
     By Satyrs and by fauns, many and few,
     Creatures who rule wild places dank with dew,   1545
     And may Atropos cut my life's thin thread
     If I am false, so trust me now instead.

222 And you, Simoïs, that as an arrow clear
     Through Troy's town runs onward towards the sea,
     Bear witness of the words that I say here,   1550
     That on the same day when untrue I be
     To Troilus, my darling, my heart's key,
     Run backwards, river, to your source and well,
     And let me, soul and body, sink to Hell.

223 But what you've said, that we should go away   1555
     And leave your friends and kin, why, God forbid
     That you for any woman so should stray,
     Especially now, when Troy has such great need
     For help. And specially you should take great heed
     Of this, if it were known, my reputation   1560
     And your honour, they'd both be lost and taken.

224 And if, as well may be, we soon have peace,
     As often, after anger, mirth and game,
     Why, lord, what great distress you'd feel, disgrace
     And woe, not to return to Troy for shame,   1565
     So, ere you risk in such a wise your name,
     Don't be too hasty in this hot affair,
     A hasty man is never without care.

225 What do you think that neighbours all about
    Would say of it? Easy to guess and read!   1570
    They'd say, and swear that it was true, no doubt
    That real love didn't make you do this deed,
    But lust, and cowardly fear, and gluttonous greed,
    Then would be lost, my love, my sweetheart dear
    Your honour, which now shines with lustre clear, 1575

226 And also think about my honesty
    Which still bears flowers, how I would smirch its bloom,
    With what foul spots its petals spoilt would be
    If in this way I went with you. My doom,
    Even if I lived to the world's end, its gloom   1580
    Would blacken my fair name eternally,
    And I'd be lost and damned perpetually.

227 So kill and cool with reason all your heat.
    Men say a patient man wins patiently.
    Who wants his love must go at love's own gait,   1585
    And make a virtue of necessity."
    By patience thinking Fortune's lord is he,
    Fearing her not, for she skips to his tune.
    Only the wretched man fears Dame Fortune.

228 You believe this, that truly, darling heart,   1590
    Before Apollo's twin, Lucina bright
    Slides from the Lion's den to Aries' cart,
    Without a doubt I will be here outright,
    May Juno, Heaven's queen, aid me with might.
    On the tenth day, unless death makes me quail,   1595
    I will see you, my love, nor will I fail."

229 "Then, so this may come true," said Troilus,
    "I'll bear my sufferings until the tenth day,
    Since now I see it must be surely thus.
    But, for the love of God, better I say   1600

It would be for us both to steal away,
To be for ever one, to live at rest.
My heart says that way would have been the best."

230   "O mercy, God, what life is this?" said she.
       "With grief you kill me, me, your love, your own.   1605
       I see quite well that you're not trusting me,
       This by your words is clearly, fully shown.
       Now, for the love of Cynthia, the moon,
       Don't doubt me without cause, for pity's sake,
       Since to be true my vow, my pledge I take.   1610

231   Think well how it is sense sometimes, my dear,
       To spend time wisely further time to win.
       Nor have I left you yet, I am still here.
       Though we've known partings, we have met again.
       Drive out those grievous fancies that are in   1615
       Your head, and trust in me, make light of sorrow,
       Or by my faith I will not see tomorrow!

232   For if you knew how this is hurting me
       You'd stop, you'd cease. God, Troilus, you know
       My self, my soul weeps, bleeds continually   1620
       To see you, whom I love most, sunk in woe,
       Knowing to Greeks, to strangers I must go.
       Were it not that I knew the remedy
       My swift return to you, right here I'd die!

233   But truly, I am not a stupid head.   1625
       I can work out, foresee and plan a way
       To come back on the very day I said.
       Who can keep fenced the beast that longs to stray?
       My father can't, though he vast plots may lay!
       So, through my planning, though I go from Troy   1630
       In a few days I'll turn our woe to joy!

234 Therefore, with all my heart I beg you now,
    If you desire to please or do my will,
    And for the love which in us both does grow,
    Before I leave you, calm yourself, be still,   1635
    Look cheerful and be happy, dearest, fill
    Your heart with hope, that you may set to rest
    My heart that almost breaks within my breast.

235 And most of all I pray you," then she said,
    "My darling heart, my root of joy and bliss,   1640
    Since wholly yours through love, by love I've made,
    While I'm away, please let no happiness
    With others drive me from your consciousness,
    For I'm so fearful—What men say is true,
    Love's full of jealous fears and terrors, too.   1645

236 For in this world there is no woman living
    Who, if you were untrue, (ah, God forbid)
    Would be as much betrayed, as sad, yet loving
    As I, who trust you so. And if I did
    Discover you were false to me, ah, dead   X   1650
    I'd be. So, love, remember and be kind,
    Don't hurt me through your body or your mind."

237 Troilus replied to these her words, and said,
    "Now God, who sees all things with his keen eye,
    Bear witness, never since I saw Criseyde   1655
    First, was I false to her, nor yet will I
    Be false to her before the day I die.   X
    Believe me, love, and at the judgement day
    You'll know these words are truth which now I say."

238 "Thank you, my darling love, for that," said she.   1660
    "And joyful Venus, let me not die until
    I can give him, my dear, such ecstasy
    In love as recompense, and to fulfil

His life with joy. And while I live I will
Do so. For true I have my true love found,   1665
Honour from this towards him shall rebound.

239   Dearest, believe me, all your royal estate
       Enticed me not, nor might, and worthiness
       In war or tournament, your prowess great,
       Your pomp, array, nobility, richness   1670
       Made me take pity on your great distress,
       But goodness, with the strong, true heart you have
       This made compassion grow and turn to love.   ✕

240   Your gentleness, the manhood that you had,
       And, as it seemed to me, your strong despite   1675
       Of everything contemptible and bad,
       Rudeness, vulgarity and trivial spite,
       Because your reason bridled, checked delight,
       This made me yours, made me love you the best,
       Yours, yours, while this my heart beats in my breast. 1680

241   Long years of time cannot kill love like this,
       Nor may all-fickle fortune this deface,
       But Jupiter, who may restore to bliss
       The saddest folk, may he grant us his grace
       Before ten days are up, here, in this place,   1685
       To meet, both lost again in happiness.
       Now, farewell, love, time now to rise and dress."

242   And after they such long complaints had made,
       After they kissed, held in each other's arms,
       The sun arose, Troilus himself arrayed,   1690
       Then looked most sadly on his lady's charms,
       Staring like one dazed, stunned by war's alarms.
       And then he knelt and begged that she would bless
       Him. How he felt I leave you all to guess.

243 For no man's mind can feel what he felt then,   1695
     Nor can imagine, nor his great pain tell.
     His grief cannot be told by tongue or pen,
     His torments were more strong than those of Hell,
     For when he saw she could no longer dwell,
     His very soul from his poor heart was rent,   -1700
     Dumb, stumbling, stunned, out of the room he went. 1701

Book Five

1 Now nearer came that fatal destiny
   Which Jove held fixed and in position,
   And to you, angry Parcae, sisters three
   He handed it, axe poised for execution.
   So Criseyde had to leave her home and town,   5
   And Troilus now would live in agony
   Until Fate cut his thread and let him die.

2 Golden-haired Phoebus high up in the sky
   Three times had brought back spring with his light's sheen,
   Melting the snows, and Zephyr, warm and dry   10
   Unfurled once more the tender leaves so green,
   Since the Prince, son of Hecuba, the queen,
   First loved Criseyde, and whose only sorrow
   Was this, that she must go from Troy tomorrow.

3 At prime all ready there was Diomed   15
   Criseyde towards the Greecian hosts to lead,
   For sorrow of which she felt her sad heart bled,
   Half dazed, not knowing what to think indeed,
   And truly, as you can in all books read,
   No woman ever had more grief and care,   20
   Or was more loath out of a town to fare.

4 Troilus, without advice, and helplessly,
   Like one who'd lost all joy and happiness,
   Was waiting on Criseyde continually.

In her was centred all his joy, no less.   25
She'd been the root of all his steadfastness.
But Troilus, now farewell to all that joy.
You'll never see your love again in Troy!

5   True it is that whilst he served her so
      His sorrow like a man he tried to hide,   30
      So folk could not detect his grief and woe.
      But at the gate through which she had to ride
      He waited, hovering, others at his side,
      So woebegone, though he would not complain,
      That he could scarce keep on his horse for pain.   35

6   With rage he shook, and anger gnawed his heart
      When he saw Diomed mount on his horse,
      And to himself he said, standing apart,
      "Ah, what a hateful thing is this, perforce.
      Why do I suffer it, not stop its course?   40
      Better at once to rescue her and die
      Than all my life in agony to lie!

7   Why don't I rouse the city, rich and poor,
      And give them work to do, before she'll go?
      Why don't I lead all Troy out with a roar?   45
      Why don't I kill this Diomed also?
      Why don't I, with a man at arms or two
      Take her away? Why do I this endure?
      Why don't I help myself to my own cure?"

8   But why he did not do so wrong a deed   50
      I'll tell you now, and why he let it go.
      He had at heart a feeling of great dread
      Lest Criseyde, in the rushing to and fro
      Be hurt or killed. This torment was, and woe,
      Else certainly, as I have said before,   55
      He would have rescued her, with no words more.

9   Criseyde, when she was ready forth to ride
    Sighed with great sorrow, and cried out, "Alas"!
    But she was forced to go, ah, woe betide.
    And so she slowly rode the gates to pass.   60
    For her no other remedy there was.
    No wonder that she felt both pain and smart
    Losing her lover and her own sweetheart.

10 This Troilus, like a courteous, gracious knight,
    His hawk upon his glove, with many men   65
    Around him, rode with her, his lady bright,
    Through the long valley facing them, and then
    Further on would have ridden, eager, when,
    Still wanting to press on and with her ride,
    He had to turn at last and leave her side.   70

11 And as he turned, there Antenor had come
    Out from the Greecian army, and each knight
    Was glad of it, and said he was welcome.
    But the sad heart of Troilus felt no light.
    He had to try with all his manhood's might   75
    To hold back tears from eyes which now grew dim,
    Yet he kissed Antenor and greeted him.

12 And with this done, his leave he had to take,
    And on her cast his eye most piteously,
    And nearer rode, his farewell now to make,   80
    And took her by the hand most soberly.
    And lord, she started weeping tenderly,
    And to her he, low voiced and secret, said,
    "Keep to your promised day, or I'll lie dead."

13 With that, he turned his courser round about   85
    With white, pale face, and unto Diomed
    He spoke no word, and likewise all the rout
    Of knights. Of this Tydeus' son took heed,

    o

Like one who knew well in such books to read,
I mean, of rage, then took her bridle rein,   90
And Troilus to Troy went home again.

14 This Diomed, who led her by the bridle,
    When he saw all the Trojans ride away,
    Thought to himself, "My time shall not be idle!
    I'll work indeed, I'll sow good words today.   95
    At least to talk will shorten much our way.
    And there's a proverb I've found a good rule.
    'He who forgets himself is a true fool'."

15 Nevertheless, he thought this well enough,
    "All my words and labour will be naught   100
    If I talk love to her, or make it tough!
    No doubt if she has lurking in her thought
    That lad who said goodbye, he can't be brought
    Out of her mind so soon. Yet I shall try
    Some way without her guessing what or why!"   105

16 This Diomed, who knew well what was good
    For him, began to talk most pleasantly
    Of this and that, and asked her if she would
    Tell him just why she rode so dismally,
    What was it so distressed her? Courteously   110
    He asked if he could help her. If she would
    Tell him, he'd ease and aid her, if he could.

17 For truly, so he swore as a true knight,
    There was no thing, if with it he could please
    Her, he'd not try with all his main and might   115
    To do, if this would her poor, grieved heart ease
    And then he begged that she'd her grief appease,
    Saying, "In truth, we Greeks feel as much joy
    In honouring you as those you've left in Troy."

18   He also said, "I know you think this strange,   120
     And it's no wonder, for to you it's new,
     The friendship of the Trojans now to change
     For that of Greeks, strangers you never knew.
     But, God knows, without doubt a Greek as true
     Among us all I'm sure that you will find   125
     As any Trojan is, and quite as kind.

19   And now, because I promised you right now
     To be your friend and helper, with all might,
     And because riding so I've grown to know you
     Better than any other stranger knight,   130
     Ask me to serve you, though it may press hard,
     To carry out your wish in deed and word.

20   And I ask, too, please, like a brother treat
     Me, do not take my friendship in despite.   135
     And though your grief may be both deep and great,
     I do not know the cause, yet my delight
     Will be to make it less, or end it quite.
     And if I cannot make your sorrow less,
     At least I'll share and pity your distress.   140

21   And though you Trojans with us Greeks are wroth,
     And have been so for a long while, truly,
     One god of Love indeed we worship both,
     So, for the love of God, my dear lady,
     Though you hate Greeks, do not turn hate to me,   145
     For truly, there's no man who longs to serve
     You, who's so loath your anger to deserve!

22   And if we were not now so near the tent
     Of Calchas, who no doubt hears all we say,
     I'd tell you all my thought and my intent.   150
     But this must wait until another day.
     Give me your hand. I am, and shall be aye

God help me, while I live and keep my nature,
Your own above all other living creature.

23 I've never spoken so to any girl   155
    Before; God knows I've never yet before
    Loved any woman, nor met such a pearl
    As you, and God knows, will do never more.
    So, lady mine, don't be my foe in war.
    I can't put my case better, for in love   160
    I'm still a learner, and ineptly move.

24 And do not be surprised, my lady bright,
    That I should speak of love so suddenly,
    For I have heard that many a noble knight
    Loved what he had not seen with certainty,   165
    And I can't struggle against Love's decree,
    But must with meekness his great power obey,
    And so your mercy and your pity pray.

25 There are so many great knights in this place,
    And you're so lovely that each one of these   170
    Will beg to stand high in your love and grace.
    But if you could my pain and longing ease,
    Take me for servant, let me work to please
    You, none will be more true, more staunch than I
    Of all these lovers, till I fall and die."   175

26 Little Criseyde said to him, nor answered,
    For she with sorrow's load oppressed was so
    That in effect his tales she never heard,
    Excepting here and there a word or two.
    She felt her heart would almost break with woe,   180
    And when far off she saw her father, well,
    Down from her horse's back she nearly fell.

27   But all the same she turned to Diomede
      Thanking him for his pains and kindliness,
      And that he'd offered friendship true indeed,   185
      She would accept it with much thankfulness.
      And wished to make return with friendliness.
      She would place trust in him. With faith so plighted
      She dropped the reins and from her horse alighted.

28   Now in his arms her father's taken her,   190
      And twenty times he's kissed his daughter sweet,
      Saying, "Dear daughter, welcome, welcome here."
      She said that she was glad with him to meet,
      And stood there mutely, courteous, mild, discreet.
      But here I leave her with her father dwelling,   195
      And now of Troilus' doing I'll be telling.

29   To Troy has come this woeful Troilus,
      In sorrow greater than all woes before,
      With frowning face and look all piteous,
      Then from his horse sprang down before his door,   200
      And through his palace, angry and heartsore
      Went to his room. Of nothing he took heed,
      And none dared speak a word to him for dread.

30   And there the grief that he had kept in check
      Welled up and over. "Death, O death," he cried,   205
      And in his frenzy, frantic, mad and black
      He cursed Jove, and Apollo and Cupid,
      And likewise Ceres, Bacchus, and, beside,
      His birth, himself, his fate, and even nature,
      And, save his lady, every other creature.   210

31   And then to bed he went, wailed there, and turned
      In fury, just as Ixion does in Hell,
      And in that wise, almost till day sojourned.
      Then with less pain his heart began to swell,

Because of tears which now began to well,   215
And piteously he called upon Criseyde,
And to himself like this he spake and cried.

32   "Where is my own sweet lady, loved and dear?
Where is her white breast, where is it, ah, where?
Where are her arms, her eyes, sparkling and clear,   220
Which last night at this time all with me were?
Now I must weep alone with many a tear,
And though I feel around, here in this place
Save pillows, there is nothing to embrace.

33   What shall I do? When will she come again?   225
I do not know. Why did I let her go?
If only God had let me drop down slain.
O, my dear heart, Criseyde, O my sweet foe,
O lady mine, I love no one but you.
To you for ever more my heart I give.   230
Unless you rescue me, I shall not live.

34   Who looks upon you now, my true lode-star?
Who sits or stands now in your sweet presence?
Who can now comfort you, soothe your heart's war?
Now I have gone, to whom give you audience?   235
Who speaks for me in my enforced absence?
I have no advocate, and it's my care
That you as sadly now as I do fare.

35   And how shall I ten whole days thus endure,
When on the first night I am suffering so?   240
And what shall she do, sad and sorrowing creature,
So tender hearted, how then will she do,
How suffer so for me? Pale, pale the hue
And pinched and wan will be your lovely face
With pining ere you come back to this place."   245

36 And when he dropped off into slumberings,
  Straightway he tossed and turned with fearful groan,
  And dreamed of all most dreadful, torturing things
  That might befall. He thought he was alone
  In horrid places, making a wild moan,   250
  Or, as it seemed, was hard beset by all
  His enemies, wounded, near to fall.

37 Then with his fear his body gave a start,
  And with that start, he sat up, wide awake,
  And such a trembling felt about his heart 255
  That in his fear he felt his body quake,
  And heard himself a noise, a crying make.
  He felt as if he fell down, down, a steep
  Height from aloft. Then, shaken, he would weep,

38 Thinking about himself so piteously   260
  That it was sad to hear his troubled fancies.
  Another time he tried so very strongly
  To cheer himself, saying it was unwise
  Without cause to give way to fantasies.
  But then his bitter sorrows came again 265
  Till everyone felt pity for his pain.

39 Who can write down correctly, or describe
  His woes, complaints, the griefs which make him pine?
  Not any author yet, dead or alive!
  Reader, you'll know this well, and can divine 270
  That woe like his my wit cannot outline.
  In vain I'd work to set such sorrow down,
  When even to think about it makes me frown.

40 In heaven still the glittering stars were seen,
  Although quite pale and wan the moon had grown, 275
  And whitely did the bright horizon gleam
  Towards the east, and in the first light shown

Phoebus within his rosy cart came down
Ready to drive in state across the sky,
And Troilus sent for Pandar hastily.   280

41   This Pandarus, who all the day before
Wanted, yet could not go his friend to see,
Though he to help and comfort him longed sore,
For with the King, Priam, all day was he
On state affairs, and so could not get free   285
Or go elsewhere, but on the morrow went
To Troilus, who'd servants for him sent.

42   For in his heart deep down he guessed quite well
That Troilus all night for sorrow woke,
And that he'd straightway all his troubles tell.   290
This he knew, without need for a book,
And so to Troilus' room his way he took,
And with a solemn face he greeted him,
Sat down upon his bed, and said "Begin."

43   "My Pandarus," said Troilus, "The sorrow   295
Which pierces me I cannot long endure,
I don't think I will live until tomorrow,
And so I'll tell you now, lest there's no cure,
How to arrange my tomb and sepulchre.
As for my goods, disperse and dispose these   300
Just how you wish, and as you think will please.

44   But of the pyre and funeral fire crackling
In which my body burned to ash shall be,
The feast, the funeral games and wrestling
At my vigil, arrange these carefully,   305
Offer to Mars my war horse piously,
My sword, too, and my helmet and my shield,
Gleaming and bright, Pandar, to Pallas yield.

45 The powder into which my burning heart
    Turns, I pray you take, preserving this   310
    Safe in a golden urn, keep it apart,
    And to my lady, whom I serve and kiss,
    And for whose love I die, deprived of bliss
    Give it, do me this last sad observance,
    Ask her to keep it for remembrance.   315

46 For now I feel, by this my malady,
    And through my dreams, today and long ago,
    Quite certainly that I am going to die,
    And the foreboding owl has warned me, too,
    By shrieking after me the whole night through.   320
    And Mercury, when you desire to fetch
    My soul, take it from me, a mournful wretch."

47 Pandar answered, and said "Troilus,
    My dear friend, as I've often said before,
    It's stupidness to sit bewailing thus   325
    Quite without cause. But why should I say more
    To one like you, who won't heed words or lore?
    It's useless offering any remedy.
    Stew here in your own juice of fantasy!

48 But, Troilus, I pray you, tell me true   330
    If you believe, before now, any might
    Have loved their girls in the same way as you?
    Of course they have, and many a worthy knight
    Has parted from his lady a fortnight,
    And he's not made one half the fuss you've done! 335
    What need for you to make so loud a moan?

49 Since you, day after day, can yourself see
    That from his sweetheart, or else from his wife
    A man must part through some necessity,
    And even though she's dear to him as life   340

He will not turn what's got to be to strife.
For you know well, my brother very dear,
Friends may not always be together here.

50   What about those who see their true loves wedded
Through friends' contriving? It can happen so.   345
Seeing them with their spouses safely bedded!
Why, they accept it sensibly, they know
There's always hope, therefore they undergo
A temporary time of fast and sorrow.
One day brings pain, yet joy may come tomorrow!   350

51   Put up with things, and let the time slide by.
Try hard to be content and light of heart.
Ten days is not long to wait patiently.
And since she's promised you to come, her part
She'll keep to, she'll not fail you for a start.   355
Don't be afraid, she's sure to find a way
To come back here again, I'll wagers lay.

52   Your dreams, and all that sort of fantasy
Drive them away and drown them in mischance,
For they spring out of dumpish melancholy   360
Which makes your sleep a hard and long penance.
A fig for dreams and their significance!
God help me, I don't give for them one bean!
No man alive can tell what dreams do mean!

53   Priests in the temple come and tell you this,   365
Dreams are the relevations of the gods.
But they say, too, (if I don't hear amiss,)
That dreams descend when Hell and the devil prods!
And doctors, that they're temperament and moods,
Or are the fruit of fast, or gluttony.   370
Who knows indeed what, when, or why they be!

54   Other men say they're due to deep impressions
      Such as when men have this or that in mind,
      And this gives rise to visions or repressions;
      And others in the books they're reading find   375
      That changing seasons cause dreams of each kind.
      And to the moon, they say, some dreams are due;
      Don't believe dreams, I say, they'll not come true!

55   All very well for old wives to have dreams,
      For them to look at omens, bug, beast, bird.   380
      (Omens can scare some folk to death, it seems.
      Boding raven, shrieking owl preferred.)
      It's false and foul to think *these* souls have stirred!
      Alas, that man in all his nobleness
      Should fear such folly, dread such filthiness.   385

56   And so, with all my heart you I beseech,
      Forget all this and drive it from your mind.
      Get up at once without another speech,
      And let us ways of new diversion find,
      How you may pass the time and make it kind
      Until she comes again, which she'll soon do.
      God help me, it is best to act just so.

57   Rise, let us talk of the good times in Troy
      We've had, and will have, to pass time away.
      And let us think of all our future joy,   395
      The bliss which we shall feel to make us gay,
      To drive away the sadness of today.
      We'll soon forget the gloom that we've been feeling
      In the sweet glow of happiness' healing.

58   This town is full of well-bred, pleasant men,   400
      It's truce time still, and has been this long while.
      Let's meet the lads, amuse ourselves with them. ᵡ
      Let's go to Sarpedon's, it's not a mile

To his place, we can there the time beguile,
Liven it up until that glad tomorrow   405
When you'll see her, the cause of all your sorrow!

59   Now get up, my dear brother Troilus,
To lie here brings no credit, certainly,
Weeping and in your bed here wallowing thus,
Indeed, and in this one thing trust to me,   410
If you lie here a day or two, or three,
People will think that out of cowardice
You're feigning sickness and you dare not rise."

60   Then Troilus answered, "Pandar, friend most dear,
People know well, who like me, have felt pain,   415
That for a man to weep with bitter cheer
Because he's agonized in every vein
Is no great wonder, and though I complain
And weep, you cannot blame me for all this,
Since I have lost the root of all my bliss.   420

61   But since I must do so, I must arise,
And will do so, as soon as ever I may.
And God, to whom my heart I sacrifice,
Send to us quickly that tenth happy day.
No bird so longed for spring, green, fresh and gay   425
As I for her, my spring, come back to Troy,
She, cause of both my torment and my joy.

62   But what do you advise?" asked Troilus.
"Where can we best amuse ourselves in town?"
"By God, my council is," said Pandarus,   430
"To join the party held by Sarpedon."
So they discussed this plan, both up and down,
Till Troilus at the last gave his assent,
Got up, and so to Sarpedon's they went.

63 This Sarpedon was rich and honourable,   435
    Lived well, was clever, full of high prowess.
    Rich wines, good foods were served upon his table,
    No matter what they cost, there in richness
    He had it for his guests, that such excess
    Generous and noble hospitality   440
    Had never yet been seen in the city.

64 Nor was there any instrument or sound
    Delightful, either wind, or string, or chord
    That any travellers or musicians found,
    Or tongue can tell of, or pen can record,   445
    Which at his parties were not seen and heard,
    Nor lovelier girls than those who nightly came
    To dance at Sarpedon's or play some game.

65 But what use was all this to Troilus,
    Who in his sorrow heeded, noticed nought?   450
    For ever more his sad heart piteous
    Busily his love, Criseyde, sought.
    She was the only thing of which he thought.
    Now this, now that he was imagining,
    And he found pleasure in no other thing.   455

66 The girls there at the party whom he met,
    Since his own lady from Troy was away
    He could not see with pleasure, but, upset
    And sad, heard all their music, saw them play,
    Yet since she was not there, who held the key   460
    To his heart's joy, he had no wish to hear.
    Music without her, that he could not bear.

67 Nor was there one hour in the day or night
    When those who were around him could not hear
    Him say, "O sweetheart, dearest lady bright,   465
    How have you been since you were with me here?

How welcome will you be, my darling dear!"
But this, alas, was only Fortune's teasing,
For him she'd malice, and no wish of pleasing.

68   The letters which Criseyde in former time   470
      Had sent him, these alone again he'd read
      Over and over between noon and prime,
      And in his mind her shape, her form indeed
      He saw, and every word and every deed
      They'd spoken or had done. So to a close   475
      The fourth day of their parting slowly grows.

69   Then Troilus said, "Dear brother Pandarus,
      Do you intend that we shall stay on here
      Till Sarpedon out on the street will throw us?
      Better for us to go whilst we're still dear.   480
      For God's sake, and for mine, yourself please tear
      Away from all this noise and revelry.
      I'm sick of it. So let's go home quickly."

70   Pandarus answered. "Have we both come here
      To get lit up, then dash back home again?   485
      God help me, for indeed I don't know where
      We could go that would better cure your pain.
      Sarpedon likes and welcomes us, it's plain,
      And if we leave like this, and homeward hie
      So suddenly, he'll think it villany.   490

71   We'd stay a week with him, that's what we said.
      Join a house-party, and then go away
      On the fourth day! He'd think it strange indeed,
      And rude to leave after so short a stay.
      So let's keep to our plan. And do obey,   495
      Keep to your promise, stay at least a week,
      And then ride home to wait her whom you seek."

72   So Pandarus, with pleading, sighs and woe
      Persuaded him to stay. At the week's end
      They took their leave of Sarpedon, and so   500
      Went on their way, back to their homes to wend,
      And Troilus said, "May God his mercy send—
      O let me find, there at my homecoming
      My Criseyde waiting." He began to sing.

73   "That's all my eye! The poor lad has been sold!"   505
      To himself softly whispered Pandarus.
      "God knows, this hot fare will grow freezing cold
      Before Calchas sends Criseyde to Troilus!"
      But covering up, he jested, saying thus,
      "No doubt it's true what hope and your heart say, 510
      And she will come as soon as ever she may."

74   When they had both to Troilus' palace come,
      They each dismounted from their horses, then
      Climbed to the prince's private sitting room,
      And until it grew dark, there sat these men   515
      Talking about Criseyde, the bright, and when
      They'd ceased, they dined upon the very best
      Troy offered, and then went up to their rest.

75   Next day, as soon as night began to clear
      Troilus sat up and shook off sleep, and said   520
      To Pandarus, his friend so close and dear,
      "For love of God, let us rise up and ride
      To see the house where once lived my Criseyde,
      For since we can't have her with us in joy,
      Let us at least look where she lived in Troy."   525

76   And with that, to deceive his knights and men
      He found excuses into town to go,
      And past Criseyde's house they rode again.
      But lord, this foolish Troilus felt such woe

He thought his sorrowful heart would break in two, 530
For when he saw her doors barred safe and sound,
With sorrow he almost fell down to the ground.

77 But when he'd gained control and could behold
How shuttered were the windows of the place,
He felt as if frost made his heart grow cold,   535
And deathly pale and ashen grew his face.
Without a word he rode at such a pace,
And, the gods helping, so fast did he ride
That no one with him his distress had spied.

78 Then to himself he said, "O desolate place,   540
O house, of all once best, most dear, most bright,
Disconsolate, empty, bereft palace,
A lantern in which quenched is the pure light,
A house once full of day, now filled with night,
You should fall down as dust, and I should die   545
Since she has gone who ruled us equally.

79 O palace, once the crown of houses all,
Illumined with the sunshine of all bliss,
O ring, from which you've let the ruby fall,
O cause of grief, who once caused happiness,   550
But since I've nothing else, I long to kiss
Your cold doors, if I could do so unseen.
Ah, farewell, shrine, where once a saint has been."

80 At this, on Pandarus he cast his eye,
His looks quite altered, pitiful to see,   555
And when he could fit time and place espy,
Riding along, he told his misery
To Pandarus, new woes, joys in decay,
So pitiful his words, so pale his hue,
Compassion all should feel for one so true.   560

81 And afterwards he rode up streets and down,
  And everything came to rememberance
  As he passed different places in the town
  Where he'd once felt both joy and gay pleasance.
  "Why, it was there I saw my lady dance, 565
  And in that temple, with her eyes so bright
  I saw her first, and loved her at first sight.

82 And over there I heard most cheerfully
  My dear heart laughing, and there joke and play
  In happiness and youthful energy, 570
  And there to me she turned her head to say
  "Sweetheart, my darling, love me well, I pray."
  And here she looked at me so lovingly—
  Remembering it, I ache with her to be.

83 And at that corner, in that very house 575
  I heard my best beloved lady dear
  So womanly, with voice melodious,
  Singing so well, so charmingly, so clear,
  That ringing in my soul I seem to hear
  That blissful sound. And yonder, in that place 580
  We first made love, she granted me her grace."

84 Then he thought this. "Cupid, joy-bringing lord,
  When all these things move through my memory,
  How you've beset me, pierced me with your sword!
  Why, men could write a book on it, a story— 585
  Why do you seek to win new victory
  Since I am yours, and in your power, so then
  What do you gain by killing your own men?

85 Lord of love, you've wreaked your rage on me,
  Most powerful of all gods, whom all must fear. 590
  Help, gracious lord, I crave your grace and mercy.
  Of all the joys your joy is the most dear.

P

I'll live and die your fervent worshipper,
And of you I will beg one single boon,
That you'll send back my Criseyde to me soon.   595

86 Make her heart filled with longing to return,
As you fill mine with longing her to see.
I'm sure she does not wish there to sojourn,
So, kindly god, do not be cruel to me,
Nor to my Trojan blood, I make my plea,   600
Not harsh as Juno to the Theban men.
Because of which they suffered grief and pain."

87 And after this, he to the town gates went,
From which Criseyde had ridden many a mile.
And up and down, and in and out he bent   605
His way, and to himself talked for a while.
"From these gates rode my love without a smile.
O that it were God's will she should come back,
And that I saw her here, whom now I lack.

88 And to the hills beyond I did her guide.   610
Alas, and there I took of her my leave,
And there I saw her to her father ride,
For sorrow of which my heart will ever grieve.
And here I came back home when it was eve.
And here I live, outcast from every joy,   615
And shall, until I see her back in Troy."

89 And he imagined, in his great distress
That he was tired, lost weight, and grew quite pale,
And that men said he must be under stress.
"What's wrong with him? Why does he pine
                       and fail?   620
What weighs on Troilus, makes him weep and wail?"
Yet all this worry was but melancholy,
Making him fancy illness and such folly.

90   And sometimes he imagined passers-by
      Who saw him walking sadly through the city   625
      Pitied him for his grief, said with a sigh,
      "Troilus is dying. Is it not a pity?"
      So days went by, and in this sort of fit he
      Spent hours and minutes, such a life he led
      As one who stands half way twixt hope and dread.   630

91   And so he wrote out poems, and tried to show
      The reason for his woe, as best he might,
      Making a song of words, concise and few
      Through which to make his sorrowful heart more light.
      And when he was alone and out of sight,   635
      In a low voice he of his lady dear
      Who was away, sang, as you now shall hear.

92   "O star, of whom I've lost the lovely light,
      With sad, sore heart I ought now to bewail
      That dark and deep in torment, night by night   640
      Towards my death, and tempest-tossed, I sail.
      And so, if on the tenth dark night I fail
      To see your guiding beams lighting my way,
      My ship and me Charybdis foul will slay."

93   When he had sung this song and written it,   645
      He fell again to sighing as of old,
      And every night, as was his new habit
      He stood, the bright moon's full face to behold,
      And to the moon his love and sorrow told,
      And said, "O moon, when you are thin and new   650
      I will be happy, if my girl is true.

94   I saw your old horns growing on the morrow
      When from this city rode my lady dear,
      Cause of my present sadness, pain and sorrow,
      For which, bright Lucina, moon goddess clear,   655

For God's love quickly turn your silver sphere.
For when your new young horns begin to spring,
She'll come, and with her all my new joys bring."

95   Days were now longer, longer every night
Than they both used to be, or so he thought.   660
And the sun took a course which was not right,
Longer, more slow than that he had been taught.
Troilus feared lest Phaeton might have caught
His father's chariot, and the sun's child
Once more drove it amok, flaring and wild.   665

96   Upon the walls in haste then he would walk,
Trying if the Greek army he could see,
And then, like this, with his own self he'd talk,
"There, yonder, is my darling, safe and free,
Or else out there, where all those white tents be.   670
And from her flows this air which is so sweet
And heals my soul that longs with her to meet.

97   And maybe this same wind that more and more
In fits and starts blows straight into my face,
Is born of my Criseyde's sighings sore.   675
I'm sure it's so, for in no other place
Through all this town, save only in this space
I've felt this breeze, sighing as if in pain,
As if to say, "Why parted are we twain?" "

98   All this long time he acted just like this,   680
Till past and gone were the ninth day and night,
And always by his side was Pandar, his
Dear friend, who sought with all his wit and might
To comfort him and make his sad heart light,
And give him hope that on the glad tenth morrow   685
She would come back, and put an end to sorrow.

99   Upon the other side was poor Criseyde
     With women few, among the Greeks so strong,
     Because of which, each day, "Alas", she cried,
     "Alas that I was born! And how I long.   690
     For death, for now it seems I live too long.
     Alas, and now I cannot put things right,
     All's much worse than I dreamed, and black as night.

100 My father will not grant me leave, instead
     He scolds. I cannot please him, nor persuade.   695
     And if I don't return just when I said,
     Troilus will think I'm false, or that I've made   ✗
     Friends of the Greeks. And I shall be repaid
     By blame, harsh words, black looks on every side.
     Alas, that I was born," the poor girl cried.   700

101 "And if I put myself in danger by
     Attempting to escape, and it befall
     That I am caught, they'll take me for a spy.
     Or else, and this I dread the most of all,
     Suppose I in the hands of some wretch fall?   705
     I'm lost, whatever happens, though I'm true.
     Pity my sorrows, gods, your grace I sue."

102 Pale, ashy pale had grown her rosy face,
     Her limbs all lean as she, throughout that day
     Stood, when she dared, and looked out at the place   710
     Where she'd been born, and lifelong, hoped to stay,
     And all that night, choking with tears, she lay,
     And so, despairing, hopeless of a cure,
     She led her life, this woeful, sad creature.

103 Often in daytime she'd sigh in distress,   715
     And in her mind forever was portraying
     Troilus, his looks, his voice, his worthiness,
     His words and all he'd said rewhispering,

Since the first day her love began to spring,
And so she set her woeful heart on fire   720
Through thinking of all she did so desire.

104   In all this world there's none so cruel of heart
Who, if they'd heard her wailing in her sorrow
Would not have wept in pity of her smart,
So much she wept and cried, both eve and morrow.   725
She did not need a single tear to borrow.
And this was quite the worst of all her pain,
She had no friend to whom she could complain.

105   Depressed and sad she looked across at Troy,
Saw the high towers, the houses and the halls,   730
"Alas," she said, "The pleasure and the joy
Which now is turned to gall, or to dust falls,
I was so happy once inside those walls.
O Troilus, what are you doing now?
On me do you one single thought bestow?   735

106   Why did I not trust you, and long before
Go with you, as you told me I should do?
I would not then be here, and sighing sore.
Who was there who could say I sinned also
To run away and with my true love go?   740
All too late comes the doctor with his cure
When in the grave the dead man lies secure!

107   Too late to talk about this matter now!
Prudence, alas, one of your three keen eyes
I've lacked since I've been here, I am too slow   745
The past I can remember, and what lies
Around me now I know, but not the ways
That lie ahead, the future. Ah, love's snare
Made me quite blind to this, so I feel care!

108   Nevertheless, whatever will betide,   750
      Tomorrow night, by east ways or by west
      I'll steal off from this army on some side,
      And go with Troilus, follow his behest.
      I'll do this thing I plan, this will be best.
      I won't fear wicked tongues, gossip, or talk,   755
      For real love's always envied by mean folk.

109   For those who of each man's advice take heed
      And rule their lives by other people's words
      Will never thrive, but be in constant dread.
      What some find fault in, hack with verbal swords, 760
      That same to others joy and praise affords.
      As for me, all this sheer variety
      Makes me find pleasure in stability!

110   And so, without more words of hesitation
      I'll go to Troy, and that is my conclusion."   765
      But God knew well, before two months' duration
      She'd very far from that intention come.
      Both Troilus and her love and Troy's fair town
      Slid like a well-greased, knotless cord right through
      Her heart. She stayed there with the Grecian crew! 770

111   This Diomed, to tell of whom I started,
      Went about, with himself still arguing
      With Grecian craftiness, most cunning hearted,
      How he could best, and without tarrying
      Into his net Criseyde's affections bring.   775
      No ending to his plans, his deep design,
      To land this fish he laid out hook and line.

112   Nevertheless, within his heart he thought
      That she was not without a love in Troy.
      For never, since he'd from that city brought   780
      Her, had she laughed or shown a sign of joy.

How could he lure her, she so cool and coy?
"Effort," said he, "A man like me won't grieve.
He who tries nothing nothing will achieve."

113   Yet he said to himself one sleepless night,   785
"Now, am I not a fool who knows well how
Her lovesickness is for some other knight,
And yet I plan to court and woo her now!
I might as well accept such love won't grow!
Wise writers in their books say, for a start,   790
You cannot court or win a woe-crazed heart."

114   But whosoever wins so fair a flower
From him for whom she pines both night and day,
He might well call himself a conqueror!"
And then that knight, bold-hearted, stalwart, gay,   795
Thought in his heart, "Whatever happen may,
I'll try to win her heart, risk life or death.
After all, I can lose but words and breath!"

115   This Diomed, as all the books declare
Forced his own way with speed and deeds courageous. 800
His voice was stern, his body brawny, square,
Sturdy, impatient, strong, yet chivalrous,
In his deeds like his father, Tydeus.
Some say he boasted—that's not here nor there—
And of Argos and Calydon was heir.   805

116   Criseyde was medium tall, and slight of stature.
Although in figure, face and looks aglow,
There could be no more lovely living creature,
And often times she'd let her long hair flow
Loosely, and just as nature made it grow,   810
Over her collar down her back behind,
Where, with a golden thread gold locks she'd bind.

117   And, save her eyebrows closely joined together,
       There was no fault in her that I can see.
       But to speak of her eyes, so bright and clear,   815
       People who saw her, with sincerity
       Say Paradise shone in her eyes' beauty,
       And with her rich, warm beauty there was store
       Of love, a goddess could not have had more.

118   She was a serious girl, modest and wise,   820
       The best of living women you could find,
       Charming in speech and voice, manners and poise,
       Charitable, well-bred, lively, kind,
       Merciful and compassionate in mind,
       Tender of heart, but variable her courage   825
       I fear I cannot tell you what her age!

119   And Troilus was well grown, manly and tall,
       Perfect in his proportions and his grace.
       So much so that he lacked nothing at all.
       Young, strong and lion-like, and fresh of face,   830
       True as steel at every time and place.
       One of the best-graced and most gifted men
       That is, or was, or shall be, now or then.

120   And certainly in stories it is told
       That Troilus was never second-best   835
       In any deeds of war which warriors bold
       Might do, or a knight undertake with zest.
       Giants alone could beat him, for the rest,
       His courage with the very foremost stood.
       However great the odds, his heart was good.   840

121   But now to tell you more of Diomed.
       It happened so that on that same tenth day
       Since he from Troy's town Criseyda had led,
       This Diomed, as fresh as branch in May,

Came to the tent where she and Calchas lay,   845
Pretending that he'd business to discuss.
But what he meant I'll tell you without fuss.

122   Criseyde, in brief, and a short tale to tell,
Welcomed him, and set him by her side.
And it was easy so to make him dwell.   850
And after this, (to cut it short I've tried.)
The servants brought them wine, and spice beside,
And sitting there they spoke of this and that
As friends do, and I'll shortly tell you what.

123   First he began to talk about the war   855
Now waged between the Greeks and all Troy town,
And of the siege he spoke, beseeching her
To tell him what was her opinion.
That done, by subtle sleights he travelled down
To ask her if she'd strange and curious thought   860
The ways of Greeks, their work, and all they wrought?

124   And also why her father tarried so
In marrying her to some good, worthy knight.
Criseyde, whose pains and sufferings you know
For Troilus, her darling love, scarce might   865
Heed what he said, though distant and polite
She answered him. But as for his intent,
It seemed as if she knew not what he meant.

125   Nevertheless, this same man, Diomede,
Had self-assurance, and spoke thus, and said,   870
"If I've heard you aright, and taken heed
It seems to me, O lady mine, Criseyde,
Since I first held your bridle rein, and led
You out of Troy on that bright shining morrow,   875
I've never seen you but in tears or sorrow.

126   I cannot guess just what the cause may be,
       Unless for love of some Trojan it were,
       And this I think is shame and great pity
       That you for any man who lives out there
       Let fall even one quarter of a tear,   880
       Or so deceive, and your dear self beguile.
       Believe me, to do so is not worth while.

127   The folk of Troy, or so all say who know,
       Are there as if imprisoned, as you see,
       And from that prison none alive shall go   885
       For all the gold in Priam's treasury.
       So do believe and put your trust in me.
       Not one of them unscathed shall leave that town,
       Not even if he's a king, and wears a crown.

128   Such a revenge for lovely Helen's rape   890
       We'll take before we leave these shores and go,
       That spirits of the slain shall stare and gape
       Aghast to see how we will lay them low.
       In future men will dread to do just so,
       No one will henceforth ravish any queen,   895
       So cruel, so harsh shall our revenge be seen.

129   And unless Calchas leads us all astray
       With double talk, ambiguous words all sly,
       'Words with two faces', that's what people say,
       You'll know quite well I don't mislead or lie,   900
       And see it for yourself with your own eye,
       And quickly, too, you don't know quite how soon
       Your Trojans all will dance to our brisk tune!

130   Why do you think that your wise father would
       Have otherwise for Antenor changed you,   905
       Unless he could forsee the city would
       Be totally destroyed? I swear it's true,

No Trojan would escape alive, he knew,
And knowing this, and driven on by fear
He dared not leave you longer dwelling there.   910

131   What more then do you want, my lady dear?
Let Troy and Trojans from your memory fade,
Drive out that bitter hope, and make good cheer,
Look gay and take your beauty from the shade
That clouds it, dry the tears which often made   915
It pale. For Troy lies in such jeopardy
It can't be saved, there is no remedy.

132   And think instead, among the Greeks you'll find
A better lover, and before it's night,
Better than any Trojan, and more kind,   920
To serve you better he will do his might,
And if you will agree, my lady bright,
I'll be that one, for you do everything.
I'd rather be your servant than a king!"

133   And as he spoke these words, he blushed quite red,   925
And his voice thickened, deepened, trembled, shook.
He looked down, hanging low his bashful head,
And paused awhile, then seemed as if he woke,
And very serious was his steadfast look
As he said, "Though it gives you no real joy,   930
I'm as well bred as any man in Troy.

134   For if my father, Tydeus," he said,
"Had lived, I would have been, long before this
King of Argos and Calydon, Criseyde.
And I still hope I'll have such wealth and bliss.   935
But he was killed, alas, pity it is,
Unhappily at Thebes, and early, too,
In battle, but his many foes he slew.

135 But, my dear heart, since I am your own man,
    Since you're the first from whom I've asked
                      love's grace,   940
    I'll serve with what sincerity I can,
    And always shall, whilst I may see your face.
    So, love, before I leave this tent, this place,
    Grant me permission to tell you tomorrow
    At better leisure all my grief and sorrow."   945

136 Why should I repeat the words he said?
    He spoke enough for one day at the least,
    There's proof enough, he spoke so well, Criseyde
    Permitted him next day, at his request
    To let him talk with her. But what his breast   950
    Burned with, she begged he would not speak of this,
    And what she said to him here briefly is.

137 She, who had set her heart on Troilus
    So deeply that none could the marks erase,
    Spoke coldly to her wooer, saying thus,   955
    "O Diomed, I love that town, that place
    Where I was born. May Jove, out of his grace
    Deliver it from some of its distress.
    God, in your power, help it to suffer less!

138 That the Greeks wish on Troy their wrath to wreak 960
    If they can do it, I know they'll not miss,
    But it shall not fall out just as you speak,
    And before God, and further, over this
    I know my father wise and clever is,
    And that it cost him much to bring me here   965
    You've told me, and for this I hold him dear.

139 That the Greeks are a great and valiant nation
    I know quite well, yet truly, men will find
    People as good in Troy, of every station,

As clever and as perfect, and as kind   970
As any in this world of ours confined,
And that you could become a worthy lover
That I believe. May some girl this discover!

140   But as for talk of love," Criseyde then said,
      "I had a lord to whom I wedded was.   975
      My heart was wholly his till he lay dead.
      And other love, so help me, maiden Pallas,
      Is not within my heart, nor ever was.
      And that you're nobly born, of great kindred
      I've heard, and so I feel for you great dread.   980

141   And knowing this, I'm filled with puzzled wonder
      That you should mock and tease a woman so.
      God knows that love and I are far asunder.
      I feel more like a creature sunk in woe,
      Weeping and wailing as to death I go.   985
      How I will feel hereafter I can't say.
      As yet, though, I've no mind to jest or play.

142   My heart is now in grief and tribulation,
      And you are busy fighting day by day.
      Hereafter, when you've won the war and town,   990
      Maybe it will fall out that my eyes stray
      In a new path and a quite different way,
      And I'll do that which I've not done before.
      This must suffice you now. I can't say more.

143   Tomorrow I'll agree to talk with you   995
      As long as you keep off this love matter.
      And, when you wish, you may call here again.
      But, Sir, before you go, I tell you here,
      (May Pallas help me with her grey eyes clear,)
      That if on any Greek I should take pity
      You shall be he, I swear this by Troy city!

144   By this I do not mean that I will love you.
        No, I don't say that, but in conclusion,
        I mean well to you, swearing that it's true."
        And as she spoke, she blushed, looked shyly down,   1005
        And deeply sighed, and said, "O Troy, my town,
        I pray the gods, may I, in peace, at rest
        See you, or may my heart break in my breast."

145   But, in effect, and to be brief, I say
        This Diomed began to plead anew,   1010
        And press his suit on her, her mercy pray,
        And after this, to tell the truth to you,
        He took her glove, for a love-token true,
        And then at last, and late, when it was eve
        And all was going well, he took his leave   1015

146   Bright glowing Venus rose, and shining, showed
        The way when Phoebus quenched his chariot's light,
        And Cynthia's horses through the dark sky glowed,
        Whirling beyond the Lion's path through night,
        And Signifer his candles showed, all bright,   1020
        When Criseyde to her rest and quiet bed went,
        Inside her father's well appointed tent,

147   Rolling within her mind, first up, then down,
        The words of this brash, sudden Diomede,
        His rank and name, the danger of Troy town,   1025
        And that she was alone, and had great need
        For help of friends. From this began to breed
        The reason why, and this is truth I tell,
        That she decided with the Greeks to dwell.

148   The morning dawned, and earnestly to speak,   1030
        Diomed came there, searching for Criseyde,
        And, to be brief, lest from my tale you break,
        He pressed his suit so well, such good things said,

That a mere nothing of her sighs he made,
And finally, to tell you what is true,   1035
He cured her pain, and made her love anew.

149   And after this, or so the story tells us,
       She gave to him the comely bright bay steed
       Which he'd once won in a fight from Troilus,
       Also a brooch, (and there was little need,)   1040
       Once Troilus', she gave to Diomede,
       And so he might his love and pain relieve
       She made him wear a pennant from her sleeve.

150   I find in stories written down elsewhere,
       That, when in war with flesh wounds, Diomed   1045
       Was hurt by Troilus, she wept many a tear,
       Seeing his wide wounds gape and sorely bleed,
       And that to nurse him then she took good heed,
       And sought to heal him of his sorrow's smart.
       Some say, not I, that she gave him her heart.   1050

151   But truly, as the written story tells us,
       There never was a woman wept more sore
       Than she, when she played false to Troilus.
       She said, "Alas, it's gone for ever more,
       My name of truth in love time can't restore,   1055
       For I've betrayed a man, the gentlest
       That ever was, also the worthiest.

152   Alas, of me and of my deeds of shame
       No good words shall be written, told or sung
       Till the world's end, and me all books will blame.   1060
       They'll jeer, and roll my name on many a tongue,
       Throughout the world my bell shall be so rung,
       And women will hate me the worst of all.
       Alas, that such a fate should on me fall.

153   They'll say that, in as much as in me is,   1065
       I have dishonoured my own sex today,
       Though I am not the first who did amiss,
       That does not help to wash my blame away.
       But since there is, I see, no better way,
       And that it's now too late for me to rue,   1070
       To Diomed at least I will be true.

154   But, Troilus, since I now can do no better,
       And since we two are parted cruelly,
       May the gods free you from love's shackling fetter.
       You are the gentlest lover, dearest, truly,   1075
       The best to serve his lady faithfully,
       The one who will his lady's honour keep."
       She with those words began again to weep.

155   "Truly, truly, hate you or scorn I'll never.
       A friend's warm love, that you will have from me, 1080
       And my good word, though I should live for ever.
       Truly, unhappy, sorry I should be
       To see you harmed, or in adversity.
       Free from all blame, all guilt are you, I know.
       But all will pass, and so I go, I go—"   1085

156   But truthfully, how much time lay between
       Her leaving Troilus for this Diomed
       No author tells, nor with these two has been.
       However hard to books you may pay heed,
       You'll find no word about the time, indeed.   1090
       In fact, though he quite soon began to woo,
       Before he won her, there was much to do!

157   Nor do I want this foolish girl to chide
       More than the story's dictates will devise.
       Her name, alas, is published now so wide,   1095
       That for her punishment this should suffice,

Q

And if I can excuse her any wise,
She felt such pain for her unfaithfulness,
In pity I'll forgive her none the less.

158   This Troilus, as I before have told,   1100
      Went on with life as well as the lad might,
      But often his heart felt first heat, then cold,
      And most of all upon that same ninth night
      Upon whose morrow she had promised right
      She would return. God knows, no rest at all   1105
      He had that night. Asleep he could not fall.

159   The laurel-crowned god, Phoebus, with his heat
      Began his upward course, golden and gay,
      Warming the eastern sea's waves, cold and wet,
      And Nisus' daughter sang to welcome day,   1110
      When Troilus for his Pandar sent straightway,
      And happily upon Troy's walls they strayed
      To look and see if they could glimpse Criseyde.

160   Till it was noonday, they stood there to see
      Who came that way, and every passer-by   1115
      That came from far they thought it must be she,
      Until they saw them coming close and nigh.
      Now Troilus' heart was dull, now it was gay,
      And so they talked and joked of nothing there,
      Pandar and Troilus, as they stood to stare.   1120

161   To Pandarus this Troilus then cried,
      "As far as I can tell, before noonday
      Back into town Criseyde will not ride,
      She's found it hard enough to get away
      From her old father, that is what I say,   1125
      And that old man will make her stop and dine
      Before she leaves. May the gods make him pine!"

162   Pandarus answered. "That may well be true,
So let us both dine, too, this I beseech.
Then in the afternoon come back here, do."   1130
So home they went, not stopping for more speech,
And then returned, but long, long may they seek
Before they find what they are looking for.
Fortune played with them, made them her catspaw!

163   Said Troilus, "I see it now, how she   1135
By her old father has been hindered so
That ere she comes near evening it will be.
Come, then, I will up to the town gates go.
The porters there are stupid, dense and slow,
And I must stop them shutting up the gate,   1140
So she may enter, even if she's late."

164   The day went fast, and then the evening came,
Yet with it Criseyde came not to Troilus.
He looked out over groves, trees, hedge and lane,
Stretching across the wall to see her thus,   1145
And then at last turned towards Pandarus.
"By God, I know what she intends to do,
Though I admit my worries sprung anew,

165   But I am sure she's planned all to the good.
Of course she means to ride back secretly.   1150
She's wise and sensible, why, by the Rood,
She'll not make folk stare at her curiously
As she returns, but creep in here softly.
By night into the town she plans to ride,
So, my dear friend, we won't have long to abide.   1155

166   We've nothing else to do now, but just this
My Pandarus, and now will you believe me,
Why, look there, there I see her, there she is!
Lift up your eyes, man, why, look, can't you see?"

Pandarus answered, "No, I can't, truly.   1160
By God, you're wrong. What's up, man, have a heart!
What I can see is but a travelling cart!"

167   "Alas, you're right indeed," said Troilus.
"And yet, in spite of that, it's not in vain
That in my heart I'm now rejoicing thus.   1165
It's good I have some hopes, some thoughts again,
I don't know how, yet since my birth, my brain
Has never been so comforted, that's flat.
She'll come tonight, I'll stake my life on that."

168   Pandarus answered, "It may well be well,"   1170
And he agreed with him in all he said,
But in his heart thought otherwise. There fell
A premonition. To himself he said
"No use you waiting. Fickle hazel shade!
The tree you trusted in is weak, I fear!   1175
Farewell, farewell the snows of yesteryear."

169   The guardian of the gates began to call
To all the folk who still outside them were,
And bade them drive within their cattle all,
Or all night long they'd have to stay out there. 1180
And far into the night, with many a tear
Troilus set out, back homeward now to ride,
For he saw it was useless to abide.

170   Nevertheless he cheered himself like this,
He thought he had not reckoned the right day,   1185
And said, "I'm sure I've counted up amiss,
That last night with my love, I heard her say
"I'll be back here with you, if yet I may,
Before the moon—O my dear heart, my sweet—
Is out of Leo and in Aries heat."   1190

171   And so she may well keep her promise yet."
      So the next day up to the gate he rode,
      And up and down, first west, then east he set
      His path, and round and round the walls he strode,
      But all in vain. His hopes deceived. A load   1195
      Of pain at night he bore, with sighings sore,
      Then homeward went, without delaying more.

172   His hope now clean out of his heart had fled.
      No longer anything on which to hang,
      But with the pain he thought his sad heart bled.   1200
      His agony was sharp, bitter his pang.
      For now he saw she stayed so long, so long,
      His mind was all confused, his thoughts were dim,
      Since she had broken all she'd promised him.

173   The third, the fourth, the fifth, then the sixth day 1205
      After those first ten days of which I told,
      Fixed between hope and dread his heart now lay,
      Still half believing what she'd said of old.
      But when he saw she'd not to her word hold,
      He then could face no other remedy   1210
      Except to steel himself for death, and die.

174   And then that wicked spirit, God us bless,
      Which men call mad, demented jealousy
      Crept through him, in this state of heaviness,
      Because of which, and as he wished to die   1215
      He did not eat or drink, in melancholy,
      And also from all company he fled.
      This was the life that all this time he led.

175   So cast down and depressed he was, no man
      Could recognise him scarcely as he went,   1220
      For he was thin and haggard, pale and wan,
      So feeble that he on a stout stick leant,

With irritable temper, shamed and bent.
Yet if friends asked him what had made him smart
He said his trouble was his ailing heart.   1225

176   And Priam often, and his mother dear,
        His brothers and his sisters questioned him
        Why he was sorrowful and full of fear,
        And what had caused his pain and sorrows grim?
        But all in vain, he'd not explain to them,   1230
        But said he felt a grievous malady
        Affect his heart, and that he wished to die.

177   So then one day he laid him down to sleep,
        And, as he slept, in dreams poor Troilus thought
        That through a forest glade he walked to weep   1235
        For love of her who all his sorrows wrought,
        And up and down as he the cool trees sought,
        He dreamed he saw a boar with tusks so great,
        Sleeping in all the bright sun's midday heat.

178   And by this boar's side, folded in its arm   1240
        Lay kissing it, Criseyde, his lady bright,
        For sorrow of which, when he saw this, alarm
        Smote Troilus, and out of his sleep in fright
        He sprang, and cried to Pandarus outright,
        "O Pandar, now I know the truth indeed,   1245
        And I will die, for sorrow now I bleed.

179   My lady bright, Criseyde, has betrayed me,
        In whom I trusted more than any born.
        She's given her heart elsewhere, this way repaid me.
        The powerful gods showed me this thing to warn.   1250
        In dreams I saw the truth, and am forlorn.
        Like this my Criseyda I did behold."
        And then to Pandarus the dream he told.

180 "O my Criseyde, alas, what subtlety,
     What new lust, beauty, wisdom or science   1255
     Lures you? What anger do you feel for me?
     What guilt of mine, or bad experience
     Has driven your love from me, and sent it hence?
     O trust, O faith, and all she did profess!
     Who can have stolen her, my happiness?   1260

181 Alas, why did I let you from me go?
     Because of this I almost went quite mad.
     How can I trust in others now? I know
     That I believed, my darling, all you said
     Was gospel truth, and out of true love led.   1265
     But who can deceive better, when he must,
     Than one in whom we have most cause to trust!

182 What shall I do, alas, my Pandarus?
     I feel now sharply and anew, such pain,
     Since there's no hope or remedy for us,   1270
     Better with my two hands to be self slain
     Than to love on, and in this way complain.
     For through my death sorrow itself would die.
     Each day I live heaps more disgrace on me."

183 Pandarus answered, "Ah, alas the day   1275
     That I was born! Why, haven't I said this,
     That dreams so often lead a man astray?
     Why so? Because they are explained amiss.
     How dare you say your lady untrue is,
     Because of dreams. It's your own fear you fear.   1280
     You can't interpret dreams. You're not a seer.

184 Because you dreamed about a sleeping boar
     Maybe it's so the dream can signify
     Her father, who is piggish, old and hoar,
     And snores there in the sunshine, near to die,   1285

And she for sorrow starts to weep and cry,
And kisses him as he lies on the ground.
This is the way you should such dreams expound."

185   "What shall I do then?" asked poor Troilus,
"To know if this is so, and what is right?"   1290
"You're talking sense at last," said Pandarus.
"My council's this, since you can well indite,
Quickly, and now, a letter to her write,
In which you can ask her the truth about
This question which is causing you some doubt.   1295

186   Now see just why the matter is quite plain.
If she's untrue, or acts unfaithfully,
I do not think that she'll write back again.
And if she does, you will quite quickly see
If to come back to you again she's free,   1300
Or if some plan hinders her for a season.
If this is so, she'll tell you what's the reason.

187   You have not written to her since she went,
Nor she to you, and it's my guess, maybe,
Something has kept her back from her intent,   1305
Something so pressing that you will agree
For her to stay may be the best, truly.
So write to her, and you will quickly know
The truth. There's nothing more that you can do."

188   When they had both come to the same conclusion,   1310
And at the same time, these two lords also,
Troilus sat down, and then in some confusion
Rolled out his thoughts, and pushed them to and fro,
Wondering how best to tell her of his woe,
And to Criseyde, his own sweetheart so dear   1315
Wrote in this manner, as I'll tell you here.

189   "My sweet, fresh flower, whose I have been, and shall
        Without a thought of others, serve always,
        With heart and body, life, thought, feelings, all,
        I, wretched man, in humble wise and ways   1320
        Will go on serving you all through my days,
        And while this world swings on through time and space,
        I recommend myself unto your grace.

190   As you will realise, my own sweetheart,
        And as you know, that a long while ago   1325
        You left me suffering bitter pain and smart
        When we were parted, and as yet there's no
        Respite, but sufferings which still grow and grow
        From day to day, leaving me racked in hell,
        For in you, love, my joys, my pains both dwell.   1330

191   And so to you, with heart anxious but true
        I write as one whose pain drives him to write,
        Of all my pain, which grows and gnaws anew,
        Complaining, as I dare or can indite,
        And what is blotted here, you'll know aright,   1335
        Is through my tears, which from my eyes now rain,
        Which would speak, if they could, of all my pain.

192   And first I beg you, with your eyes so clear,
        Don't think this letter foul, spotted, defaced,
        And above all, Criseyde, my lady dear,   1340
        Please read my letter, don't deem me disgraced,
        And by that parting, which we lovers faced,
        It stupified me, so my blundering
        Sweetheart, forgive it, and my poor writing.

193   If any lover dares, or should, by right   1345
        To his dear mistress piteously complain,
        Then I feel I should be that very knight,
        Because you have for two months caused me pain

By tarrying, when you said you'd again
Be with me here after ten days sojourn.   1350
Yet in two months you still do not return.

194   But as I must, through love's decrees, agree
With all you do, I dare not complain more,
But humbly, and with sighs, pledge loyalty.
Now from my letter learn my sorrows sore,   1355
From day to day desiring ever more
To know in full exactly how you fare,
How you have been, and what you've done while there.

195   Your welfare and your health may God increase,
And may you prosper so in each degree   1360
That all goes well for you, and will not cease,
May you have all your heart's desire, lady,
And as you wish your life, so may it be.
Yet in compassion think of me, since I
Am true to you throughout eternity.   1365

196   And if it pleases you, my love, to know
How I do, my distress cannot be told.
I can't say more. In me all sorrows grow.
As I write this, I'm living, yet so cold
And near to death, my struggling soul I hold   1370
Back from the grave to wait your healing words.
Your letter life and hope to me affords.

197   My eyes, through which in vain I look for you
With tears of sorrow now are brimming wells.
I cannot sing, my words are sad and few.   1375
My good's all gone, my happiness grown hell's,
My joy is lost in woe, I can't say else.
All's turned contrary, and all's weariness.
All pleasure faded into dreariness.

198 Which with your coming home again to Troy   1380
     You can put right, and more, a thousandfold
     Than I felt yet, increase my bliss and joy.
     For never yet did heart, through woe made cold
     Rejoice at life returning, as I, bold
     And gay at your return. So, though you feel   1385
     No mercy, think of me, pity and heal.

199 So, if my failings death and doom deserve,
     If you no longer wish to love or see me,
     In recompense for love, the years I served
     You, sweetheart dear, I beg you truthfully   1390
     When you get this, write and be frank with me,
     For love of God, my lodestar and my dear
     Then death will end my sorrow, pain and fear.

200 If any other reason makes you dwell
     Among the Greeks, then comfort me and write,   1395
     For though to me your absence is a hell,
     I'll bear it patiently like a true knight,
     And through your letter feel some hope, some light.
     Now write, my darling, let me not complain.
     Give me some hope, or kill me, please be plain.   1400

201 Indeed, my own dear heart, most sweet, most true,
     I think that when you next your Troilus see,
     I have so lost my health and ruddy hue
     That scarcely will my Criseyda know me!
     Yes, my heart's dayspring, my sweet lady free.   1405
     My heart so thirsts your beauty to behold
     That scarcely can it life and life's blood hold.

202 I say no more. All that I have to tell
     To you is well more than to say I may,
     But whether you give life to me, or kill,   1410
     I'll pray the gods you live in joy each day.

So now, farewell, my fresh, sweet girl I say.
You are the one who life and death may give,
And in your truth, your love I hope to live,

203   With health and hope, which only you give me,   1415
Health, which, unless you come, I shall not have,
It rests with you, if you wish this to be,
To lay me in the covering of my grave,
Or grant me life, for you alone can save
Me from the agony of pain and smart.   1420
And now farewell, my own, my dear sweetheart.
                                        Your Troilus."

204   This letter then was sent unto Criseyde,
To which her answer in effect was this.
Most pityingly she wrote again, and said
As soon as she could do so, she'd be his,   1425
She'd come and mend all that had gone amiss,
And at the last she wrote and told him then
That she would come, but still could not say when.

205   But in her letter she wrote flattering things
That made one wonder, said she loved him best,   1430
Which he found unreal, light words plumed with wings.
Ah, Troilus, you can now, eastwards or west
Pipe on an ivy leaf, make a vain quest.
This way the world wags. God keep us from harm!
And prosper those who speak the truth
                                        with charm!   1435

206   Now flourished woe and grief from day to night
In Troilus' heart for Criseyda's delaying.
And now his hopes ebbed with his strength and might,
Because of which in bed he soon was laying.
He did not eat, drink, sleep, no word was saying,   1440
Imagining that she had grown unkind,
For which he almost went out of his mind.

207   This dream of which I told you all before
       He could not drive from his rememberance,
       Always he thought he'd lost his love therefore,   1445
       And that Jove, with his foresight, in advance
       Showed him in dreams the full significance
       Of her betrayal, his unhappiness,
       And that boar as a sign of his distress.

208   Because of which he for his sister sent,   1450
       A sibyl she, Cassandra was her name,
       To ask about this dream and its intent.
       He begged her tell the meaning of the same,
       What did the strong tusked boar denote? She came
       In a short while to tell him what the dream   1455
       Foreshadowed, and the sadness in it seen.

209   She smiled a little, saying, "Brother dear,
       If you are sure you really wish to know,
       You first must old and hoary stories hear,
       How Fortune through her wiles can overthrow   1460
       Great lords in olden times, from which I'll show
       What this same boar denotes, and of what kind
       He is. Men can in books this meaning find.

210   Diana once grew angry, full of ire,
       Because the Greeks would not make sacrifice,   1465
       Nor throw sweet incense on her altar fire,
       So, as the Greeks this goddess did despise
       She sought revenge in a most cruel wise,
       And with a boar, huge as an ox in stall
       She wrecked their corn and fruitful vines and all.   1470

211   To kill this boar was all the country raised,
       Amongst which crowd there came, this boar to see
       A maiden, for her beauty widely praised,
       And Meleager, lord of that country,

So loved that fresh, sweet maiden, fair and free,   1475
That he in manhood killed the monster dead
Before he'd done, and sent his love its head.

212   From which deed all the old books tell to us
Arose a dispute, argument and envy,
And from this prince descended Tydeus   1480
In line direct, or else these old books lie.
But how this Meleager came to die
All through his mother, that I cannot tell
You now, for it would take too long a spell."

213   Before she ceased, she told how Tydeus went   1485
Up to the walls of Thebes to claim the crown
For Polynices, that was his intent.
Eteocles, his brother, held the town
Most wrongfully, doing his kinsman down.
But Tydeus meant to see the upstart fail.   1490
So, point by point, she told the lengthy tale.

214   She told him how Haemonides escaped
When Tydeus slew fifty sturdy knights.
She told the prophecies, how these were shaped,   1495
And how the Seven Kings, in feints and fights
Beseiged the city round by days and nights,
And of the holy serpent and the well,
And of the Furies, all this she did tell.

215   Of Archimones' funeral pyre and games,   1500
And how Amphilochus fell through the ground.
How Tydeus, lord of Argos, died in pains,
And how Hippomedon was shortly found
Drowned, and Parthenopaeus dead of his wound,
And also how Capameus the proud   1505
By thunderbolts was slain, though he cried loud.

216 Cassandra also told how either brother,
     Eteocles and Polynices, too,
     In skirmishing each felled and killed the other,
     And of Argia's weeping and great woe,
     And how the town was sacked she did then show,   1510
     And so through all the family tree she led
     To modern times, and told of Diomed.

217 "Now this same boar betokens Diomede,
     Tydeus' son, who straight descended is
     From Meleager, who made the boar bleed.   1515
     And your sweetheart, with whom you had great bliss,
     Diomede has her heart, and she has his.
     So weep now if you will, for out of doubt
     This Diomede is in, and you are out!'"

218 "What you say is not true, you sorceress!   1520
     All your false spirits you call prophecy!
     You think yourself a great interpretess!
     Now don't you see that foolish fantasy
     Is all too apt in female laps to lie!
     Get off," said he, "And may Jove give you sorrow, 1525
     And all you say be shown as false tomorrow!

219 You might as well have run down fair Alceste
     Who was, of all women, unless men lie,
     One of the kindest, truest, loveliest, best,
     For when her husband was in jeopardy   1530
     And near to death, unless for him she'd die,
     She chose to take his place and go to Hell,
     And perished there, as the books to us tell."

220 Cassandra went, and he, with furious heart
     Forgot his woe in anger at her talk,   1535
     And from his bed leaped with a sudden start,
     As if a doctor's art had made him walk.

And day by day he asked, peered, pried and sought
The truth of what she'd said with pains and care,
And living so, himself he did not spare.   1540

221   Fortune, who has the charge and permutation
       Of things committed to her charge and care,
       Through Providence, and by the dispensation
       Of Jove, and who'll sit in the royal chair
       Or who'll be toppled down, this she'll prepare,   1545
       Now plucked the brilliant plumage out of Troy
       Day after day, till it was bare of joy.

222   And with all this, the end of Hector's life
       Was now in sight, and now the time was near
       When Fate should loose his soul and end his strife. 1550
       The ways, the means were all prepared and clear.
       No use to try from such a rock to steer.
       On the appointed day to fight he went
       And met the death which gods and Fate had sent.

223   Because of which I think that every wight   1555
       Who uses arms should mourn him and bewail
       The death of one who was so noble a knight,
       For as he gripped a king by the ventail,
       Achilles struck and pierced him through the mail,
       Running him through the body. So the breath   1560
       Left this most worthy knight, and he met death.

224   For whom, as all the old books tell to us
       Such grief was made that this no tongue can tell.
       Especially the woe of Troilus,
       Who, next to Hector, was the fount and well   1565
       Of virtue. And in grief his heart did swell,
       So, what with sorrow and love and such unrest
       He felt his heart would break within his breast.

225   Nevertheless, although he felt despair,
And dreaded that Criseyde was untrue,   1570
In hope, in thought still to her did repair,
And as all lovers do, he tried anew
To get her back, his darling, bright of hue,
And made excuses for her in his heart.
Calchas, he said, had kept them both apart.   1575

226   And often he was on the point of dressing
Himself in pilgrim's clothes to seek Criseyde,
But knew he could not keep wise people guessing,
They'd know him soon enough. He could not ride
Disguised among the Greeks. He would be spied.   1580
If captured, what excuses could he make?
And so he wept, from this last dream awake.

227   He wrote to her time after time anew
Most piteously, he was not slothful now,
And begged her, since he loved her and was true,   1585
That as she'd promised she'd return, and show
Pity. And she, I think, was sorry, too,
And wrote to him again of this matter,
And what she wrote I'll tell, and you shall hear.

228   "Child of true love, seemly, good, valiant, dear,   1590
O sword of knighthood, source of gentleness,
How can a creature in torment and fear,
And hopeless, too, send you comfort or gladness?
I, heartless, sick, unhappy, in distress?
Since you with me, nor I with you may meet,   1595
I cannot send you love, nor healing sweet.

229   Your letters full, the very paper weighed
With pain, arouse and stir my heart's pity.
I've seen the marks of tears, and how you said
If only I would come again—Truly,   1600

R

This is not possible, this cannot be.
But why, I cannot tell you now, for fear,
In case this letter should be found, my dear.

230   Tormenting to me is your great unrest
And your impatience. This, the gods' decree   1605
It seems you won't accept all for the best.
Nothing, it seems, is in your memory
Except what pleased you or made you happy!
But don't be angry, this I do beseech.
What keeps me here is gossip, wicked speech.   1610

231   For I have heard more than I could believe
About us two, and just the way things stand,
Which I'll put right with scheming, do not grieve.
So don't be angry. I do understand.
You've kept me on a string, a bird in hand!   1615
Never mind, for now I see in you
Nothing but truth and gentleness all through.

232   Indeed I'll come, but I'm in such a plight,
Such a sad state, that what year or what day
I will come back I can't tell you, nor write.   1620
But, in a word, I beg you that I may
Count you a friend, and that for me you'll pray.
For truly, while my sad life lasts, I'll be
Your friend, and you may count on me truly.

233   And now I beg that you won't take it ill   1625
That it's so short, this that I write to you.
Where I am now, I daren't write much or well.
I never could write very well, it's true.
But much can be packed into words quite few.
The thought counts in a letter, not the length.   1630
And now goodbye. God guard you with his strength.
                         Your own Criseyde."

234   Troilus thought this letter very strange
       When he had read it. Sorrowfully he sighed.
       He thought it was a portent, foretold change.
       Yet he could not believe, although he tried   1635
       That she'd not keep her promise, that she lied.
       For though he's sad, he who in love is true
       Cannot think ill, or ill and evil do.

235   Nevertheless, men said that at the last
       Clear and unveiled reality we'll see,   1640
       And so it happened, and it happened fast,
       That Troilus saw and understood that she
       Was not as kind or true as she should be.
       And finally he knew, beyond all doubt
       He'd lost the jewel he'd worked so hard about.   1645

236   He stood then one day wrapped in melancholy,
       Poor Troilus, in doubt and in suspicion
       Of her for whom he'd thought in grief to die.
       And so it happened throughout all Troy town
       As was the custom, they bore up and down   1650
       A coat of armour, so runs the old story,
       In sign of Deiphebus' victory.

237   The which same coat of armour Lollius
       Tells Deiphebus won from Diomede
       That very day. And when poor Troilus   1655
       Saw it, he soon began to take much heed
       Of it, measured the length, the breadth, indeed
       Admired the workmanship. Then suddenly
       His heart went cold with pang of agony,

238   As he upon the collar found pinned fast   1660
       A brooch, the one he gave Criseyde that day
       When she was torn from Troy and him at last,
       To wear in grief, for love and memory,

And she had promised in fidelity
To keep it always. But quite well he knew   1665
He could not trust her now, she was untrue.

239   So he went home, and then at once did send
For Pandarus, and of this happening,
And of the brooch he told him to the end,
Of her changed heart and her untruth complaining, 1670
His love unchanged, his truth and his enduring.
And then he called for death, without words more,
To give him back his peace, and rest restore.

240   And then he said, "O lady mine, Criseyde,
Where is your faith, your promise made to me?   1675
Where is your love, your plighted troth?" he said.
"Now Diomede gives you love's ecstasy.
Alas, I would have thought at least to me
You'd be less cruel, and even if not true,
You would not drag me like a bear in tow.   1680

241   Can one have faith or trust in any now?
I would not have believed, before all this
That you, Criseyde, could have been changed so.
Even if I had sinned or done amiss
You should not have been cruel. As it is   1685
You'll kill me. For your love and your good name
Have gone, and I am left in grief and shame.

242   Was there no other brooch for you to let
Fall in the hands of your new love?" said he,
"But this same brooch, which with my own
                                    tears wet 1690
I gave you as remembrance of me?
You had no reason, only cruelty
To give him this, or else because you meant
By such a gift to show your true intent,

243   Through which I see that clean out of your mind   1695
      You've cast me, yet I neither can nor may
      For all the world power in my own heart find
      To unlove you a quarter of a day.
      Accursed was my birthday, yet I say
      That you, who make me all this grief endure,   1700
      I still love more than any other creature.

244   I only pray the gods may grant me grace
      To meet and fight against this Diomede,
      And truly, if I have the strength and space
      I hope I'll live to make his black sides bleed!   1705
      O God," he said, "You, who should take good heed
      To punish wrong, the good and true to bless,
      Why do you not smite down such wickedness?

245   O Pandarus, you who so often said
      I was to blame for trusting in a dream,   1710
      Now you can see how we were all misled,
      How true she was, Criseyde, who bright did seem!
      In different forms the gods reveal a gleam
      Of what's to come, both joy and misery
      Through dreams. My dream came true,
                                    most certainly.   1715

246   And so, without more words, or much ado,
      Henceforth, with all the boldness that I may
      I'll seek my death in battle, even so
      I do not care how soon comes that dark day.
      But truly, sweet Criseyde, this I say,   1720
      I, who with love and life you ever served,
      Have not this fate you've heaped on me deserved.

247   Poor Pandarus, who all these sad things heard
      And knew quite well he spoke the truth in this,

Not one word back to Troilus answered,   1725
So sorry for his friend's great grief he is,
And shame he feels that his niece did amiss,
And there he stands, half stunned, his wits away,
Still as a stone. Not a thing could he say.

248   Then at the last he spoke again, and said,   1730
"My brother dear, I can help you no more.
What can I say? I hate, I loathe Criseyde,
By God, I'll hate and loathe her evermore,
Yet all those things you begged me do of yore
I did them not for honour, profit, rest,   1735
Nor for reward, but only for the best.

249   If I did anything that could please you
It gave me joy. And so her treason now
God knows, it hurts, sorrows and shames me, too.
If heartease in your sad heart I could grow   1740
I'd sow it there, if only I knew how.
So from this world, almighty God, I pray,
Take her, the wretch! More than this I can't say."

250   Great were the griefs and groans of Troilus,
But Fortune still to the same course did hold.   1745
Criseyde loved the son of Tydeus,
And Troilus must weep in care so cold.
Such is the world, and whoso may behold
Sees that in each estate no heart's at rest.
God help us then to take all for the best!   1750

251   In many cruel battles, out of dread
Of Troilus, this same most noble knight,
As you in ancient books yourself may read,
Men saw his prowess and his valiant might
His anger and his bravery, day and night,   1755
And the Greeks safety very dearly bought.
But in each skirmish Diomed he sought.

252 And oftentimes I find that bloodily
     These two assailants met with boastful word.
     Each tried to see how sharp their spears could be.
     God knows, with bitterness and whirling sword   1760
     Troilus beat on his helmet, but the cord
     Of life he could not cut. The Fates deny
     That by the other's hand either should die.

253 And if I'd undertaken to write out   1765
     The deeds of arms of this most worthy man,
     I'd list his battles, every fight, each bout,
     But since in this same story I began
     With love, his love, I've said all that I can
     About his warlike deeds. Who wants to know   1770
     About them, read what Dares has to show.

254 And so I beg each lady, bright of hue,
     Each gentlewoman, whoso e'er she be,
     That although Criseyda was so untrue,
     That for her guilt she'll put no blame on me.   1775
     In other books than mine that guilt you'll see,
     And better pleased I'll be to write for you
     Of good Alceste and Penelope true.

255 Now I don't speak like this for men alone,
     But most for women who have been betrayed   1780
     By false and wicked folk, (God make them moan!)
     Who with great wit and cunning on them preyed.
     This makes me angry, and my rhymes I've made
     To warn them. Women, to you all I pray,
     Beware of men, listen to what I say!   1785

256 Go, little my book, go, little my tragedy,
     God grant your maker may, before he die
     Have strength to shape some witty comedy.
     But, little book, no verse-making envy,

But be subject to greater poetry,   1790
And kiss the steps up which you see them pace,
Virgil and Ovid, Homer, Lucan, Stace.

257   And, because there is such diversity
In English, and in writing our own tongue,
Pray God there will be no mistranslating be,   1795
Nor scansion all amiss through speaking wrong.
And that wherever you are read or sung
Men may still understand, that I beseech.
But now back to the point of my first speech.

258   The anger, as I first began to say,   1800
Of Troilus the Greeks paid for most dear.
Thousands his hands and sword made die that day,
For he among the knights had not his peer,
Save Hector in his heyday, as I hear.
But oh, alas, because it was God's will,   1805
Unpitying Achilles Troilus did kill.

259   And when he had been slain in this manner,
His light ghost all in bliss aloft was sent
Up to the hollowness of the seventh sphere,
Passing through every other element,   1810
And there he saw and knew, in full content,
The erratic stars, and heard their harmony,
Chords full and rich with heavenly melody.

260   And then he contemplated from that place
This little spot of earth, which with the sea   1815
Is all embraced, and scorned its silly face,
This wretched world, and held all vanity
Compared to so much pure felicity
Which is in heaven above. And at the last
To where he'd died his downward glance he cast.   1820

261   And in himself he laughed then at the woe
    Of those who wept there for his death so fast,
    And he condemned our deeds in following so
    Lust's blindness, fires that cannot, will not last,
    When we should all our heart on Heaven cast.   1825
    And then he went, as I'll be brief to tell,
    Where Mercury decreed that he should dwell.

262   Such ending had this Troilus for love,
    Such ending had his fame and worthiness.
    Such ending had his rank on earth, above.   1830
    Such ending for his joy and nobleness.
    Such ending has all earthly brittleness.
    And so began his great love for Criseyde
    As I have told, and in this way he died.

263   O young, O young, fresh folks, both he and she,   1835
    In whom love springs and grows up with your age,
    Repent and leave all worldly vanity,
    And of your heart upcast the fair visage
    To God, who made you after his image,
    And think that all you see is but a fair,   1840
    This world, which fades as soon as flowers most fair.

264   And set your love on Him, who for true love
    Upon a Cross, our souls through this to buy
    First died, then rose and sits in Heaven above,
    For He plays false with no one, I dare say,   1845
    Who will his heart's devotion on Him lay.
    Since He is best to love, and the most meek,
    What need false, frail, pretended loves to seek?

265   Look, here, at pagans' cursed and ancient rites,
    Look, here, at all their fragile gods avail.   1850
    Look, here, at wretched worldly appetites.
    Look, here's reward and ending for travail

Which the old gods give out, through which they fail!
Look, here the words and sense drawn from the old
Poets. You'll find it in the tales they've told.   1855

266   O erudite Gower, this book I direct
To you, and to the philosophical Strode,
To vouchsafe, where there need is, to correct
Our of your kindness, and your zeal so good.
And to the Christ we trust, who died on Rood,   1860
With all my heart I ever for mercy pray,
And to the Lord himself I speak and pray.

267   O Lord, the Father, Son and Holy Ghost,
Who ever living, ever one, reign still
Unbounded, yet bind those, by bleak storms tossed, 1865
Who are the prey of spirits dire and ill,
Defend us, and extend Thy mercy still.
Fit us, Lord Jesus, for Thy grace divine,
For love of her, Thy Mother, Maid benign.   1869
                                        Amen.

Appendices

APPENDIX A. THE DOMESTIC BACKGROUND OF TROILUS AND CRISEYDE

Quite a clear picture can be formed of the houses in which Criseyde, Troilus and Pandarus lived. Chaucer imagined them as large town houses, such as the Savoy, in which John of Gaunt, Duke of Lancaster, lived and where Phillipa, Chaucer's wife, served the Duchess of Lancaster as lady in waiting.

Criseyde's house had a paved floor, at least in the parlour where she received her uncle. This was of stone or chequered tiles, and such floors were only found in the most modern and luxurious residences. Stairs led down into an enclosed garden, probably with walls and trellis around it. The plants grown there are not mentioned, but contemporary illustrations and descriptions show that Criseyde might have grown a variety of roses, (the summer flowering kinds, such as damask, centifolia, alba and sweetbriar), lilies, iris, carnations, marigolds, violets, herbs of various kinds, and a few salad vegetables. The sanded walks were shaded by pleached trees, perhaps apple and pear, or vines trained over wires.

On the lower floor there was a large dining hall, probably with a dais for the upper table, where the mistress of the house and her principal guests sat to eat. Close to the hall there seems to have been a private room, perhaps a study or withdrawing room, into which Criseyde went to read her love letter from Troilus. And upstairs, looking out on to the street, and with other houses facing it, (one newly painted and done up!) was a pleasant parlour with a bay window and some elegant furniture. (Criseyde pulled up a stool of jasper with a richly embroidered golden cover on it.) Her own bedroom seems to have overlooked the garden. There was a cedar tree outside, and in it was her great curtained bed. Shutters to the windows, and a sturdy door, probably with great metal hasps, were other features, for Troilus saw these closely shut when Criseyde had left Troy. The windows may have been glazed. Glass windows were expensive, and only to be found in very great houses, but Criseyde was evidently a wealthy widow, whose husband had left her so well off that she was involved in constant lawsuits!

Troilus, as prince of Troy, lived in an even larger palace, though less is told about it. He and Pandarus dined in a large hall, but the only place in which they could talk in privacy was Troilus' own bedroom. This was a large room, with a number of windows, probably of the casement type, with shutters. Both Troilus and Pandarus sat on the bed, for mediaeval bedrooms, even those of wealthy folk, had little furniture other than the bed, a rail over which clothing could be hung, and a chest in which linen, blankets and clothes could be stored. Some well-appointed rooms had a small basin and ewer for washing hands, held in a metal stand. Troilus also had a truckle bed, which could be pushed out of the way beneath the big bed. On this his servant could sleep, and Pandarus made use of it when he stayed overnight.

Pandarus also lived luxuriously. He entertained Criseyde in a dining hall, they danced and amused themselves in a parlour; Troilus was hidden somewhere in a small closet or pantry, and Criseyde was put to bed in a quiet inner room, dark and curtained, where she could not hear the rain storm. Outside this room was an antechamber where her waiting women slept, and Pandarus had his bedchamber beyond this room. The beds themselves were like little rooms, for they had a canopy overhead, curtains all round, and cupboards and shelves in the headboard. Wealthy people slept on several mattresses of wool or down, and had comfortable pillows, linen or silken pillow covers and sheets, and blankets and coverlets of wool, fur or rich fabric. Walls were cosily covered with tapestry hangings, very necessary when the houses were stone built and exceedingly draughty and cold.

Criseyde, Troilus and Pandarus ate very well. Chaucer gives us no particulars, only points out that nothing was lacking at their tables. A normal mediaeval banquet, such as the one given by Deiphebus, or the party, at which Pandarus entertained Criseyde, would consist of at least three courses of meat or fish, and at each course there would be a choice of five or six main dishes, meats baked, boiled, stewed or done up in rich sauces, or minced and mixed with costly fruits and spices. Spices were often necessary to disguise the flavour of 'high' meat or fish, but the mediaeval palate liked rich and spicy things. Between each course a 'subtlety' was carried in, a masterpiece composed by the chef, of spun sugar, marzipan or pastry, a castle, maybe, or a bird or heraldic beast, part of the arms of the guests, or even a tableau consisting of a scene from the Bible or some popular story. The banquet ended with dessert, creams, pastries and sweets of all kinds, nuts and fruit, and was, of course, accompanied by wines, plain or spiced, in variety.

Criseyde started the day early, at six in the morning, or even earlier, taking a breakfast snack of bread and wine. Dinner was at about ten in the morning, supper at four or five in the afternoon, and a snack with cups of spiced wine would be taken at bedtime. People usually went to bed early, for the only method of giving artificial light was by expensive candles, ineffective rushlights, smoky torches, or a fire. Pandarus took a candle to read a romance by the fire as the lovers talked, and he and Criseyde probably amused themselves after dinner in the parlour by torch or firelight.

Criseyde wore, under her tight-fitting furred bodice and flowing skirt, a smock; petticoat and vest all in one. She may have worn long hose, kept up by garters, but no pants, and no other underclothes, though she may have given herself an elegant small waist by binding a linen band round her body as a form of corset. In her bedroom she would have worn a rich 'nightgown', that is, a dressing gown, but would have slept naked, except perhaps for a neat nightcap. Chaucer says that she wore her hair loose, flowing down her back, or tied in a form of 'pony-tail,' although this is the type of hairstyle adopted by unmarried girls. When Pandarus first visits her, she wears a barbe and widow's veil, the type of close-fitting wimple and pleated chin and neck covering familiar from memorial brasses and monuments of the Fourteenth Century. Presumably she dressed in this way, and wore a dark brown dress when Troilus first saw her, and this showed up her dazzling fair skin, fine eyes and elegant figure!

Troilus and Pandarus probably dressed much alike, in a short tunic, embroidered and befurred; tightfitting hose, like modern tights, and shoes with long pointed toes. In the house Pandarus, as a slightly older man, might have worn a long, dignified gown, and out of doors he wore a hood. Under their tunics the men had a shirt of linen or silk. Pandarus cast a furred cloak around Troilus as he shivered in his shirt and underclothing whilst waiting in the closet. Both men probably had neatly trimmed beards, for few in Chaucer's day were clean shaven, and their hair would be long and curled, probably by curling tongs! Criseyde also had wavy hair, but whether this was natural, or crimped by curl papers or heat no one knows!

As a prince, Troilus affected jewellery, a brooch, which he later gave to Criseyde as a love-token, and rings, one of which he exchanged with his beloved. In battle he wore armour of the fourteenth century type, for Chaucer sees him as a knight of his own day on a fully accoutred war horse.

Troilus has often been criticised by modern readers for his "effeminate" behaviour. But Pandarus weeps plentifully, too, and even the 'sudden Diomede' blushes and is bashful. In fact, in mediaeval times, and up to the late Eighteenth Century people were much more emotional, unrestrained and uninhibited in behaviour. They wept when sad, laughed when merry, were amorous, quick tempered, fiercely alive in every way, and more like the volatile inhabitants of the continent than today's more inhibited and disciplined English men and women. So Troilus gives way to his feelings, and probably never suffered from neuroses or ulcers, though he may have given himself a headache from banging his head on the wall in grief or temper! He is brave, virile, and a real man despite his tears, with all the steadfast qualities we still admire, of loyalty, faithfulness and human warmth. Pandarus had these, too, and one of his most endearing traits, is the ready sympathy and understanding he shows. Pandarus is the sort of friend everyone would like to have, unselfish and tireless in his efforts to please, even if he is somewhat too ready to moralise! His wit makes up for this, and he is as ready to poke fun at himself as to make jests to amuse other people.

Criseyde is a charmer, too, and Chaucer quite clearly thinks so, and is anxious that we should forgive her human failings. For she is timid, daughter of a traitor, and all alone in the city her father betrayed. Like all human beings, she longs for love. She was probably married young, a marriage of convenience arranged by her father, although it seems to have been reasonably happy.

She is certainly intelligent and well educated. Her quick wit and repartee show this, and like most women, she has a very practical side to her nature. One notices the plans she makes for returning to Troy, and the clear way in which she tells Troilus of the alternative ideas for outwitting her father. She can read and write, and presumably knows Latin and the language spoken by the Greeks. (Although the scene is Troy, obviously we must regard Criseyde, Troilus and Pandarus as English nobles, Troy as a walled English city, the Greeks as Frenchmen, and the dress and locale as modern times, Chaucer's modern times.)

Chaucer stresses Criseyde's breeding, grace, kindness and charity. It is her 'pity', that virtue, half sympathy, half sexual warmth, and also very real human kindness, which makes her love Troilus, and also give way to Diomede. 'Pity' is pricked on by fear. She is a conventional girl, afraid of what people will think; afraid, too, of what may happen to her if she offends powerful noblemen like Troilus and Diomede. And she is human in liking admiration; self analytical and honest, too. Although the portrait is mediaeval, for Criseyde is a Fourteenth Century lady, subscribing to the conventions of Courtly Love, (see Appendix B) she and all her friends are as real and as delightful and as consistently human in their behaviour as any people we may meet today.

APPENDIX B. COURTLY LOVE

The lovers in Chaucer's Troilus and Criseyde are two warmly human people, behaving as men and women always have done and always will do, but they are also a man and woman of noble birth living in the Fourteenth Century, and therefore subject to the conventions of a particular code, that which is usually called Courtly Love.

This particular code might be called an attempt to reconcile man's sensual and animal appetites with his longings for romance and a more sensitive sensuousness. It clothes lust in the silken trappings of love, and places it in a chivalric and feudal setting. So, many of our modern ideas of what is right and proper in love, the whole paraphernalia of romance, the sighs and longing of hopeless love, the 'decorations' of sex, are derived from the conventions of Courtly Love, in which the Beloved, the Lady, was queen, unattainable, almost divine, and the Lover her humble servant, a victim of hopeless passion. She was 'dangerous', that is, proud and distant in her purity, enjoying sexual power, merciless in her beauty. So Chaucer addresses a real or imaginary mistress as follows—

> "So hath your beaute fro your herte chased
> Pitee, that me n'availeth not to plaine
> For Danger halt your mercy in his cheyne."

It was right and proper for her to behave in this way, and throughout the centuries it has been correct for a lady to be unobtainable, and for a lover to burn, to feel love strike him through like a dart, to lie sleepless, and to 'change his hue', grow pale and wan, thin and pining in the throes of hopeless passion. Yet love ennobled, it was a refining fire. Love was spring, joy, happiness, but like all things mortal, subject to Fortune's whim. A lover must be content to sigh and to fight for his lady, to wear her glove or a sleeve from her gown, or a rose given by her hand, as a love token, and to expect no other gift or guerdon. He might serve her, without further reward, for years, as Pandarus tells Troilus he may have to do. (Book 1, Stanza 116.)

This does not mean that sexual satisfaction was not possible within the Courtly Code. The lady could, and often did, show mercy, but the relationship still continued as one of Sovereign and Servant, and did not usually lead to marriage or domestic felicity! Marriage, in the Middle Ages, had little to do with love, it was an arrangement made between families, often governed by the desirability of combining estates, or strengthening some feudal allegiance, and so was a practical or even mercenary matter. Marriages were often arranged between children, and though they were often happy enough, (that of Criseyde herself seems to have been one of real affection, if not romantic,) a wife was subject to her husband, who literally owned her and all she possessed.

Love, however, was a religion, with its rites and sacraments, and so when Troilus enters upon Love's service, and takes Criseyde for his mistress within the Code, he does not envisage marriage, or being 'happy ever after'. He does think of asking his father for Criseyde, but this seems to be a desperate measure, and it is the practical woman, Criseyde, who sees that this cannot be. It would be the end of the carefree "dance of love", the elaborate and joyful ritual of youth and pleasure.

So, much of the love of Troilus and Criseyde is courtly and correct. Troilus behaves as a young nobleman should; it is right and proper for him, as a lover, to weep and feel hopeless. Criseyde, too, as his Sovereign Lady, must reject him, think of her own virtue and power, and the image which she presents to the world.

Yet, despite the conventions, these two lovers are human, real, and act as individuals, and as two people genuinely in love. Criseyde may have many of the attributes of the heroine of romance, with her long sides, elegant small fingers, white skin, arched eyebrows and wavy golden hair, but she is also a real and very individual woman, warm, human, and wholly delightful. Troilus, too, is the conventional hero, tall, brave, faithful, but he is also human, young, vulnerable, so pathetically anxious to seem correct as a lover. (See in particular Stanzas 89 and 90, Book V, where he is sure that he is pining away, although to all beholders he looks perfectly fit.)

It should be noticed that Criseyde is a widow, and therefore sexually experienced, yet her niece takes it for granted that she does not know what love is. (See Book II, Stanzas 885 and 886.) She is independent, and has no wish to marry again, for in marrying she would become wholly subject to her husband. She is no green girl, but a lady with a robustly practical knowledge of the world and of the ways of men. (See in particular Book II, Stanzas 112, 113 and 114.)

Troilus, too, rejoices in his freedom, he is a gay bachelor, who scorns love, jeers at his friends who are in love, and has no wish to be like them, yet when he is smitten, then

> "Glad was he if any wight wel ferde,
> That lover was, whan he it wiste or herde."

It is Pandarus, wily, practical, experienced, who is the truly involved Lover, emmeshed in the chains of Love, serving a disdainful Mistress who has no pity for him. Yet he, in spite of his own unhappiness, wants to help and give happiness to others.

The reactions of Troilus and Pandarus to Criseyde's betrayal are interesting, too. Troilus cannot 'unlove' her for even a quarter of a day, but Pandarus, the true romantic, condemns her out of hand; he hates Criseyde, and wishes she may die, for she has betrayed not only Troilus, but Love and the Code.

To watch the movements of these three people is indeed like watching one of the stately, distant, yet intensely sensual dances of the Middle Ages, to the throbbing music of pipe, tabour and lute. And yet, as we read on, they become our friends, and indeed ourselves. The Code may be different today, but the 'olde dance of love' still goes on.

Those who wish to know more about the Courtly Code should turn to Professor C. S. Lewis' *Allegory of Love,* the first chapter of which deals with Courtly Love, how it arose, how its lovers moved and behaved, and how its intricacies and delicacies inspired and excited the writers of the Middle Ages and the Renaissance.

Chaucer's views on Courtly Love, half mocking, half involved, should also be studied in *The Parliament of Fowles,* where through the falcons and the lesser fowls he parodies with exquisite humour the Court, where Richard II, Anne, his newly married bride and all their retainers move in the rite and dance of love, a sophisticated world within the earthly, commonsense outer world of London, with its burghers and artisans, like the ducks, geese, sparrows and finches of the bird world. In this poem, in *The Knights Tale,* and in *Troilus and Criseyde* the two worlds are contrasted, one romantic, decorative, sophisticated, the Court, the Code; the other earthy, sensual, unchanging human nature, and the syncopation, the impact of one upon the other makes tension, tragedy and great poetry. Chaucer's world is the *whole* world, he takes it like an apple, "with an easy hunger", in Laurie Lee's words, welcoming

> "— the ripe, the sweet, the sour
> the hollow and the whole."

APPENDIX C. DATES AND EVENTS IN THE LIFE OF CHAUCER

1340-4 Geoffrey Chaucer born. (The exact date is not known.)

1357   Geoffrey Chaucer is given an outfit of black and red hose as a page in the household of Elizabeth, Countess of Ulster, daughter-in-law of Edward III.

1359-60 Geoffrey Chaucer serves as a soldier in France with Lionel, Duke of Clarence, husband of Elizabeth.

1360   Chaucer is taken prisoner, and ransomed on 1st March for £16. (In those days a considerable sum.) He probably begins to translate the *Romance of the Rose*.
In the negotiations for peace, the Treaty of Calais, he probably helps in a minor capacity.

1366   John Chaucer, the poet's father, dies, and his mother, Agnes, remarries. Geoffrey himself may have married Phillipa de Roet, whose father was a Court official.

1367   Edward III grants Chaucer an annuity of 20 marks as Valet.

1368   Lionel, Duke of Clarence, dies. In July Chaucer is sent to France on official business, with two hackneys and gold to pay for expenses.

1369   France repudiates the Treaty of Calais, and war is renewed. Queen Philippa, wife of Edward III, and Blanche, wife of John of Gaunt, Duke of Lancaster, both die.

1370   Chaucer is sent abroad from July to October on diplomatic business for the King. He writes the *Book of the Duchess*, a tribute to Blanche of Lancaster, in 1369 or 1370.

1371   The Black Prince returns from active service gravely ill. John of Gaunt marries Constance, a Spanish princess. Phillipa Chaucer is given a pension of £10 for her services to the new Duchess of Lancaster at the palace of the Savoy.

1372   Chaucer is appointed member of a trade commission to go to Genoa, and sets out for Italy in December.

1373   Chaucer is back in England, and is sent to Dartmouth, where the Mayor has been accused by an Italian merchant captain of piracy and robbery. (Chaucer is evidently considered to have a way with Italians, and to be skilled in diplomacy of all kinds!)

1374   Chaucer is granted an annual gift of wine by the King, and in June is made Controller of the Wool, Skin and Hide Customs, with a house over Aldgate, one of the main gateways into London.

1376   Chaucer is sent on a secret mission to France.

1377   In February he catches a smuggler on the Thames red-handed. Later in the year he is sent abroad on some diplomatic mission. In June, Edward III dies and is succeeded by his ten year old grandson, Richard II.

1378   Chaucer is sent to negotiate with the powerful rulers of Milan, the Visconti.

1380   Phillipa Chaucer is given a gift of a silver gilt cup for her services to John of Gaunt, and is given further presents in 1381 and 1382.

1381   The Peasants' Revolt.

S

1382   Richard II marries Anne of Bohemia. Chaucer probably writes
        the *Parliament of Fowles, The Legend of Good Women,* and
        part of *Troilus and Criseyde.* He is made Controller of the
        Petty Customs.
1384   He is allowed to appoint a deputy at the Customs House. Prob-
        ably at this time he moves from Aldgate to Greenwich in Kent.
1385   He is made a J.P. for the County of Kent.
1386   He is appointed Knight of the Shire of Kent, to represent them
        in Parliament. (This does not mean that a knighthood was con-
        ferred upon Chaucer, but that he was a Member of Parliament.)
1387   In February Phillipa Chaucer is inducted as a member of the
        Fellowship of Lincoln cathedral. In July Chaucer goes abroad,
        to Calais, and sometime after Midsummer Phillipa dies.
1387-8 Chaucer is writing the *Canterbury Tales,* probably still living
        at Greenwich, having left the Customs.
1389   In July Chaucer is appointed Clerk of the Works.
1390   He surveys the walls, drains, ditches, bridges and sewers on the
        banks of the Thames between Woolwich and Greenwich.
        In May he is in charge of preparing lists and seating for jousts
        held before Royalty at Smithfields.
        In July goes to supervise repairs to St. George's Chapel, Windsor.
        In September is robbed several times by highwaymen when on
        official business.
1391   Chaucer is appointed Forester at North Petherton, Somerset.
1394   Queen Anne dies at Sheen Palace, and King Richard has it
        pulled down. Constance, Duchess of Lancaster, dies, and a little
        while after John of Gaunt marries Katherine Swynford,
        Chaucer's sister-in-law, who has been his mistress for many years.
        Richard II also remarries, taking as his bride Isabella, Princess
        of France, aged 8.
1397   The pitcher of wine granted as an annual gift to Chaucer by
        the King is increased to a tun!
1398   Chaucer is sued for debt. In March John of Gaunt dies.
1399   Chaucer is given an additional pension of 20 marks, and takes a
        house in Westminster, within the Abbey precincts.
        In September, Henry IV comes to the throne, deposing Richard.
        He confirms Chaucer's annuity. Chaucer writes his Complaint
        to his purse.
1400   October 25th, Geoffrey Chaucer dies.

Notes

BOOK I

STANZA 1, LINE 2

Priam or Priamus was the only surviving son of Laomedon, the King who employed the sun god, Apollo, and the sea god, Poseidon, as labourers to build the walls of Troy, and by not paying their wages, offended them unforgivably. Priam inherited the city of Troy after it had been swept by Poseidon's floods, and suffered from the attacks of the hero, Hercules, to whom Laomedon had also broken his word.

Priam married Hecuba, and had by her a huge family of sons and daughters, of whom Troilus was one.

LINE 3

"Adventures", the Middle English word used by Chaucer, is difficult to translate. It means more than our modern word "Adventure"; it signifies the whole of life's doings and happenings, all Troilus tries and attempts in life. Adventure has perhaps too much of 'derring-do' and excitement about it. For Troilus "Adventure" included sorrow, disappointment and pain, as well as extreme happiness, excitement and success.

LINE 5

In the original, Chaucer writes "Ere that I part fro ye," "Before I part from you all," that is, from the audience gathered to hear him. Chaucer's poem is written for reading aloud to a courtly audience. This is why the various rhetorical devices are used so dramatically, and why the poet so often addresses the Reader, who is, in fact, an attentive Audience, of which many members may know him personally.

STANZA 2, LINE 6

Tisiphone, (Thesiphone) was not a Muse, but one of the Eumenides or Furies, goddesses of vengeance, and so, Chaucer felt, appropriately invoked at the beginning of a tragedy. He may also have had in mind the mourning and sorrowing attributes given them by Dante in the *Inferno*. He envisages his poem as a tragedy, 'Litel my tregedie', a 'dite of prosperitie for a tyme that endith in wretchednesse' as Boethius defined tragedy and as Chaucer translated him, or, as the Monk in his Prologue, (*Canterbury Tales*) says:

> 'Tragedie is to seyn a certeyn storie
> Of him that stood in greet prosperitee
> And is y-fallen out of high degree
> Into miserie and endeth wrecchedly.'

STANZA 9, LINE 63

Helen, daughter of Leda and Jove, and sister of Clytemnestra, married Menelaus, King of Sparta.

Paris, the second son of Priam, King of Troy, for a time tended his father's flocks on Mount Ida, and was chosen by the three goddesses, Hera, wife of Jove, Athena, goddess of wisdom, and Aphrodite, goddess of love, to act as judge in a beauty contest between them, the winner's prize to be a golden apple. Each goddess promised Paris appropriate rewards, Hera, sovereignty, Athena wisdom and renown, and Aphrodite, the loveliest woman in the world as wife. Paris gave the apple to her, and she directed him to Sparta, where Menelaus welcomed him as guest with lavish hospitality. Treacherously breaking the sacred laws of hospitality, Paris persuaded Helen to leave her husband, and taking gold and jewels with them, they set sail for Troy. In revenge, Menelaus, his brother, Agamemnon, (married to Clytemnestra, Helen's sister) and the other Kings and chieftains of Greece, set sail for Troy and beseiged it. Homer's Iliad tells the story of this ten years' war, and the final fall of Troy is related in the *Aeneid* of Vergil.

STANZA 10, LINE 66.

Calchas was a soothsayer who, through his art, foresaw the fall of Troy, though in the *Iliad* he is a Greek. Chaucer gives him some of the characteristics of Chryses, a priest of Apollo, whose daughter was captured and held slave by Achilles. He also follows Guido delle Colone, who, in his *Historia Trojana,* makes Calchas Trojan, not Greek.

STANZA 11, LINE 71

Chaucer has "Whan this Calkas knew by calculation", and I have retained his pun.

LINE 76

Chaucer has the word 'sort', meaning magic divination, but the type of divination used by a crystal gazer or clairvoyante. He is scornful of, and dislikes Calchas, with good reason!

LINE 77

"Wolde who-so nolde" in the Middle English.

LINES 88 TO 90

In reported speech in the original, but I think sufficiently dramatic to justify a change to direct speech.

STANZA 15, LINE 99

Criseyde is not found in the original Troy story. She is a mediaeval character, developed from Briseis, Archilles' slave girl, and Chryseis, daughter of Chryses, a priest of Apollo, both of whom appear in Homer's *Iliad.*

STANZA 16, LINE 110
Hector was the eldest son of Priam and Hecuba, and was the great champion of Troy.

STANZA 20, LINE 139
Compare what the Monk says at the beginning of his Tale, (C.T.)

> "For certein, whan that fortune list to flee
> Ther may no man the cours of hir witholde;
> Lat no man truste on blind prosperitee."

This is one of the main 'themes' of *Troilus and Criseyde*. Chaucer, like so many of his learned and thoughtful contemporaries, was deeply impressed by Boethius, the late Roman philosopher, (470 A.D. to 524 A.D. approx.) whose great work, *De Consolatione Philosophiae*, was translated by Chaucer. In this work, the fickleness of Fortune is stressed, and problems of freewill and predestination are debated, as they are throughout *Troilus and Criseyde*. It is the helplessness of the lovers, as 'star-crossed' as are Romeo and Juliet, which moves us so greatly. (Some interesting close parallels to Shakespeare's tragedy will be noticed, and the character of Pandarus has the healthy, earthy sensuality and the practical commonsense of Juliet's Nurse.)

STANZA 21, LINE 146
Chaucer gives as his sources for the Troy story, Homer's *Iliad,* and Dares, the Phrygian, and Dictys, or Dyte, as Chaucer calls him, a Cretan. These two were supposed to have been eye witnesses of the Trojan war. Benoît de Sainte-Maure, a French poet of the Twelfth Century, wove their apocryphal tales into a story of Troy, the *Roman de Troie*. Guido delle Colone, a Thirteenth Century Italian writer, embroidered it further, and using these sources, Boccaccio, (about 1338) composed *Il Filostrato,* the tale of the loves of Troilo and Criseida, helped by Criseida's cynical young man-about-town cousin, Pandaro.

STANZA 22, LINE 153
The Palladium was a very ancient and extremely holy statue of Athena. As long as it remained in Troy, the city could not be captured.

STANZA 23, LINE 156
April is not loved by Chaucer solely on account of its beauty as the month of flowers and showers. Spring to people in the Middle Ages meant even more than it does to us, it meant deliverance from the discomforts of winter, being pent in stuffy houses, dependent on candles, rushlights, firelight, having to go early to bed, and getting up to darkness and cold. It meant long days in the open air, salads, green vegetables and fresh meat and fish after living on short commons and perhaps 'high' meat, salt fish and other unpleasantnesses. And it meant, too, that

clothes could be washed, people could bathe in rivers and streams, get exercise and out of doors recreation. Spring was re-creation in every sense.

STANZA 24, LINE 161
The Trojan temple is very much a mediaeval church or cathedral, open and without pews or seats, like some continental cathedrals today. People came and went during the services, ladies paraded their fashionable dresses, prostitutes picked up clients, gallants eyed the girls, even business might be conducted discreetly as the service continued. A modified form of this can still be seen going on in many Italian churches, a cheerful hum of busyness within the house of God, heaven and the world well mixed!

STANZA 25, LINE 171
This is probably a delicate compliment to Anne of Bohemia, the princess whom Richard II had just married.

STANZA 26, LINE 182
"Debonaire" is perhaps left unchanged. As can be seen, it is a French word, and means 'elegant', 'well-bred', 'poised'. Criseyde was completely mistress of herself and of her situation, she was a noble mediaeval lady, well educated, beautiful, skilled in all the necessary arts and courtesies. "Debonaire" is a compendium of a word, which conveys in nine letters all her courtliness, elegance and breeding.

STANZA 30
Here, in a sense, Troilus commits the sin of 'hubris', that is, a sin of blasphemous pride. Love is a god, and the rites of Love, within the Courtly Code, are religious, sacred, and to be broken at peril. All through Troilus and Criseyde, Chaucer stresses the religion of Love, and uses phrases and words which emphasize this. It is right, too, from the human point of view, that the insufferable smugness and arrogant self-satisfaction of Troilus should be properly punished!

LINE 210
At this date, peacocks were not only looked on as decorative, but also as delectable birds. They were frequently served up at banquets and as a rule the plucked plumage was put back, and the roast served 'in his pride' with the fan of feathers beautifully arranged.

STANZA 32, LINE 218
Chaucer has 'Bayard' as the name of the lively horse. This was a common name for horses in the Middle ages. The original Bayard, ('Tall bay horse') was Renaud's horse, given to him by Charlemagne. The tale of the champion and his steed is told in many 13th Century French chansons, and in Boiardo's Orlando Innamorato.
A charming picture in the Luterell Psalter seems to illustrate this

scene, and shows frisky horses harnessed tandem fashion, skipping up a hill as if evading the carter's whip. Horses were often driven in traces, tandem wise, and so were more free to prance and play up than those driven in shafts.

STANZA 43, LINE 300
The Middle English reads:—

> "He was tho glad his hornes in to shrink,
> Unnethes wiste he how to loke or winke."

that is, "He was glad to pull in his horns, and hardly knew quite how to look about him." I think that Chaucer had in mind the shy, hesitant progress of a tender horned snail. Compare Shakespeare's simile in *Venus and Adonis.*

STANZA 48. LINE 336
'Your order is ruled in good wyse.'
Troilus here regards the Servants of Love as members of a Religious Order, or possibly as members of a Guild or Club, banded together for a common purpose, and subject to rules and a code of behaviour. He is, of course, thinking of the Code of Courtly Love, with its obligations, rites and rituals.

STANZA 55, LINE 381
Mews were orginally places in which hawks were kept when moulting. (To mew meant to moult.) Afterwards the term was used to describe places in which hawks were kept and trained, and afterwards the word was used for stable buildings in general, hence mews behind dwelling houses in cities.

STANZA 57, LINE 394
No one knows who Lollius was. Chaucer may have mistranslated or misunderstood two lines from one of the *Epistles* of Horace, referring to 'maxime Lolli'. Some authorities think he used the name as a pseudonym for Boccaccio, or wished to make his own poem seem more authoritative by giving it a source, an 'author' whom he followed. There are various other theories, none of which can be substantiated. The important thing is, Chaucer wished us to believe that Lollius existed and used him as a firm, friendly 'auctor', under whose shield and protection he could write his story. A good Latin name gave this weight and authority!

STANZA 60. LINES 419 and 420
The rhetorical device or figure of Oxymoron, contradictory terms used to convey the extremes of love, is commonly used in mediaeval literature, and continues to be a favourite in Tudor times and indeed right up to and beyond the 18th Century.

STANZA 63, LINE 441

To lose his colour was the correct behaviour for a true lover, following the Code of Courtly Love, but here Chaucer does seem to be poking fun at the Code and its conventions.

STANZA 65. LINE 455

Polyxena was sister to Troilus, a daughter of Priam and Hecuba, and noted for her beauty and charm.

STANZA 79, LINE 548

Pandarus is among the Trojans mentioned by Homer in the Iliad, and was famed for his archery. Nothing in the Iliad links him particularly with Troilus. It is in Boccaccio's *Filostrato* that he becomes Criseyde's relative, and Troilus' friend, but there he is a contemporary, a young man-about-town, and a cynical, sophisticated character. Chaucer's character is quite different, and the portrait he draws is one of the finest pieces of comic characterisation in all literature.

STANZA 90

Pandarus is very fond of using proverbial phrases, colloquial cliches which he trots out sententiously, yet with kindness and an earthy humour!

STANZA 94, LINE 653

Oënone was a nymph living on Mount Ida, who loved Paris, and was loved by him until he was lured by Aphrodite to hanker for a more beautiful bride.

These lines are a translation or adaptation from Ovid's *Heroides,* (*Epistolae Heroidum*) Book V, which is probably a late interpolation, and not Ovid at all.

LINE 664

The reference to Admetus and his daughter is puzzling, for although Apollo was often unlucky in love, there seems to be no legend of his rejection by *this* girl. Admetus, King of Pherae, was Apollo's master and friend. The sun god had been bound to him by Zeus as a servant, as reparation for the killing of the Cyclopes, the armour bearers of Zeus. Apollo helped Admetus to win the princess Alcestis as his wife, and when in later life she sacrificed her life for her husband, it was Apollo who intervened with the Fates, who were seeking to destroy Admetus. (See note on Stanza 219, Book V.)

STANZA 100, LINE 699

Niobe, mother of six sons and six daughters, boasted about her large family, and taunted Leto, who was mother of only two children. But these two were Apollo and Artemis, who, outraged at the insult to their mother, killed all Niobe's children. Niobe was turned to stone, but stone which wept tears continuously for her bereavement.

Stanza 105, Line 730
Pandarus is remembering lines from Boethius' *Consolations of Philosophy*, in Chaucer's own translation, "Artow lyke an asse to the harpe? Why wepestow, why spillestow teres? Yif thou abydest after help of thy leche, thee behovest discovere thy wounde."
Pandar, a well-read man, over and over again quotes tags from, or incorporates the ideas of Boethius with his many admonitions and advisings.

Stanza 107
Chaucer may here be referring to the response of a well-managed or schooled charger, disciplined or 'governed' in the mediaeval equivalent of 'haute ecole'. A war horse had to be fully responsive to all the 'aids', that is, indications given by his rider through bit or rein, or movement of hand and leg. The life of horse and rider might well depend on the intelligent response of a horse to these. So, at a touch, a well-schooled horse would advance or flee, spring, swerve, bound, rear or kick, and the Haute Ecole movements of levade, ballotade, capriole and so forth, familiar in a debased form from circus acts, are derived from the essential and practical education of a horse used in war.

Stanza 112, Line 780
I have retained Pandarus' exclamation, Benedicite, which is much the same as our 'Bless you!'

Stanza 113, Line 786
Tityus was a giant cast into Hades for his presumption in attacking Artemis. He was tormented by snakes and vultures who fed continually upon his liver.

Stanza 120
Fortune and her wheel, (see note to Stanza 20) is a favourite subject in mediaeval art and literature. There are some particularly beautiful illuminated M.S.S. in the Wallace Collection, showing Fortune turning her wheel, to which are tied men of various ranks and professions, all alike whirled from prosperity to pain. Chaucer again follows Boethius here in stressing mutability, the tragedy of change and decay, the powerlessness of the individual and the mightiness of Fate.

Stanza 123, Line 859
Cerberus was the many-headed hound who guarded the entrance to Hades, the Greek underworld.

Stanza 131, Line 916
The wretched lovers were suffering from 'greensickness". Those 'sick for love', and particularly those who were true lovers, keeping to the Rules, had to be pale.

STANZA 133, LINES 927 and 928

The lovers at whom Troilus jeered were people who thought that they could guard against failure by attacking, trying everything all at once!

STANZA 147, LINE 1024

Pandarus calls him "The churl in the moon", for in folk-lore the Man in the Moon is a countryman carrying a bundle of sticks, who was tossed up into the moon as a punishment for working on the Sabbath.

STANZA 153

Chaucer borrowed the comparison of Pandar with a man about to build a house from a Latin poem by Geoffrey de Vinseuf, but he would of course have watched and talked with architects and masons. Richard II was always having work done to the royal palaces, and later in his life, Chaucer was to become Clerk of the Works, responsible for directing the various royal architects and workmen, and for being extremely careful about plans, materials and all to do with building.

STANZA 154. LINE 1073

Troilus rides a bay horse, deemed the best colour for a horse. (Bayard, the famous charger of romance, was a bay; see note to Stanza 32.) Virgil, in the *Georgics,* (Book III) commends bay and iron grey as the best colours, particularly for a charger. Even to this day, bay is thought to be the best colour for a horse, and grooms look with disfavour on chestnut, (hot tempered) and a white grey, (weak). In bay, the four elements, earth, wind, fire and water, (and so the humours) are perfectly blended.

BOOK II

STANZA 2, LINE 8

Clio was the Muse of History. The nine Muses were goddesses of the liberal arts.

STANZA 8, LINE 55

Taurus is the Sign of the Zodiac which rules from April 21st to May 22nd. The planet associated with this Sign is Venus.

On May 3rd the sun would have reached the 20th degree of Taurus. May 3rd seems to have been a special, and possibly disastrous day for Chaucer! In the *Knight's Tale,* Palamon escapes from prison on May 3rd, and in the *Nonne Preestes Tale* it is on May 3rd that Chantecleer has his dispute with Reynard the Fox!

STANZA 10, LINE 64

Procne and Philomela were the daughters of King Pandion. Philomela married Tereus, King of Thrace, and had a son, Itys. Tereus later fell in love with his sister-in-law, Procne, ravished her and cut out her tongue so that she could tell no one what had happened to her. She wove the story into a tapestry and gave it to Philomela, and together the sisters plotted a terrible revenge. Philomela killed Itys, and served Tereus with his own child's flesh at a meal. The outraged father pursued the sisters with an axe, but the gods, in pity, turned them all into birds. Tongueless Procne became a swallow, and ever since she has chattered around the eaves of houses, telling everyone of her sad fate. Philomela became a nightingale, and sings all night of love and sadness. And Tereus became a hawk and continues to hunt down the swallow and the nightingale.

STANZA 11, LINE 74

This was quite usual practice. No one would dream of undertaking any serious business until they had found out whether the stars were favourable. Pandarus could have consulted a Lunarium, or Moon Book, showing whether or not the phases of the Moon were propitious.

STANZA 11, LINE 77

Janus was the two-headed Roman god of gates, the porter of Heaven, and the god who, as guardian of entrances and exits, also had charge of travellers.

STANZA 12, LINE 84

Criseyde was listening to the *Thebaid*, by P. Papinius Statius. (Chaucer's Stace.) This was a heroic poem in twelve books, very popular in the Middle Ages, which dealt with the legends of Thebes. First the death of Laius was related, then the coming of Oedipus, his marriage to Jocasta (legends which are the basis for Sophocles' great play, *Oedipus Rex*), then the quarrels which arose between the sons of Oedipus, Eteocles and Polynices, culminating in the expedition against Thebes of the Seven heroes, Polynices and his comrades. (See notes to Stanza 15 and to Stanza 214, Book V.)

The fact that Criseyde possesses a book, and possibly has a small library, shows the extent of her wealth. Printing had not been invented in Chaucer's lifetime, and books, written by hand, often beautifully bound and illustrated were extremely costly.

In the Middle Ages it was a usual practice for books to be read aloud, and most poems, Troilus and Criseyde included, are written with this in mind. Serious works of piety and edification, histories, romances were read during meals (as the Scriptures, spiritual or theological works are still read at mealtimes in the refectories of Religious communities). And in noble households a well-educated girl would be given the task of reading to her companions as they spun, wove or embroidered. Criseyde and her nieces are all literate, they read and write, are skilled in music and singing, and are, in fact, extremely well educated young women.

STANZA 17, LINE 104

Amphiorax is the Greek, Amphilochus. He was a seer or prophet, so

Chaucer makes him a bishop! He was one of the descendents of the
Seven against Thebes, heroes who banded with Polynices, prince of
Thebes, in an attempt to depose Eteocles, his brother. The attempt
failed, but the descendents of the Seven, known as the Epigoni, amongst
whom was Amphilochus, took Thebes, and razed it to the ground.

STANZA 16, LINE 110
"Do wey your barbe" in the original. This was a covering for the
neck and chin, worn with a coif or veil over the head, and usually of
pleated linen. It was the correct, modest and discreet costume for a
widow.

STANZA 17, LINE 114
The views about women in the Middle Ages were oddly confused. At
one moment they were all daughters of Eve, wicked temptresses of
stalwart men, and as Chaucer's Wife of Bath points out:

> " . . . it is an impossible
> That any clerk wol speke good of wyves,
> But—if it be of holy seintes lyves."

At another moment they almost shared the exalted position, worshipped
and apart, that was held by the Virgin Mary herself; they were the object
of man's adoration, superior in love, Courtly Love; refined, delicate,
almost ethereal beings, like Criseyde, who on her first appearance seems
so spiritually beautiful that she is like

> "— A heavenish perfit creature
> That down were sent in scorning of nature."

(Further information about the position of women in the Middle Ages
will be found in a chapter by Eileen Power in *The Legacy of the Middle
Ages*, edited by D. G. Crump and E. F. Jacob, O.U.P.)
Girls, wives and widows all had to use great circumspection in their
behaviour, and as a widow's position made her particularly vulnerable,
she had to be extremely discreet. San Bernardino of Siena, the great
preacher and saint (1380-1444) advised widows as follows: "You should
behave like the Jewish women who, when their husband dies, bury all
their goods with him. If you used to wear headdresses with ornaments,
pretend that you have buried them, and so with your clothes and other
vanities. And bury your eyes, too, with him; keep them modestly cast
down." (See *The World of San Bernardino*, by Iris Origo. Cape. 1963.)

STANZA 17, LINE 118
An Anchoress was usually a solitary Religious, a female Hermit, who
took the threefold vows of Poverty, Chastity and Obedience, yet lived,
not in a community, but in a room or cell, often one attached to a
church. The *Ancrene Riwle* was compiled about 1210 as a Handbook

for Anchoresses (in this case for three pious ladies who set up their Anchorage at Tarence Kaines, or Kingston, in Dorset.)

From this Rule, which tells the ladies they may keep a cat but no other pets, we learn that Anchoresses must not wear laced hose, nor fashionable wimples, and when they give advice or help to the villagers who are sure to come asking for it, they must speak from behind a curtain and be particularly discreet if a man asks their advice. Some Anchoresses seem to have given not only spiritual, but also practical help in medical matters and problems, very like an early Citizens' Advice Bureau or problem page in a paper! (There is a translation of the *Acrene Riwle* available, by M. E. Salu, Burns Oates. 1955.)

STANZA 34. LINE 232.
Minerva is the name given by the Romans to Athena, the goddess of Wisdom.

STANZA 45, LINE 310
Chaucer has "Com of and tel me what it is."
Strictly speaking this is a hunting or hawking term, a command to "get on with it". I could not resist the use of the modern idiom, which conveys Criseyde's playful impatience.

STANZA 50, LINE 344
In the Middle Ages and earlier, gems were not only valued for their beauty and their rarity, but for various magical, mystical and medical properties they were thought to possess. These beliefs linger on, hence

> "As a compassionate Turcoyse which doth tell
> By looking pale, the wearer is not well."

(John Donne, *The Anatomie of the World, The First Anniversarie.* Lines 343-4.)
A gem, however, to be effective had to be perfect of its kind, and one flawed was valueless, its magical properties had leaked out of it. (For 17th Century views about the properties of precious and semi-precious stones see Chapter V, Book II, of Sir Thomas Browne's *Vulgar Errors.*)

STANZA 55, LINE 384
The Middle English reads: "So lat your daunger sucred be a lyt.'
'Daunger' is a word which has a variety of meanings, difficult to explain. It can mean 'disdain', the immaculate remoteness of chastity, and the fear and fastidiousness that go with this. It can carry the connotation of ungraciousness, but at times can mean power, the almost magical power of the virgin, to whose bright purity the White Unicorn is drawn. In the Courts of Love the Lady is daungerous, imperious, disdainful, hard to get, and she has to be so, for she is the Princesse Lointaine, the quintessance of immaculate femininity, even if later she is found to be a very warm and human woman (as is, in fact, Criseyde).

STANZA 57, LINE 393

Compare Pandarus' words with Herrick's lines:

"Gather ye rosebuds while ye may . . . "

Both are echoing the famous lines of Ausonius,

"Collige, virgo, rosas, dum flos novus et nova pubes.
Et memor esto aevum sic properare tuum."

(Maiden, gather the roses whilst they and you are young, for you and them, life is fleeting and brief.)

STANZA 58, LINE 400

Fools were essential members of most wealthy households. They could be professional jesters, or mental defectives whose simplicity and crude jesting or uncouth antics were thought entertaining.

These words, which seem to be those of a cynical and professional satirist, anticipate those of Shakespeare in *Hamlet*, Act V, Scene 1, where Hamlet, seeing Yorick's skull, seems to remember his mockery of the ladies of the Court.

"Now get you to my lady's chamber, and tell her, let her paint an inch thick, to this favour she must come; make her laugh at that."

STANZA 61, LINE 425

Criseyde calls upon Pallas Athene, the Virgin Goddess, who was always ready to protect women whose virtue was in danger.

STANZA 63, LINE 435

Pandarus, as a knight, and a man of war, calls upon Mars, god of war, and helper of the valiant soldier.

STANZA 64, LINE 443

Neptune, or Poseidon, god of the sea, and god, also, of horses. In the *Aeneid*, he was offended by the Trojans, especially by their priest, Laocoon, who was suspicious of the great Wooden Horse which had been pushed close up to the walls after the Greeks had apparently retreated. Sinon, a Greek spy, told the Trojans it was an offering which the Greeks were anxious to make to Neptune, and if the Trojans honoured it, the god's favours would be granted to them. In fact, as everyone knows, Greek warriors lurked inside the horse. Laocoon, a seer like Calchas, foresaw disaster, and told the Trojans to beware of Greeks, especially when they came bringing gifts. The Trojans took no notice of him, and dragged the horse inside the city walls. As Laocoon stood sacrificing at Neptune's altar, he and his sons were crushed to death by sea serpents as a sign of the god's wrath. So, for Pandarus to swear by Neptune, god of the changing sea, and a deity inimical to Troy, is an augury of disaster.

STANZA 65, LINE 449

Fear is the extremely human yet tragic flaw in Criseyde's nature. It is fear which stops her returning to Troilus after she has been sent to her father and the Greeks, and fear again which makes her listen to Diomede, and to give way to his importunate love making. Fear, too, plays its part in her love for Troilus. He is a powerful prince, and could make things very difficult for her, alone in Troy, if she repulsed him. Yet, at the same time, as a young widow, with a timid disposition, Criseyde has good reason for her fear, and one feels that, as daughter of an unstable man like Calchas, she must have suffered from a deep seated sense of insecurity.

STANZA 66, LINE 461

Here Chaucer shows the least pleasant, yet again very human side of Criseyde, her worry over what other people will think. There is shallowness in her, yet great warmth, much gentleness and charm, and a humorous self-awareness which is most appealing.

STANZA 69, LINE 477

"I nil not holden him in hand," that is, "I will not lead him on, promise what I do not intend to do."

STANZA 73, LINES 506 ONWARDS

This sudden, as if improvised on the spot, explanation by Pandarus, is typical of the way in which he schemes. His stories are always somewhat involved and penduious. Compare his intricate plan for getting the lovers together, and his story of why Troilus has come to his house, in Book III. It must have been his charm, and the convincing way in which he talked, rather than the skill of his invention which made people believe in his tales!

STANZA 75, LINE 525

Troilus here uses the phrase, "Mea Culpa", which he would have used in making his Confession to a priest.

STANZA 76, LINE 530

"Desesperaunce", wanhope, the ebbing away of spirit which is almost Accidie, a sin of despair and sloth, despair of God's love, but here of the god of love, a god easily offended. (Compare Henryson's *Testament of Cressid*, a poem by a Scottish poet living a little later than Chaucer, in which Aphrodite and Cupid behave with extreme touchiness when Cressid, in her grief and despair, blasphemes against them.)

STANZA 89, LINE 618

It could be the gateway of the road leading to Dardanus, a city neighbouring Troy, or the gate named after Dardanus, ancestor of the Trojan people, and founder of the city named after him. He was the grandfather of Troas, who gave his name to the city of Troy.

Stanza 90, Line 630
The phrase "Cap-a-pie" probably comes from a Spanish phrase "Capa y paza", helmet and sword, that is, properly equipped, though some think it is the French "Cap a pie'." It is commonly used by mediaeval and later writers. (See *Hamlet,* Act I, Scene 2. "Armed at all points exactly cap a pé.')
Chaucer sees Troilus as wearing a full suit of Fourteenth century armour, and carrying a great shield with an outer covering of toughened hide. He himself had served in the army, and knew weapons and armour from practical experience.

Stanza 93, Line 651
"Who yaf me drinke?" This could mean, simply, that she felt a glow, like that which comes after a draught of wine, or it could refer to a love potion. The most famous instance of a love potion is that found in the story of Tristan and Iseult. Here I think Chaucer wants his readers to sense the tingling and sudden shock of love at first sight. He qualifies this in Stanza 97 by explaining that it was not after all so sudden.

> "I sey nought that she so sodeynly
> Yaf him hir love, but that she gan enclyne
> To lyke him first . . . "

The whole incident is completely in character, and worked out with great understanding of human psychology.

Stanza 98, Line 681
Astrologically the sphere of the Heavens is divided into twelve parts. Chaucer's own Book of the Astrolabe, which he wrote for his little son, Lewis, shows how to reckon these divisions or "houses". (Part II, chapter 37.) They, like the Zodiacal 'Houses' had influences and properties, and the First 'House' which crossed the Eastern horizon, and the Seventh, that above the Western horizon, were propitious.

Stanza 108, Line 754
Chess was a popular, yet aristocratic, game in the Middle Ages, and one which noble ladies often played.

Stanza 117, Line 816
Not the famous Antigone, daughter of Oedipus. Chaucer probably chose these charming Greek names for their musical sound and metrical convenience!

Stanza 118, Line 820 onwards
Criseyde's garden was a typical mediaeval one, with dry sanded paths and alleys over which branches had been trained to make shady walks, as in the little garden near Kensington Palace, in London In the *Legend*

of Good Women Chaucer describes his own garden, and its seats made from fresh turf.

> "In a litel erber that I have
> Y-benched newe with turves fresshe y-grave
> I bade men shulde me my couche make."

It is a charming idea, though possibly somewhat conducive to rheumatism, especially as Chaucer describes sleeping on the turf seats!

STANZA 119, LINES 827 ONWARDS
Antigone's song owes something to the French poet, Guilliame de Machaut's *Paradis d'Amour*. Chaucer read and admired Machaut, for he often echoes him.

STANZA 124, LINE 867
The mediaeval version of 'People in glass houses shouldn't throw stones."

STANZA 130, LINE 905
This self mockery is typical of Chaucer. He takes off himself and all other poets, as in the *Franklin's Tale* (lines 1017-8) or in the *Ballad of Sir Topas*. (Chaucer's own tale in the *Canterbury Tales,* where, as G. K. Chesterton points out, Chaucer, the maker of all the Tales, is told by the Host that his tale is 'rym dogerel', and has to tell a 'litel thing in prose'.)

STANZA 132
Philomela, the nightingale, is the bird of love. In the 13th century poem, *The Owl and the Nightingale,* it is she who extols pleasure, beauty and love, especially the graces and refinement of Courtly Love, whilst the Owl is cold, calculating Reason, a disciplined and puritanical bird.

STANZA 137, LINE 954
The Middle English is "Don thyn hood", that is, "Put on your hood or hat", in other words, "Shut up and get going!"

STANZA 138, LINE 964
"Hameled", the word Chaucer uses, means mutilated. A poaching dog was 'hameled' to stop it from hunting; either the dew claws were cut, or the paw amputated.

STANZA 148
In other words, "Don't harp on one string!"

STANZA 158, LINE 1105-6
Compare this with the Wife of Bath, who was an adept in Love's
T

dance. The mediaeval dances were, in fact, extremely sensual, despite their formality and discipline.

STANZA 162, LINE 1130
"Don't put it in writing." Criseyde, at this stage, does not want to be committed, or to face up to the reality of the situation. She is still very much on the defensive, thinking about her reputation, and that of a young widow was particularly vulnerable.

STANZA 164, LINE 1145
As Capaneus was, in the *Thebaid*, which Pandarus knew so well. Jove struck him down as he scaled the walls of Thebes. (See note to line 1492, Book V.)

STANZA 172, LINE 1201
This line could be translated, "I'll sew the letter up", that is, seal or sew up the parchment.

STANZA 172, LINE 1202
Pandarus made a gesture of entreaty in a somewhat theatrical manner, threw up his hands, and then let them drop on his knees. Some authorities have translated this as 'knelt down', but this does not seem quite in character at the moment.

STANZA 176, LINE 1229
The stool had a seat of some rich fabric embroidered with gold thread.

STANZA 189, LINE 1320
"Look at all this black writing", an excellent description of closely scrawled mediaeval script. Probably Criseyde's writing was large and sprawling, too. She owns later that she, like so many of us, does not find it easy to write letters!

STANZA 191, LINE 1345
Troilus probably tried, by magic and folklore, to see how his luck in love would turn out, perhaps throwing the peel of an apple over his shoulder to see if it would form a C; reading cards; throwing dice, or the various other age-old tests used by those who long to read the future.

STANZA 201, LINE 1402
Deiphebus was one of the many sons of Priam and Hecuba. Chaucer makes the relationship of Pandarus to Deiphebus that of a noble who owes allegiance to a great Prince, who is at the same time his clan kinsman and friend. The relationship is very close to the Anglo-Saxon 'brotherly' relationship of Lord and Retainer, a comradeship akin to the Celtic clan relationship, or the 'blood brotherhood' of primitive tribes.

STANZA 208, LINE 1450
Hector is the elder brother, and higher in rank.

STANZA 210, LINE 1467
Chaucer may have formed the name Poliphete from Polites, one of the younger sons of Priam.

STANZA 211, LINE 1474
Aeneas, son of Anchises and Aphrodite, and a grandson of Troasm the founder of Troy. He was, therefore, a second cousin of Troilus. It is, of course, Aeneas who will become the hero of Vergil's *Aeneid,* as father of the Italian people.

STANZA 220, LINE 1535
Tryst here is used in the sense of the hiding place of a hunter. In mediaeval times drives of deer were arranged, beaters and hounds to flush the game were used to drive the deer past tristes or 'hides'.

STANZA 223, LINE 1556
Helen, in Chaucer's poem, is a charming and sympathetic character, with a warm heart and almost motherly nature, not the hard beauty which she so often is in the imagination of other writers.

STANZA 223, LINE 1557
Prime was at nine, the time of the religious service of that name. An hour after Prime is ten, the mediaeval dinner time, the first main meal of the day, breakfast being a mere snack or break fast.

STANZA 229, LINE 1598
In the correct order according to rank. Even in a private household due precedence was kept, and guests would walk into the dining hall, and seat themselves in the correct order due to their rank and status.

STANZA 248, LINE 1735
"And in the vertue of corounes tweyne". This is a very obscure and difficult line. Chaucer may be referring to chaplets of flowers used to crown a bride and groom, marriage crowns (like those still used at weddings in the Russian Orthodox church). Pandarus may be reassuring Criseyde that Troilus is 'honourable in his intentions', though this would be a hint that his love was true, rather than that he intended marriage! It may simply mean "Don't betray this man, not even if you gain a double crown, or reward, for doing it." Or the meaning could be "Don't betray him, even if by doing so you win earthly reward and a heavenly crown (for virtue)".

STANZA 250, LINE 1750
"Come off", the cry used in hunting to encourage hounds, or to call

them from their quarry, but I have used it in the modern idiomatic sense, as this does not seem inappropriate for Pandarus, informal, colloquial and teasing as he is with his niece.

BOOK III

STANZA 1, LINE 1
   The invocation is to Aphrodite (Venus), as goddess of love, and as the planet Venus. As the first, she is daughter of Jove, and as the second, a planet of the third heavenly sphere and companion of the sun. Later, Aphrodite, sexual love, seems to take on a more Christian aspect, and to be a force of divine and unifying love.

STANZA 3, LINE 16 and 17
   Jove (Zeus) was often in love with one mortal woman or another, in whose pursuit he disguised himself in some different shape; as bull to woo Europa, as a shower of gold to make love to Danae, and as a swan to win Leda.

STANZA 4, LINE 22
   Mars (Ares), god of war, was the lover of Aphrodite, for whom he doffed his terrifying armour.

STANZA 5, LINE 35
   Literally, "Why this fish and not that one comes to the weir," that is, why some are chosen, others not!

STANZA 7, LINE 45
   Calliope was the Muse of Epic poetry, and Chaucer invokes her because now his tale begins to approach its climax.

STANZA 9, LINE 60
   Troilus was lying in a mediaeval canopied bed, closely curtained.

STANZA 11, LINES 71 and 72
   Criseyde here behaves very much like Philosophy, who visits Boethius in his prison bed. Chaucer translates as follows: "She leide her hand softly upon my brest." But alas, Criseyde is *not* Philosophy, and will not bring rest or long lasting consolation to Troilus!

STANZA 13, LINE 87
   This mediaeval phrase, "Make it tough", that is, 'make things difficult', or even behave aggressively, swagger, put on airs, seems to be capable of translation into modern slang usage, which can take the same meaning, 'make difficult' and behave aggressively, like a present day Mod or Rocker!

STANZA 13, LINE 88

Compare the proverb, "Fools rush in where angels fear to tread".
Troilus did not speak without thinking. The Middle English, 'To singe
a fool a masse" is probably proverbial, meaning to do something ex-
tremely stupid.

STANZA 19, LINE 133 ONWARDS

Troilus is here asking Criseyde to make him her Servant in the
Courtly Code of Love. He will then be bound to do her will, declaring
himself her champion, accepting all her decrees, and executing all her
commands cheerfully, and without hope of further reward. Pandarus had
been servant to *his* lady for many years, and progressed no further in the
formal Dance of Love.

STANZA 22, LINE 150

Jove, as creator god, presided over birthdays, so this could mean "by
the feast of Jove, who blesses birthdays and beginnings". Criseyde, by
condemning Troilus to death, will offend the god of life.

STANZA 29, LINE 198

The phrase, 'to bear the bell' is often used in mediaeval literature,
and may refer to the wearing of bells by cattle, team horses, or a bell
wether leading a flock of sheep. More probably the reference here is to
a trained hawk, which often 'bears the bell', attached to the tail. The
smaller hawks, such as the merlin, hobby and goshawk, were usually
furnished with bells when actually being used in the field. The bell was
heard when the hawk soared, and again when she pounced to make her
kill.

It is possible that "to bear the bell" meant to win the prize, often a
a bell, in a race or game of skill, but I feel that the reference is more
probably taken from falconry.

STANZA 33, LINE 229

Pandarus made use of a truckle bed, small and easily moved, on which
servants could sleep when required. When not in use, such beds were
pushed under the big curtained bed.

STANZA 42, LINE 493

Scholars are very divided about the age of Pandarus! Boccaccio, in
Il Filostrato, made Pandaro, Criseida's cousin the same age as Troilo,
but Chaucer's Pandarus seems to be 'young middle-aged', and this, in
mediaeval times might well be the early thirties. He is a little older
than Criseyde, and head of the family since Calchas deserted to the
Greeks. Yet nothing about him suggests a very ripe age. He may be
experienced, but he is full of energy, fun, and romantic hope, even for
himself, and after much ill luck in love. I cannot agree with the various
authorities who call him old, or even elderly, and cynical. At times

Pandarus seems younger than his niece and her lover, and this is part of his charm.

STANZA 43, LINE 295
These continual digressions of Chaucer, his asides, interpolations, and the proverbs and 'saws' and long-drawn out tales his characters tell, may seem tiresome to modern readers, but a mediaeval audience demanded them. They liked 'sententiae'; wise words, plenty of advice and admonition. Digressions were welcome, and the longer a story went on, and the more stories within stories, classical allusions, quotations from poets (preferably Latin), the better! Chaucer was giving his public exactly what it wanted.

STANZA 54, LINE 374
Troilus was, in fact, slain by Achilles, who had previously killed Hector, his brother.

STANZA 55, LINE 379
Chaucer was once a prisoner of war himself. In 1359 or 1360, whilst serving as a soldier in France under Prince Lionel, son of King Edward III, he was taken prisoner, and in March, 1360, the King paid for him a ransom of £16, a very large sum of money in those days. Geoffrey Chaucer's imprisonment was not at all likely to have been as uncomfortable as the experience Troilus imagines, but he may have heard, from fellow soldiers, of captivity as harsh as that described here.

STANZA 58, LINE 404
Troilus here displays his education. He seems to have studied philosophy, for he is distinguishing between likeness and identity of substance, as taught by Aquinas and other mediaeval philosophers. (See also Boethius, Book III, Prose XI, in Chaucer's translation.) Troilus later on shows that he, too, has a good knowledge of Boethius (Book IV, Stanzas 138 onwards).

STANZA 59, LINES 409 and 410
Troilus means that he thinks so highly of Pandarus that he'd gladly give him any one of his sisters or sisters in law as a mistress.

STANZA 78, LINE 542
The sweet laurel, or Daphne, was the tree sacred to Apollo, and sometimes used in divination.

STANZA 85, LINE 592
Pluto was the god of the underworld, or Hades.

STANZA 85, LINE 593
Tantalus was a king who betrayed the secrets of Zeus, and in punish-

ment was thrown into Hades, and there tormented by raging thirst. Water receded from him when he attempted to drink it, and fruit above his head also vanished when he tried to pick it.

STANZA 86, LINE 601
"A stewe", that is, a small room, perhaps a store room, in which Troilus was "mewed".

STANZA 88, LINES 614-5
Chaucer has "He tolde tale of Wade". Wade may be the same warrior hero as Wayland, a legendary, giant-like figure, dating back to pre Anglo Saxon days. Evidently Pandarus is retelling an old yet popular, ballad-like, tale, in which there are elements of magic and romance, very fitting for a stormy night!

STANZA 90
Chaucer's audience would know, on hearing this stanza, that the astrological influences, the moon in conjunction with the planets Jupiter and Saturn, were those likely to produce darkness, storm and disastrous happenings. These planets may have been in such a position in May, 1385, which could also be the date of the poem's composition. (See introduction and notes to *Troilus and Criseyde*, in the *Complete Works of Geoffrey Chaucer*, edited by F. N. Robinson. O.U.P.)

STANZA 96, LINE 671
Mediaeval people usually drank a cup of spiced wine as a nightcap, to help them to sleep.

STANZA 102, LINE 716
Mars and Saturn were planets inimical to love. Troilus invokes them as gods, and also as planets whose influences affected created things.

STANZA 102, LINE 721
Adonis was the lover of Venus, and was slain by a wild boar.

STANZA 104, LINE 726
Apollo loved the nymph, Daphne, who fled from him, and praying to Artemis, his virgin sister, was changed into a laurel tree.

STANZA 105, LINE 729
Mercury, or Hermes, god of heralds, of eloquence and skill, loved Herse. Her sister, Agraulos tried to come between the lovers. Athena's anger against Agraulos was not only because of this, but because the girl opened a magic chest in which Athena had hidden the hero, Erich-thonius, her particular servant and worshipper, later to become King of Athens.

Stanza 105, Line 733

The Parcae, or Fates, who spun, wove and then cut the thread and stuff of each man's life.

Stanza 114, Line 797

Horaste seems to be a name invented by Chaucer, much as Pandarus invents it!

Stanza 122, Line 850

"Allas, that were a fayr!", that would be a fine affair. Pandarus is being sarcastic.

Stanza 123, Line 860

Pandarus mixes his illustrations, from straw burning in a house, we suddenly find he is talking of a fieldfare! "And fare-wel feldefare". (This bird is a winter migrant, whose departure means that spring has come.)

The reference to a candle falling in the straw reminds one that fires caused by such accidents must have been common in the Middle Ages, when floors were strewn with rushes, which quickly became dry and inflammable.

Stanza 127, Line 885

Criseyde wishes to give him a blue ring, because blue is the colour that symbolises truth, honesty and hope.

Stanza 128, Line 890

Pandarus here uses a phrase which he repeats later (see Book V, line 505: :" 'Yea, haselwode' thought this Pandare"). There is no exact modern equivalent for "Hasel wodes shaken." Hazel bushes are light, tremulous plants, with no strength about them. They move easily, betraying bird or beast to the hunter, so any reference to hazel wood has in it a note of derision or mistrust. Pandarus means "That's all my eye", or "A fat lot of good that is!"

Stanza 133, Line 930

"At dulcarnon, right at my wittes ende."

Criseyde, that well-educated woman, is referring to the Forty-seventh proposition of the first book of Euclid! She is pinned on the horns of a dilemma, in the terms of logic; that is, in everyday terms, in a proper fix!

Stanza 150, Line 1046

Troilus is ready to undergo any trial or test of his integrity, to swear (on oath) to be tried by ordeal, or for Criseyde to test him by drawing lots.

STANZA 156

It is quite correct and not at all unmanly for a lover to faint in moments of great stress, and Troilo, in Boccaccio's story, does so much more publicly!

STANZA 172, LINE 1203

The seven 'joyful gods' are the seven planets whose influences, astrologers taught, governed the lives of men.

STANZA 180, LINE 1255

Cythera, one of the names of Aphrodite, after an island sacred to her.

STANZA 180, LINE 1258

Hymen, god of wedded love.

STANZA 196, LINE 1369

The rings the lovers exchanged were probably 'posy' rings, with vows, promises or the lovers' names inscribed on them.

STANZA 198, LINE 1384

"They shul forgo the whyte and eke the rede", that is, "They won't get Love's red and white wine", they will not experience the full richness of love.

STANZA 199, LINE 1389

Midas was the richest of all kings, yet, when he did a good turn to Dionysus, and was told by the god to ask for whatever he wanted as a reward, Midas begged that whatever he touched should be turned to gold. And so it was, and he almost starved to death, for all food and drink became solid gold as it reached his mouth. He besought Dionysus to take the gift back, and the god heard his prayer, but Midas still had not learned sense. When Apollo asked him to judge in a musical competition between Pan and Apollo, Midas preferred the inferior music of Pan, and straightway his ears grew into those of an ass!

STANZA 199, LINE 1391

Marcus Crassus was a Roman general and politician, noted for his love of money, a profiteer and speculator in property, land, mines, and even in military expeditions. He finally met his doom in a war against the Parthians, his head was cut off (in B.C. 53) and Orodes, the Parthian King, had molten gold poured into his mouth.

STANZA 203, LINE 1415

Compare the 15th Century lyric:

> I have a gentle cock
> Croweth me day:
> He doth me risen erly
> My matins for to say.

STANZA 203, LINE 1417
Lucifer is the morning star, the planet Venus.

STANZA 203, LINE 1420
Jupiter's planet—Fortuna Major, according to Prof. Skeat's interpretation is Jupiter, but there are other authorities who think the term is used to describe a group of six stars from the constellations of Aquarius and Pisces, propitious, bright stars which, at this time, May 1385, would have been showing in the morning sky.

STANZA 204, LINE 1428
Alcmena was the wife of Amphryton. Zeus fell in love with her, and disguising himself as her husband, made love to her. The night he spent with her was prolonged by his mighty power, so that the moon rose and set three times.

STANZA 208
Troilus composes an 'aubade', or aube, a dawn song of reproach made by lovers whose bliss is ended by the day. Late versions of this traditional 'lament' are Donne's 'Busy old fool, unruly sun," and Act III, Scene v of *Romeo and Juliet*.

STANZA 210, LINE 1466
Aurora or Eos, was the goddess of the dawn. In mythology her husband was Tithonus, who is here confused with Titan, a name for the sun god, Hyperion, Apollo's predecessor.

STANZA 224, LINE 1565
The Fox, in the mediaeval Beast Fables, is the cunning betrayer, who always deceives the more innocent beasts. (See and compare the *Nonne Prestes Tale*.)

STANZA 255, LINE 1784
Here it is just possible that Chaucer has in mind the popular identification of the goshawk with a flirt, wanton or faithless girl. (The goshawk was the hawk used by a yeoman. A knight flew the peregrine, a lady the merlin, and priests had to make do with a sparrow hawk. Goshawks were fine birds, but extremely temperamental, difficult to train, readily 'going wild.' See T. H. White's book, *The Goshawk*, Constable. 1951.)
Criseyde seems to be thinking of herself as a hawk in Book IV, Stanza 188, and in Book V, Stanza 1615, where she blames Troilus for 'holding her in hand', like a hawk on the glove.
For the tradition about the goshawk, and folk songs based on this, see see *The Idiom of the People*, James Reeves. Heinemann, 1958, and *The Everlasting Circle*, James Reeves. Heinemann, 1960. It is quite common for play to be made upon symbols of this kind in mediaeval poetry (i.e.

the play made by Chaucer on the word fiddle in the Canterbury Tales;
on pears and grafting in the 15th Century lyric, 'I have a new garden',
and the innuendo in the early 15th century poem, 'I have a noble cock'.
James Reeves' notes on the Lingua Franca in *The Everlasting Circle* are
particularly interesting in this connection.)

STANZA 259, LINE 1807
Aphrodite, whose mother was the sea nymph, Dione.

STANZA 259, LINE 1809
Mount Helicon, in Boetia, was the home of the Muses, who sometimes
frequented Parnassus, a mountain above Delphi, the shrine of Apollo.

BOOK IV
STANZA 4, LINE 22
Chaucer calls the Furies Herines, his version of Erinyes, or Eumenides,
the Kindly ones, those terrible goddesses of retribution and vengeance.
In Aeschylus' play, *The Eumenides,* they appear to be a multitude of
implacable and terrible creatures. Later writers mention three of them
by name, those listed by Chaucer.

STANZA 4, LINE 25
Chaucer has "Sire of Quiryne". Quirinus was a Sabine word, meaning
'spear 'and was one of the names given to the deified Romulus, founder
of Rome, and son of Mars. Mars himself is sometimes given the name
Quirinus.
But likewise Quirinus could be P. Sulpicius Quirinus (an eminent
soldier, and so Son of Mars), a Consul of Rome at the time of Augustus.
He was 'cruel' because he accused his wife of misconduct twenty years
after divorcing her, and met with general censure for this.

STANZA 30, LINE 32
Hercules' lion is Leo, the astrological sign which governs approximately
23rd July to 23rd August. One of the labours of the hero Hercules was
the killing of the terrible Nemean lion, whose skin he wore ever after-
wards.

STANZA 8, LINE 50
Antenor is called by Homer one of the wisest men of Troy. It was he
who received Menelaus and Ulysses when they came as ambassadors to
Troy, and he advised the Trojans to give back Helen. In fact, he later
became a traitor to his city, and so was spared by the Greeks when they
sacked it. The capture of Antenor in battle, and his exchange with
Criseyde is a later version of the story.

STANZA 8, LINES 51-4
Most of these heroes are Trojans mentioned by Homer. In Chaucer's

Middle English they are called Polydamus, Monesteo, Santippe, Sarpedon, Polynester, Polyte, Dan Ripheo. Phebusco, however, seems to
have been someone invented by Chaucer, as he appears nowhere else!

STANZA 9, LINE 60

Chaucer himself was held to ransom after having been made a prisoner
of war. In the Middle Ages, bargaining with prisoners was one way in
which Exchequers depleted by war could be filled! The capture of an
important or noble prisoner was not only of strategic value, it meant
a pledge in pawn, an investment which would repay dividends of gold.

STANZA 10, LINE 65

Here one has to picture Calchas bursting in upon a parliament such as
the one in which Chaucer himself served (1386), and which met in the
Chapter House of Westminster Abbey.

STANZA 14, LINE 96

'In hire sherte', literally, in her smock or underclothes, without having
time to dress.

STANZA 17, LINE 115

To foretell the future, Calchas had consulted the oracle of his god
(presumably the Oracle at Delphi). He also used the stars, that is astrology rather than true astronomy, the casting of lots, and true augury,
that is, watching the flight of birds as the augurs did in ancient Greece
and Rome.

STANZA 18, LINE 124

Laomedon was Priam's father, who cheated Poseidon and Apollo of
their promised wages when, by the decree of Zeus, they had to serve
him as labourers to build the walls of Troy.

STANZA 20, LINE 138

Here Chaucer mentions King Toas, or Thoas, who was also to be
exchanged with Criseyde. I have omitted him from the translation, as
he does not appear again, has no bearing on the story, and complicates
the metre!

STANZA 27

Some authorities have seen here a reference to the Peasants' Revolt,
which took place in the summer of 1381. As Chaucer was working in
the city at that time, he would have been in the thick of things, must
have seen the horrors of that uprising, and does in fact make several
references to the Revolt in his poems. (For instance, in the *Nonne
Preestes Tale,* lines 1483-7, *The Man of Law's Tale,* lines 645-650, and
The Clerk's Tale, lines 995-1001.) Here the image of the flames in the
straw could be a pun on the name of Jack Straw, one of the peasant
leaders.

Stanza 29, Line 97

The reference to the Tenth Satire of Juvenal, the First Century Roman poet, whose work was extremely popular in Chaucer's day.

Stanza 30, Line 210

"Thus seyden here and howne", that is, "So they all said". It could be "hare and hound", the whole lot, but there are conflicting opinions about this curious and obscure phrase. The sense, however, seems clear.

Stanza 43, Line 300

Oedipus, son of Laius, King of Thebes, and Jocasta. When the child was born an oracle told that he was doomed to kill his father and marry his mother. So Laius ordered a servant to take the child and leave him on the mountains to die, having first pierced his feet to prevent him from crawling away. A shepherd found the baby and took him to King Polybus of Corinth. He and his wife Merope adopted the baby, calling him Oedipus, Swollen Foot. Taunted by other boys with being a foundling, Oedipus consulted the Delphic oracle, and heard that he was fated to kill his father and commit incest with his mother. In horror he left Corinth, and crossing the mountains, met an arrogant old man in a chariot, who insulted him. Oedipus, not knowing this was his real father, killed him. Coming to Thebes, he was waylaid by a monster, the Sphinx, who had been terrorising the city, asking every traveller a riddle, and then killing them if they could not answer it. Oedipus gave the correct answer, killed the Sphinx, and was hailed as a deliverer by the joyful Thebans. They crowned him as king, and he married Jocasta, since her husband did not return. Outraged by the incest and parricide which Oedipus had unknowingly committed, the gods sent plague to ravage Thebes. On consulting the oracle, Oedipus was told to find and punish the murderer of Laius. Told by Teresias, the blind seer, that he was the man, Oedipus at first refused to believe him, then discovered from the old shepherd who had saved him, that he was indeed the son of Laius. Jocasta hanged herself, and in horror at his own sin, Oedipus blinded himself. He was exiled, and his daughters Antigone and Ismene went with him. The sons, Eteocles and Polynices remained, eventually fighting over which should inherit the throne of Thebes. (See notes to Book V. line 1494.)

Stanza 56

Compare this with Book II, Metre 1 and Prose 2 of Chaucer's translation of Boethius.

Stanza 60, Line 414

Zanzis may be Zeuxis, a sage in the Story of Alexander, and so a name for a wise man. The line itself is proverbial. Zanzis was in reality an Athenian painter, living about 424 B.C.

STANZA 66, LINE 461

If one is stung by a nettle, the cure is to rub with the leaf of a dock, and to drive away the sting by saying "Nettle in, dock out, Dock in, nettle out."

STANZA 66, LINE 462

"Now foule falle hir, for thy wo that care!" Probably a reference to Pandarus' unkind mistress. Troilus means "May bad things happen to her, who may yet take pity on you."

STANZA 68, LINE 474

Proserpine, or Persephone, goddess of spring, was daughter of Ceres, the goddess of harvest, growth and abundance. She was abducted by Pluto, god of the underworld, as she picked flowers on the plains of Enna. Ceres searched vainly for her daughter, and the earth was visited with perpetual winter as she mourned. At last finding Persephone, Ceres pleaded with Pluto, who agreed to let the girl go. As she had tasted food (the seeds of a pomegranate) whilst in the underworld, Persephone had to spend half the year in the dark lower regions, half with her mother in the world of sun and air. When she goes back to Hades, winter reigns, when she returns to earth, it is once more spring.

STANZA 75, LINE 520

An alembeck or alembic was a glass still, or retort, used by mediaeval chemists. Liquid heated in it condensed on the sides, and ran out down a narrow spout.

STANZA 79, LINE 548

Stories included in the Troy legend tell of more than one rape. The first abduction was that of Priam's sister, Hesione, taken to Greece by Telamon, and the capture of Helen by Paris was therefore in part a revenge.

STANZA 95, LINE 659

Compare the Stage Direction in *Henry IV*, Part 1, "Rumour painted full of tongues", and the speech following. The image comes from the *Aeneid*, Book IV, line 173 onwards.

STANZA 109, LINE 762

No one knows who this lady, Argyre, was; Chaucer seems to have invented her.

STANZA 112, LINE 783

Criseyde means that she will live like a nun in a religious order, obeying a strict and penitential Rule.

STANZA 113, LINE 791

Orpheus, the poet and musician, followed his dead wife Eurydice into

Hades, and so delighted Pluto with his sweet music that he promised to restore Eurydice if Orpheus went on ahead and did not look back as he left the underworld. At the last moment, anxious to see that his wife was following, Orpheus disobeyed, and Eurydice was snatched back into the shadows. Some legends say that the lovers were united after death in Elysium. Virgil, in the *Aeneid,* Book VI, mentions Orpheus in the abodes of the blessed, as does Dante (Canto IV, *Inferno*). A mediaeval version of the Orpheus legend makes him a King of Winchester, who lost his wife through the enchantment of fairies, but was finally reunited with her and lived happily ever after.

STANZA 119, LINE 829

"Cause Causyng", the Primary cause in Logic, a branch of learning often included, under Rhetoric, as the first part of the Trivium, studied at School and university, and leading to an Arts degree. Again this shows Criseyde's learning.

STANZAS 137 ONWARD

This whole section, to Stanza 154, is a somewhat confused recollection by Troilus of much of the Fifth Book of Boethius' *Consolations of Philosophy,* in particular Prose III. It should be compared with Chaucer's translation of Boethius. Troilus, in agony of mind, and at the best, a man of action and sentiment rather than intellect, gets himself and the reader tied into knots over freewill, predestination, Providence, Divine intervention, and other philosophical and religious questions. At times it is curiously reminiscent of Bishop Berkley, especially the stanzas about the man on the seat, and one is reminded of Monsigneor Ronald Knox's immortal limerick composed upon Berkleian philosophy.

> "There once was a man who said 'God'
> Must think it exceedingly odd
> If he finds that this tree
> Continues to be
> When there's no one about in the quad."

and the anonymous, but pertinent, reply :

> "Dear Sir,
>   Your astonishment's odd.
> *I* am always about in the quad.
> And that's why the tree
> Will continue to be
> Since observed by
>   Yours faithfully,
>   God."

STANZA 143, LINE 996,
> "Eek this is an opinioun of somme
> That han hir top ful heighe and smothe y-shore."

Troilus is alluding to the tonsured pates of mediaeval scholars, most of whom were clerics, and therefore shaved and shorn. I have transferred the allusion to modern highbrows!

STANZA 163, LINE 1138
Chaucer gives myrrh a capital letter, because he is alluding to the legend of Myrra, changed into a tree with bitter bark because she had committed incest. The bark of the tree burst when Myrra's son, Adonis, was born.

STANZA 173, LINE 1208
Atropos was the Fate who cut the thread of life.

STANZA 174, LINE 1216
Some texts give Cupide, some Cipride, but whichever deity is named, it is Love in one form or another to whom Criseyde gives thanks.

STANZA 201, LINE 1401
'His sort'. Criseyde means any way in which her father foretells the future, so I have given some modern equivalents. Earlier in Book IV it was seen that Calchas used oracles, augury, lottery and astrology, so he was evidently skilled in all types of haruspication!

STANZA 202, LINE 1410
In Benoît's version of the Troy story, Calchas had gone from Troy to Delphi to consult the oracle, and there met Achilles, who had come for the same reason. So when the oracle told that Troy would fall, Calchas prudently returned with Achilles, instead of going back to his own people.

STANZA 208, LINE 1454
There are a number of mediaeval illustrations of dancing bears with their leader. Troilus is here thinking of an occasion when, watching an unruly dance, some of the crowd applaud the agility of the bear, others the skill of the trainer, not knowing quite who is leading whom! Sometimes it is the bear who seems to drag his master, rather than the man having the mastery!

STANZA 208, LINE 1456
Probably a reference to some game like He or Blind Man's Buff.

STANZA 209, LINE 1459
Chaucer has "sleighte as Argus yed." Argus was the many-eyed watch-

man set by jealous Hera to guard Io, the nymph beloved of Jove, who had been turned into a heifer. Argus slept, Jove released Io from her beastly shape, and in punishment Hera turned the somnolent watchman into a peacock, with a hundred open eyes upon its train.

Stanza 220, Line 1538

Juno, or Hera, consort of Jove, and goddess of marriage, childbirth and children, was daughter of the Titan, Cronos, with whom the Romans identified their primaeval earth god, Saturn. Criseyde here thinks of Juno as the guardian of faithful love.

Stanza 220, Line 1539

Amathas was King of Orchomenus, in Boeotia, and offended Hera (Juno), by forsaking his goddess wife, Nephele, for a mortal. In revenge he was smitten with madness.

Stanza 221, Line 1541 onward

Criseyde swears by every possible deity, the major Olympian gods and goddesses, and by the various minor powers, nymphs, satyrs, and fauns, the guardian spirits of woodlands, pastures, flocks and herds, all the attributes of nature.

Stanza 222, Line 1548

Simois was a river running through the city of Troy, and with Scamander, another river, an important feature of Homer's Iliad.

Stanza 228, Line 1591

Lucina is one of the names given to Artemis, the moon goddess, sister to Apollo.

Stanza 228, Line 1592

Criseyde means "Before the moon passes through that part of the heaven which is governed by the sign of Leo, and reaches that ruled by Aries, the Ram."

Stanza 230, Line 1608

Cynthia, another of the names given to Artemis, who was born near Mount Cynthus, on the island of Delos.

BOOK V

Stanza 2, Line 10

Zephyr, the spirit governing the west wind.

Stanza 3, Line 15

Diomedes, son of Tydeus, King of Argos, one of the foremost of the Greek heroes. Homer tells in the Iliad how he wounded Aphrodite, who had come down to fight, somewhat ineffectively, for the Trojans against the Greeks. It may be this incident which led the mediaeval writers to make him the man who hurt a Trojan prince by depriving him of his beloved.

STANZA 15, LINE 101

Here 'Make it tough' means 'behave with too much freedom', scare her by being too bold in love. "Sudden Diomede" is holding himself check.

STANZA 31, LINE 212

Ixion violated the sacred laws of hospitality by killing his father-in-law. Later he committed an even greater crime, he attempted to make love to Hera at Jove's own table. For this he was cast into Hades and bound to an ever-turning wheel.

STANZA 34, LINE 232

The Lode-Star was the guiding star used by the pilot of a ship in plotting or steering a course.

STANZA 44, LINE 308

Pallas Athene, goddess of wisdom, was also a warlike goddess, particularly honoured by skill in arms and courage and honour in war. She is usually shown wearing a helmet and carrying a shield. So these are appropriate offerings to make to her.

STANZA 45, LINE 319

In folklore the hooting of an owl is often supposed to be a sign of approaching death.

STANZA 45, LINE 321

Mercury, or Hermes, as well as being herald to the gods, was entrusted with the task of escorting souls of the dead to the underworld.

STANZA 52, LINE 362

Compare Guillaume de Lorris' *Roman de la Rose,* in Chaucer's translation:

> "Many men seyn that in sweveninges (dreams)
> There nis but fables and lesinges (lies)
> But men may somme swevenes seen
> Which hardily ne false been
> But afterward ben apparaunte."

Dreams are a common feature in mediaeval poetry, and Chaucer makes use of them again and again. He is continually falling asleep and having a wonderful vision which is the subject of the poem.

STANZA 58, LINE 403
Sarpedon appears in the Iliad as an ally of the Trojans, a valorous prince of Lycia, who is killed in battle by Achilles' friend, Patroclus.

STANZA 70, LINE 485
Literally, 'Have we come here to get fire, and dash back home with it?'

STANZA 73, LINE 505
"Ye haselwode", Pandarus' favourite expression of doubt, incredulity or derision. (See also Book III, line 890, and Book V, line 1174.)

STANZA 92, LINE 644
Charybdis, the clashing rocks through which Ulysses had to steer on his homeward journey from Troy to Ithica.

STANZA 95, LINE 663
Phaeton, the son of Phoebus Apollo, was allowed by his father to drive the chariot of the sun, but steered it too close to the earth, with disastrous results.

STANZA 107, LINE 744
Prudence had three eyes, one to look back into the past, one for seeing the present, one to stare into the future.

STANZAS 115 to 120
These portraits of Diomede, Criseyde and Troilus are typical of mediaeval courtly and romantic poetry, and Criseyde, in particular, is painted as the 'ideal heroine'. Her colouring is that required by the rules of Rhetoric, she has the requisite golden hair and beautiful eyes. The joined eyebrows are included in her description in all the sources, Dares, Benoît, and Guido. Some authorities say that eyebrows of this type are the sign of a passionate nature, and even today they are supposed to denote quick temper or sullenness.

STANZA 128, LINE 892
'Manes', a term used for souls of the departed, but souls who are worshipped, ancestral spirits, so Chaucer calls the Manes "gods of pain".

STANZA 134, LINE 932
Tydeus, father of Diomede, was one of the Seven against Thebes, and fought heroically there, but perished in the battle.

STANZA 139, LINE 971
"As between betwixen Orcades and Inde", that is, anywhere between the Orkneys and India, anywhere in the world.

Stanza 146, Line 1020
Signifer is the complete Zodiac, the sign-bearer.

Stanza 149, Line 1043
Criseyde gives Diomede her hanging sleeve (often made separately and laced or buttoned on to the bodice), to be worn on his armour as a love token or device, a form of decoration, flag or pennant. It will be remembered that he had already taken her glove for such a token. Ladies often gave their own knights such mementoes, a scarf, jewel, glove or other personal posssession, to be worn as an open acknowledgment of the relationship of Lady and Servant Knight.

Stanza 159, Line 1110
Scylla, daughter of Nisus, fell in love with Minos, and to gain his love, betrayed her father, and native city, which Minos was beseiging. In disgust, Minor refused to have anything to do with her, and sailed away. Despairingly Scylla jumped into the sea and swam after him, whereupon she was changed into a sea bird, or, some say, a lark. Nisus became a hawk, and for ever pounces on her.

Stanza 168, Line 1174
See Book III, line 890, and Book V, line 505, for other examples of this favourite saying by Pandarus. "From hasel-wode there joly Robin pleyde' is what he says this time, and again there may be a reference to the flickering, quivering hazels who betray every movement, this time probably the stir of Robin Hood in the greenwood.

Stanza 168, Line 1176
Compare this nostalgic line with Villon's famous—

'Mais ou sont les neiges d'antan',

which is the refrain to his *Ballade des dames du temps jadis*. Both Chaucer and Villon (born 1431) are using a proverbial phrase.

Stanza 169
This lovely stanza may well be written from personal observation and experience. Chaucer, from about 1374 lived in rooms over Aldgate, and must have watched the herdsmen driving in their flocks and herds at night from the Mile End fields.

Stanza 208, Line 1451
Apollo loved Cassandra, sister of Troilus, and promised her the gift of prophecy if she would let him make love to her. When she had been granted this gift, Cassandra broke her promise, and in fury Apollo ensured that no one should believe her prophecies. So Troilus doubts her like all the rest. Chaucer calls her a sibyl because of her occult gifts,

for the Sibyls were prophetic priestesses, and the Sibyl at Delphi was the mouthpiece of Apollo.

STANZA 211, LINE 1464

Oeneus, King of Calydon, forgot to sacrifice to Artemis (Diana) and enraged, she sent a huge boar to lay waste the country, noted for its fertile cornfields, vineyards and olive groves. Meleager, the King's son, killed it after the great Calydonian hunt. Atalanta is the 'fresh maiden', and she, a huntress and follower of Artemis, gave the boar its first wound, and was presented with the hide and head by Meleager. His companions were enraged that a woman should be given these coveted trophies, and Meleager slew them. His mother, Althaea, whose brothers were among these huntsmen, in fury and sorrow took out of the chest where she had hidden it, a charred piece of wood. This had been burning on the fire when Meleager had been born, and the Fates, appearing like evil Fairy Godmothers, had decreed the boy should die when the wood was consumed. Althaea saved it, only to burn it and kill her son because he had slain her brothers.

STANZA 212, LINE 1484

After this stanza Chaucer inserts, in Latin, the Argument of the Twelve Books of Statius' *Thebaid*. Translated, it runs as follows:

> The first book tells of exiled Polynices
> And Tydeus, how they together met.
> The second tells of Tydeus' embassy
> And of the ambush. Then the third book sings
> Of Haemonides and the tales of doom.
> The fourth, the Seven Kings marching to war.
> Then the fifth book relates the anguished rage
> Of the Lemnian. In the sixth we read
> Of Archemorus' funeral pyre and games.
> Within the seventh book the shades close round
> The Greeks, and Thebes, and the prophetic priest.
> In the eighth book Tydeus, hope and life
> Of the Pelasgian people, is cut down.
> In the ninth book Hippomedon is slain,
> Parthenopaeus at his side killed too.
> In the tenth book a thunderbolt strikes down
> Capaneus. The brothers slay each other
> In the eleventh book, the twelfth describes
> Argeia's grief and the high funeral pyre.

This, and Stanzas 215 and 216 of Troilus, tell of the expedition of the Seven against Thebes.

Archemorus was son of Lycurgus, one of the Seven, and was killed by a dragon (Chaucer's holy serpent) near a well, where the heroes had paused on their march towards Thebes. The Nemean games were instituted in his honour.

Hippomedon was another of the Seven, and was killed during the siege, together with Parthenopaeus. Capaneas, also one of the Seven heroes, was scaling the walls of Thebes when Zeus struck him down by a thunderbolt because of his defiant pride. Haemonides is Chaucer's version of Meon, son of Haemon, one of the fifty knights who waylaid and killed Tydeus. And Argeia was the wife of Polynices.

STANZA 219, LINE 1527

Admetus, King of Pherae, did not sacrifice to Artemis when he married Alcestis, and she was enraged. Apollo, the brother of Artemis, placated her and persuaded the Fates, who were ready to cut the King's thread of life, to spare him if his parents or wife would die in his place. Alcestis offered herself, and died, but was brought back from Hades by Hercules. Chaucer intended to include the story of Alcestis in his *Legend of Good Women,* which he wrote to 'make up' for telling the story of an unfaithful lady in Troilus! His prologue to the *Legend* makes many references to his offence against Love in telling the tale of Criseyde. The *Legend* was not finished, and the tale of Alcestis remained untold. (See also note to Stanza 95, Book I.)

STANZA 222, LINE 1548

Hector was killed by Achilles before the walls of Troy, after he had had a strong premonition of his death.

STANZA 223, LINE 1558

The 'ventail' or Aventail, was the armour which protected the knight's neck and chin, so Hector was evidently grasping by the throat the King he was attacking when Achilles ran him through.

STANZA 231, LINE 1615

"Held me in hand", that is, "kept me like a hawk on its jesses", kept me on a string. Compare the modern "stringing me along".

STANZA 236, LINE 1650

Chaucer evidently sees the fight between Deiphebus and Diomede as a joust, in which the victor strips the armour from the vanquished, rather than a Homeric encounter of life and death. Diomede is not slain, but has to yield his full suit of armour to the Trojan prince.

STANZA 254, LINE 1778

He hoped to do so in the *Legend of Good Women.* Penelope was the wife of Ulysses, who, despite rumours of his death at Troy, and the importunity of many suitors, remained waiting chastely and faithfully for him. But in fact Chaucer did not use the stories of these ladies, for he never finished the *Legend.*

STANZA 256, LINE 1792

These are the great poets of Rome, the last being P. Papinius Statius, whose poem about Thebes Criseyde was reading, with much anachronistic pleasure, when Pandarus first visited her.

STANZA 259, LINE 1809 ONWARDS

The mediaeval conception of the universe, following Ptolomy, was that it consisted of seven spheres, each moving round each, to which were attached the sun, the moon, the erratic stars or planets, and the fixed stars. As they circled, they gave out a celestial harmony, the 'music of the spheres'. God, the Prime Mover, Himself silence and stillness, set all this dance and harmony into motion, and was praised by the intricate dance and celestial music. Milton, in '*At a solemn music*', Addison, in his hymn, "The spacious firmament on high", and many other poets, up to T. S. Eliot, with his dance about the still centre, develop and delight in this conception of the divine dance of all creation.

STANZA 260, ONWARDS

These last stanzas of *Troilus and Criseyde* have in them much of the calm, contemplative maturity of Dante in the close of the *Paradiso*. Chaucer had undoubtedly read, and greatly admired Dante. He does not echo him verbally, as he does Boetheus, or the French 'romance' poets; it is the 'feeling' of Dante, the contemplative calm and the grandeur which now colours and shapes Chaucer's poetry, and gives the end of Troilus its nobility and essential goodness, a balanced humanity, beauty and full maturity of genius.

STANZA 266

John Gower, Chaucer's friend, was the author of *Confessio Amantis, Vox Clamantis, Speculum Menditantis,* long and erudite poems in English, Latin and French, all of which were extremely popular in their day. Chaucer calls Gower 'moral', but to him the world meant wise, well-instructed and capable of instructing.

Ralph Strode was a lawyer living in Aldersgate, at the same time that Chaucer lived at Aldgate. He may have been that Ralph Strode who afterwards became a fellow of Merton College, Oxford. Some scholars have identified him with the author of *Pearl*, an extremely beautiful religious poem. The one definite thing about him is that he was Chaucer's friend, a man of philosophical and poetical turn of mind, and that to these two friends Chaucer dedicated *Troilus and Criseyde,* his Tragedy, a work of high seriousness and religious depth, as well as passion and humanity.

Bibliography and suggestions for further Reading

TEXTS

Chaucer's works. Edited by Walter W. Skeat. Oxford University Press. 1933.

The complete works of Geoffrey Chaucer. Edited by F. N. Robinson. Oxford University Press, 1957.

Troilus and Criseyde. Edited by John Warrington. Everyman Library, 1953.

The Andren Riwle (Specimens of Early English). Edited by Richard Morris. Clardendon Press, 1895.

(Modernisation by M. E. Salu. Burns Oates, 1955.)

LITERARY CRITICISM AND ANTHOLOGIES

The Allegory of Love. C. S. Lewis. Oxford University Press, 1936.

The Discarded Image. C. S. Lewis. Cambridge University Press, 1964.

The Age of Chaucer. Boris Ford. Penguin Books, 1959.

Chaucer and the Fifteenth Century. H. S. Bennett. Oxford University Press, 1947.

Chaucer. G. K. Chesterton. Faber and Faber, 1932.

The Characters of Love. John Bayley. Constable. 1960.

The Poet Chaucer. Neville Coghill. Oxford University Press, 1949.

Chaucer the Maker. J. Spiers. Faber, 1951.

Mediaeval English Lyrics. Edited and annotated by R. T. Davies. Faber. 1963.

Mediaeval Latin Lyrics. Helen Waddell. Constable, 1929.

GENERAL BACKGROUND

The legacy of the Middle Ages. Edited C. G. Crump and E. F. Jacob. Oxford University Press. 1936.

The world of San Bernardino. Iris Origo. Jonathan Cape. 1963.

Mediaeval People. Eileen Power. Methuen. 1963.

Chaucer in his time. Derek Brewer. Nelson. 1963.

Chaucer and his England. G. G. Coulton. University Paperbacks. 1962.

Mediaeval Panorama. G. G. Coulton. Fontana Library. 1961.

Life in mediaeval England. J. J. Bagley. Batsford. 1960.

A history of everyday things in England. 1066-1499. Majorie and C. H. B. Quennell. Batsford. 1920.

Life and work of the people of England. D. Hartley and M. M. Elliot. Batsford. 1928.

English wayfaring life in the Middle Ages. J. J. Jusserand. T. Fisher Unwin. 1891.

Mediaeval costume and life. D. Hartley. Batsford. 1931.

A short history of costume and armour. F. Kelly and R. Schwabe. Batsford. 1931.

A history of the English people. R. J. Mitchell and M. D. R. Leys. Longman. 1950.

Mediaeval English Verse. Translated by Brian Stone. Penguin Classics. 1964.

MYTHOLOGY

Gods of the Greeks. C. Kerényi. Thames and Hudson. 1951.

Greek Myths. Robert Graves. Cassell. 1958.